Minority Report

EVALUATING POLITICAL EQUALITY IN AMERICA

JOHN D. GRIFFIN AND BRIAN NEWMAN

The University of Chicago Press
Chicago and London

JOHN D. GRIFFIN is assistant professor of
political science at the University of Notre Dame.
BRIAN NEWMAN is assistant professor of
political science at Pepperdine University.

The University of Chicago Press, Chicago 60637
The University of Chicago Press, Ltd., London
© 2008 by The University of Chicago
Printed in the United States of America

17 16 15 14 13 12 11 10 09 08   1 2 3 4 5

ISBN-13: 978-0-226-30867-8 (cloth)
ISBN-13: 978-0-226-30868-5 (paper)
ISBN-10: 0-226-30867-7 (cloth)
ISBN-10: 0-226-30868-5 (paper)

Library of Congress Cataloging-in-Publication
Data

Griffin, John David, 1968–
    Minority report : evaluating political equality
in America / John D. Griffin and Brian Newman.
       p. cm.—(American politics and political
economy)
    Includes bibliographical references and index.
    ISBN-13: 978-0-226-30867-8 (cloth : alk. paper)
    ISBN-10: 0-226-30867-7 (cloth : alk. paper)
    ISBN-13: 978-0-226-30868-5 (pbk. : alk. paper)
    ISBN-10: 0-226-30868-5 (pbk. : alk. paper)
    1. Political participation—United States.
2. Minorities—United States—Political
activity. 3. Representative government and
representation—United States. 4. Proportional
representation—United States. 5. Pluralism
(Social sciences)—United States. 6. United
States—Politics and government. 7. United
States—Race relations. 8. United States—Social
conditions. I. Newman, Brian, 1975– II. Title.
    JK1764.G743   2008
    323'.042080973—dc22   2007050136

♾ The paper used in this publication meets
the minimum requirements of the American
National Standard for Information Sciences—
Permanence of Paper for Printed Library
Materials, ANSI Z39.48-1992.

Contents

Figures

Tables

Acknowledgments

Over the past four years as we have thought about political equality, we made many false starts, explored several dead-end alleys, and followed many a blind lead. To the extent that we finally got it right, we owe a great debt to the many people who corrected our path, pointed us in fruitful directions, and encouraged us to continue working on the important questions relating to political equality. Of course our thanking them does not implicate them in our errors, which are entirely ours. We are grateful to the careful readings, comments, conversations, and encouragement provided by Chris Achen, John Aldrich, Barry Burden, David Campbell, Dennis Chong, Martin Gilens, Paul Gronke, Zoltan Hajnal, Rodney Hero, David Lublin, Paula McClain, David Nickerson, Marvin Overby, Gary Segura, Jennifer Victor, Nicholas Winter, Christopher Wlezien, and Christina Wolbrecht. We also received helpful feedback from the participants of the Northwestern University American Politics Workshop, the University of Notre Dame American Politics Workshop, and the University of California–San Diego Legislative Studies Workshop. We are especially indebted to Larry Bartels, David Canon, Ben Page, and another anonymous reviewer for reading vast parts or all of the manuscript at one time or another. Their insights and encouragement were invaluable. As junior scholars, we are privileged to garner such attention and support from leading scholars. We also appreciate the efforts, encouragement, and assistance of John Tryneski and Rodney Powell of the University of Chicago Press.

While working on this project, we received generous support from the University of Notre Dame Office of Research, the Institute for Scholarship in the Liberal Arts, for undergraduate research assistance and for summer funding; the University of Notre Dame Dean of Arts and Letters, for undergraduate research assistance; the offices of the Provost and the Dean of

Seaver College at Pepperdine University; and Duke University's Program in Democracy, Institutions, and Political Economy.

We are grateful to the several individuals and institutions for making their data publicly available. Without their efforts, we would have had much less to say. Thanks to Jeff Lewis and Keith Poole, the National Annenberg Election Survey, the Leadership Conference on Civil Rights, the League of Conservation Voters, and the National Hispanic Leadership Agenda. Thanks also to Mallory Brown and Darlene Luebbert for expert research assistance.

Portions of our analyses were published in "The Unequal Representation of Latinos and Whites," *Journal of Politics* 69(4): 1032–46 (2007).

Brian thanks his whole family for unending support and prayers. To Dina, thanks for everything, from giving me all the time in the world to hatch this project in Elma to the bigger challenge of carving out time for me to carry it through in Malibu. Thanks for listening, reading, watching, walking, and thinking with me. To Caleb and Alexander, born in the midst of this project, all my love—more each day.

John thanks his parents for encouraging him to think about inequality from an early age. To Natalie, Jack, and Elizabeth, thanks for the bike rides to school, hugs at the door, and playing with me in the yard. And to Amy, thank you for living through the many ups and downs of this long project, and for providing the advice, nudging, and support to make it happen.

Thinking About
Political Inequality

ONE

Minority Groups and Political Equality in America

In late summer 2001, four American passenger planes were hijacked by terrorists, resulting in the destruction of the World Trade Center in New York City, extensive damage to the Pentagon building in Washington, D.C., and a plane crash in western Pennsylvania. All told, 3,043 people died as a result of these actions. Among those killed in New York, 76% were white, 9% were Latino, and 8% were African American.[1] Eleven days after these tragic events, Congress created the September 11th Victim Compensation Fund. In total, the fund distributed more than $7 billion to survivors of 2,880 persons killed in the attacks and 2,680 persons injured by them (Feinberg 2004, 1). The average award to families of victims killed in the attacks was greater than $2 million. The average award to injured victims was more than $400,000.[2]

In late summer 2005, Hurricane Katrina, a category 4 tropical storm, struck the coast of the Gulf of Mexico. Its storm surge breached the levee system that protected New Orleans from Lake Pontchartrain and the Mississippi River, and most of the city was subsequently flooded. This and other major damage to the coastal regions of Louisiana, Mississippi, and Alabama made Katrina the most destructive natural disaster in the history

---

1. Schwartz et al. 2002. See table 1 at the Web site of the Centers for Disease Control Weekly Morbidity and Mortality Weekly Report, at http://www.cdc.gov/mmwr/ preview/mmwrhtml/ mm51SPa6.htm#tab1. These data include foreign-born victims, so the domestic racial composition of the September 11th victims likely was even more skewed toward whites.

2. Private contributions boosted the average compensation level even higher. According to a report by the RAND Corporation, families of civilians received an average of $3.1 million in government and charitable awards, while families of those who died in uniform received an average compensation award in excess of $4.2 million (Dixon and Stern 2004).

of the United States, with property damage totaling approximately $125 billion.[3] The storm's official death toll exceeded 1,300, with one estimate from the Louisiana Department of Health showing that 49% of the state's deceased storm victims were African American, and 45% were white.[4] More than a million people were displaced—a humanitarian crisis on a scale unseen in the United States since the Great Depression. As of November 22, 2005, the federal government estimated that it had provided more than $4.4 billion to 1.4 million families affected by the hurricane, or about $3,100 per family.[5]

These were rather different kinds of disasters, but many drew important comparisons between the two. Several African American leaders, for example, criticized what they saw as disparate federal responses to these tragedies. Jesse Jackson, president and founder of the RainbowPUSH Coalition; Marc Morial, president of the National Urban League; Bruce Gordon, former president of the National Association for the Advancement of Colored People (NAACP); and the Congressional Black Caucus all called for the creation of a government fund similar to that which compensated September 11th victims. In a press release, Gordon argued, "You got people who lost their jobs, homes and had all of their assets depleted. In some cases, families lost their bread winner. If the victims of 911 deserved compensation, and they did, then certainly these victims deserve no less to help restart their lives."[6] Morial said in a press release, "As it did then, Congress must take immediate and decisive action to begin compensating American citizens whose lives have been disrupted by this major national tragedy."[7] These spokesmen for the African American community were asking, in the words of the September 11th Compensation Fund Special Master Kenneth Feinberg, "Why should Congress provide very generous compensation to a very limited number of individuals while excluding other victims of life's misfortunes?" (Feinberg 2004, 78).

3. See "Money" at the *USA Today* Web site: http://www.usatoday.com/money/economy/2005-09-09-katrina-damage_x.htm.

4. See the Web site of the Louisiana Dept. of Health and Hospitals at http://www.dhh.louisiana.gov/offices/news.asp?ID=145&FromSearch=1&Detail=746.

5. See the news release on the Federal Emergency Management Agency (FEMA) Web site: http://www.fema.gov/news/newsrelease.fema?id=20818.

6. See the NAACP Virginia State Conference Web site: http://www.virginianaacp.org/news/cco/victimsfund.htm.

7. See the page for 2005 press releases at the Web site of the National Urban League: http://www.nul.org/PressReleases/2005/2005PR222.html.

OUR PROJECT AND ITS SIGNIFICANCE

This is not a book about September 11th or Hurricane Katrina. However, in the aftermath of the disparate federal response to the twenty-first century's two most significant disasters in the United States, many are asking questions about the federal government's even-handedness in constructing public policies that affect different racial groups. Is the response to Katrina merely the tip of the iceberg? Is it an indication of widespread inequality in Washington's day-to-day operations? We do not have to look very hard to identify other recent policies that reflect apparent inequality in racial groups' political clout. In 2005 alone, African American opposition was unable to block passage of new voter identification requirements in Georgia; an overhaul of the nation's bankruptcy system that leaves the underprivileged exposed to predatory lending; cuts in entitlement spending, including Medicare and Medicaid in the fiscal 2005 budget—and the list goes on. Whether these policies are good or bad is a matter for debate. What is clear is that African American opposition to these policies did not stop them from being enacted.

In this book we ask, "Which groups govern?" That is, which groups get what they want from government? How much more does government action respond to the demands of the majority white population than it does to minority group demands? This is a critical question to ask in the United States, a racially and ethnically diverse nation that has been challenged by deep racial divisions since before its inception. We will also investigate various avenues to equalize groups' representation.

Of course, American society is not simply made up of African Americans and whites. The U.S. Census 2005 American Community Survey estimates that Latinos comprise 14.5% of the nation's population, a proportion that is growing quickly. To understand politics in the United States today, we analyze whites, African Americans, *and* Latinos, now America's largest minority group. Since studies of minority politics are only beginning to examine more than one or two groups at once (e.g., McClain and Karnig 1990; Kaufmann 2003; Meier et al. 2004), we have much to learn about the ways multiple racial and ethnic groups in the United States relate politically. We assess the extent to which government action and policy reflect these three groups' preferences. In particular, we gauge these groups' representation *relative to each other*, asking how much more whites are represented in political outcomes and examining the conditions under which minorities and whites are more equally represented. In analyzing

the relative representation of these groups, we look at various points in the American system, including roll-call votes in the House of Representatives and the Senate, and the content of federal public policies forged across the system.

We begin by exploring exactly what political equality means. Defining equality turns out to be no easy task. We identify three different standards of political equality that have influenced political theory and governmental practice in the United States. First, equality may mean that each group's likelihood of being on the winning side of political decisions should be proportional to its size. This *proportionality* standard is clearly illustrated by the principle of "one person, one vote." On the other hand, equality may require that minority groups should be better represented in outcomes than their numbers would suggest. We call this the *race-conscious egalitarian* standard. Although it is the most stringent standard and is often controversial, the federal government has adopted it from time to time, and some prominent legal and political minds continue to argue for its application. Finally, equality may mean that various groups in society are better represented in areas of unique importance to them. This is the *pluralist* standard, one that has deep historical roots in the United States. As we might expect, our assessment of the degree of equality changes as we alter the standards of evaluation. Taking these three standards as our benchmarks, we examine the extent to which whites and minority groups are equally represented in American politics.

Scholars have been concerned with the representation of minority groups for decades. Many have examined the factors that might heighten or depress the political clout of minority groups, including the racial and ethnic composition of electoral districts, the race and ethnicity of elected officials, and the degree of minority participation allowed or mobilized in electoral contests. Rarely, however, have studies explicitly examined the representation of various groups in relation to each other. In the pages that follow, we report direct measures of the extent to which white citizens are better represented in political outcomes than are Latinos and African Americans, as well as how various factors affect these relationships.

From one perspective, our research documents considerable inequality of representation in American politics. Our analyses show that congressional votes and the ultimate content of public policy generally are much more in line with white Americans' preferences. In fact, in many cases minority groups are not better represented even where they make up a larger proportion of electoral districts, suggesting that minorities as individuals are unequally represented.

However, there is much more to the story. Three factors can boost minorities' political representation, sometimes enough to rival that of whites. First, African Americans and Latinos make gains relative to whites and are sometimes even better represented than whites on issues that these groups care about more than whites do. Second, when represented by members of their group (i.e., when minority constituents are descriptively represented), Latinos and African Americans are represented just as well as whites, at least under some conditions. Third, getting out the vote can provide a small boost to minorities' relative political representation in certain contexts. However, voting by itself does not enhance minorities' relative representation enough to produce equality. These three findings hold important implications for strategies to achieve greater equality of representation among these three groups. In short, as we shall show, the story of political equality in America is nuanced, multifaceted, and depends in many ways on one's chosen definition of political equality.

We believe that improving our understanding of the extent and causes of disparities in political representation is essential. For, while Americans widely value the abstract principle of equality (e.g., McClosky 1964; Hochschild 1981), when it comes to the details, "disparities in political influence, even if deplored, [are] widely tolerated" in American politics (Verba and Orren 1985, 20). Yet there are a number of reasons to be concerned about the equality of minority groups' political representation. First, equal representation is central to democracy (Dahl 1961). According to a leading scholar of political participation, "the equal consideration of the preferences and interests of all citizens" is "one of the bedrock principles in a democracy" (Verba 2003, 663). Stated less stringently, "[d]emocracy implies a certain degree of political equality—if not full equality of political representation among citizens, at least some limit to political inequality" (Verba and Orren 1985, 8).

As the Katrina experience shows, another reason that we might strive for equal political representation among citizens is that political representation can protect citizens' other basic rights. Political equality is tied to other forms of equality, such as economic and social equality. If minority groups are not politically equal, it is more difficult for them to protect their economic and other interests. Given these stakes, it is not surprising that minorities care deeply about equality in various forms. For example, in the NAACP's mission statement, the first "primary objective" listed is to ensure "the political, educational, social and economic equality of all citizens."[8]

8. See the NAACP Web site at http://www.naacp.org/about/mission.

Finally, measuring and explaining the political equality of minority groups is important if we are to fashion public policies to enhance political equality. That is, we must know how much political inequality exists and its sources in order to formulate strategies to promote greater equality.

There is some disagreement over appropriate terms to use when referring to African Americans, Latinos, and whites. Throughout the text, we generally refer to African Americans as a "racial" group and Latinos as an "ethnic" group, though we realize these are imperfect categories. We try to be sensitive to the diversity within all the groups, reporting, for example, differences among Latinos of different national origins. In general, we have attempted to strike a balance between precision and avoiding excessive wordiness, sometimes using "minority groups" or "minorities" to refer to both African Americans and Latinos. We also note that we treat these categories as mutually exclusive. We provide further details on the specific operationalization of these groups in later chapters.

WHAT LIES AHEAD

The next chapter lays the conceptual and theoretical groundwork for the rest of the book and summarizes what we do and do not know about political equality in America. Specifically, we define what we mean by political representation, introduce the sphere of political equality in which we operate, and elaborate on the three standards of equality introduced above. We also explain from a theoretical standpoint why minority groups might be unequally represented and why this may change as the racial and ethnic composition of districts varies, as we look at different issues, and as we consider factors like voter turnout.

Part 2 (chapters 3–5) describes differences in the political representation of African Americans, Latinos, and whites evaluated against the standards of political equality we have articulated. Chapter 3 lays a foundation for this by showing that these groups often have different policy preferences and priorities, and that these different attitudes are not reducible to income differences among the groups. Different preferences create the possibility that some groups are better represented than others. Different priorities create the possibility that these groups' representation depends on the relative salience of issues across the groups.

Chapter 4 asks how much more often whites obtain their preferred policy outcomes than do African Americans or Latinos. It shows that when the groups disagree about the direction of federal policy, whites are

more likely to see their preferences implemented on most issues. These analyses show that minorities are not as well represented as whites and therefore are politically unequal under a strict, race-conscious egalitarian standard.

Chapter 5 probes whether differences in the representation of the groups' opinions in policy are tied to differential representation in legislators' roll-call votes. It shows that whites are better represented than minorities in legislators' roll-call votes in most issue areas. In this chapter we also investigate the degree to which the proportionality standard is met by examining whether minority groups are equally represented when they comprise a substantial share of an electoral district's population or nearly half of the population. We demonstrate that larger African American populations in electoral districts do not improve African Americans' relative representation, which violates the proportionality standard. However, we find some evidence that Latinos are equally represented under the proportionality standard.

Part 3 (chapters 6–8) examines three ways to narrow the gaps in political representation. In chapter 6, we move to the third standard of political equality, pluralism. In contrast to chapters 4 and 5, where we focus on issues that are equally salient to the three groups or are less salient to the minority groups than to whites, in chapter 6 we look at issues that are more salient to minority groups than they are to whites. In these policy domains, we find that minority groups' representation often rivals that of whites, both in terms of legislators' decisions and government policies. Therefore, the pluralist standard is generally satisfied.

Chapter 7 examines a second way to close the representation gap: electing minority representatives, thereby establishing descriptive representation. This chapter shows that descriptive representation sometimes levels the disparities in representation, yielding political equality. However, although descriptive representation brings representation gains in some contexts, in others it offers few gains beyond the benefits minorities enjoy from being represented by Democrats.

Finally, chapter 8 asks how political participation affects the groups' political representation. In general, political activity increases one's political representation (Griffin and Newman 2005). However, we find evidence that African Americans and Latinos generally garner fewer rewards for voting than do whites. There are some conditions under which the rewards of voting are equal among the groups, but these tend to be the exceptions rather than the rule.

We close in chapter 9 by pulling together the various findings. Our analyses point to some tentative predictions about the future of political inequality in American politics. They also hold important implications for strategies and policies designed to enhance the political equality of minority groups.

TWO

Which Groups Govern?

There is nothing more dangerous than to build a society, with a large segment of people in that society, who feel that they have no stake in it.

DR. MARTIN LUTHER KING JR.,
1965 commencement address at Antioch College

For a group to have a stake in a political system, it must believe that it has some clout in the system's decisions. Otherwise, little would be lost if that manner of organizing the society's decisions were replaced with another. Do African Americans and Latinos have a stake in the U.S. political system, in the sense that their interests are converted into governmental action? Is this stake equal to that of whites?

This chapter defines some of our key terminology and lays the theoretical groundwork for our subsequent empirical investigations. We spend much of the chapter delineating the concepts of representation and political equality. We introduce various spheres of political equality and identify the type of political equality in which we are most interested—the equality of intermediate and final political outcomes. Thereafter, we describe three standards of political equality by which to judge whether African Americans, Latinos, and whites are appropriately represented in these outcomes. This allows us to place our investigation in the context of prior work and to develop theoretical expectations about relative representation among these groups. We close the chapter by pointing out the unique contribution our study makes by focusing on the relative equality of these three groups.

SPHERES OF REPRESENTATION AND POLITICAL EQUALITY

Representation, a fundamental element of democracy, is a rich and multi-faceted concept. Scholars have penned entire books outlining the various aspects of this concept (e.g., Pitkin 1967; Manin 1997). We focus on one dimension of representation, the confluence between what actors in the government do and what citizens want them to do. *If a citizen's preferred course of action for the government is consistent with what the government subsequently does, we conclude that the citizen is well represented, that is, better represented than a citizen whose preferences are not reflected in governmental action.* Our focus is on describing how well citizens' views on policy are represented in the outcomes of the political process: the actions of elected officials and the policies they enact.

We assume, safely we think, that any group of citizens would prefer to see policy outcomes reflect its views. We also note that to be represented in this sense does not require either that a group of citizens affirmatively attempt to change the direction of public policy or that elected officials be aware of and give special weight to the preferences of a group for the group to be represented. It only requires that the group's views prevail when the government makes decisions. For instance, if citizens tend to vote for like-minded representatives, and officials merely consult their own preferences when they vote, officials' decisions will tend to reflect voting citizens' preferences. We consider this representation, even though these citizens may not have directly caused their representatives to reflect their views by bringing pressure to bear on the representatives when it comes time to cast a roll-call vote. Although we may want to know why some citizens are better represented than others (indeed, we examine this question in later chapters), from a citizen's perspective, so long as the government or its actors are making decisions with which the citizen agrees, the citizen benefits.

Equality of representation in political outcomes is just one important form of political equality. Most generally, "political equality refers to the extent to which citizens have an equal voice in governmental decisions" (Verba 2003). More precisely, political equality demands first of all that individuals possess equal legal rights to participate in the "inputs" of the policy process: elections and other means of communicating their preferences to government officials (Verba, Schlozman, and Brady 1995; Verba 2003).[1]

1. A more demanding requirement is that all citizens have equal *ability* to participate in conveying their preferences to elected officials, requiring much greater parity in citizens' resources (Verba 2003).

America has a long history of denying this type of political equality to minority groups. African Americans were not guaranteed the franchise until the ratification of the Fifteenth Amendment, and the Jim Crow laws severely limited voting by African Americans in the South until the 1965 Voting Rights Act (VRA) (Kousser 1974 and 1999). Many Latinos in the American southwest also were effectively disenfranchised until the passage of the Voting Rights Act. The struggle for this type of political equality is ongoing. For example, felon disfranchisement laws in some states disproportionately prohibit African Americans from voting; a recent Georgia law requiring photo or digital identification to vote was overturned as racially discriminatory; efforts to challenge voters' eligibility often appear to be targeted at African American and Latino localities; and renewal of the VRA, parts of which were set to expire in 2007, sparked some controversy (e.g., Lyman 2006).[2]

Political equality also demands the equal consideration of citizens' inputs—none should be "weighted" more than others by the rules of politics.[3] For instance, the U.S. Senate's apportionment scheme and, by extension, the electoral college both give greater "voting weight" to the citizens of less populated states, which means that politically relevant groups concentrated in more populated states, including African Americans and Latinos, are disadvantaged in these bodies (Dahl 1956; Lee and Oppenheimer 1999; Griffin 2006). Institutional features of the political system like these that give greater per capita influence to some citizens on arbitrary grounds also create political inequalities among citizens (Verba 2003).

A final requirement of political equality relates more directly to citizens' relationship to governmental "outputs." Namely, political equality demands "equality in [governmental] response" (Verba 2003, 665). In this book, we focus on this final type of political equality among groups—whether they are equally represented in the decisions made by elected officials and the government as a whole. Of course, on any single policy decision, "equal treatment for all is not possible, since individuals and groups have different needs and preferences, and policies favoring some are less favorable to others" (666). However, across multiple policy decisions we can weigh

---

2. One commentator went so far as to argue that African Americans should be sure to vote in the 2004 elections, saying, "If you don't vote on Nov. 2, you may not get another chance." See "8 Reasons Why Black People Should Vote," at http://www.blackamerica web.com/site.aspx/bawnews/impacto4/reasons.

3. This is reflected in the "one person, one vote" principle. See *Wesberry v. Sanders*, 376 U.S. 1 (1964).

whether some groups are on the winning side more often than others, or whether some are better represented in terms of outputs.

STANDARDS OF POLITICAL EQUALITY

While there is general agreement that citizens should have equal opportunities to participate in politics and that these inputs should be weighted equally, what it means for African Americans, Latinos, and whites to be equally represented in government action is contentious. As Verba, Schlozman, and Brady (1995, 12) note, "If political equality is hard to achieve, it is almost as hard to define." How often should these groups get what they want before we can conclude that they are politically equal?

There is no obvious answer to this question. At least there is no consensus on which answer is best. Various theorists have offered different answers. Therefore, even though many may believe that minority groups are unequally represented in the United States, these impressions assume a standard of equality that others may not share. As we will see, our conclusions about the extent of political inequality change depending on what is meant by political equality.

What may seem to be the simplest formulation of equality, that each group should be equally represented, is actually deeply problematic because minority groups by definition are numerically smaller than the majority white group. If groups are to be strictly equal, this would require representatives in states or congressional districts where minorities make up only 5% of the population to represent minorities and whites equally well. For example, in North Dakota, where African Americans, Latinos, and whites make up 0.8%, 1.4%, and 92% of the population, respectively, strict equality across groups would require North Dakota's Senators to represent these groups equally.[4] But few would argue that groups consisting of less than 2% and 92% of the constituency ought to be equally represented. Moreover, few would expect reelection-minded representatives to act in such a way. What then might it mean for groups to be politically equal in terms of outputs?

Various political theorists, legal scholars, and politicians have argued for three different standards to evaluate equality of representation—standards that we and they have termed proportionality, race-conscious egalitarianism, and pluralism. A first standard by which we might judge the

4. Percentages are based on the 2005 American Community Survey, North Dakota Fact Sheet, U.S. Census (Washington, DC: U.S. Govt. Printing Office).

political equality of government decision making is that of *proportionality*. "The basic characteristic" of proportionality is that "all groups influence a decision in proportion to their numerical strength" (Steiner 1971, 63; Mansbridge 1999, 634). By extension, proportionality requires that each *individual* should be equally represented regardless of the racial, ethnic, or other group to which that person belongs. As Sidney Verba described this standard, "Political equality refers to the extent to which [individual] citizens have an equal voice in governmental decisions" (2003, 663; see also Achen 1978, 497). We see the "input" side of this notion most clearly enshrined in the principle of "one person, one vote" established by the Supreme Court in *Wesberry v. Sanders*. Although that case dealt specifically with the size and shape of legislative districts, the general principle of the equality of individuals at its core is a central principle in American political thought.[5] Our study pertains to the less-often studied equality of government outputs, or whether outcomes are also proportional.

In this view, evidence that whites' preferences are generally better reflected in government action than are the preferences of minority groups may suggest, but does not prove, that the groups are politically unequal. Instead, the proportionality standard requires evidence that *individual* African Americans or Latinos are less well represented than *individual* whites, or that whites' representation as a group is disproportionate to its group size.[6] As applied to the relative representation of minority groups, the proportionality standard requires that where the African American or Latino share of an electoral district's population is large, representation of African Americans or Latinos should move toward equality with whites. Ultimately, according

5. Putting this another way, one legal scholar argued that "when [majoritarian] institutions . . . produce outcomes that result in differential provision of public goods and services to political minorities (for example, in the rural South fewer roads being paved in the black side of town)—it seems difficult to resist the conclusion that Madison's nightmare of 'majority factionalism' has become a reality" (Pildes 2000, 119–20). In other words, a proportional view argues that the *ratio* of paved roads to unpaved roads ought to be the same in "the black side of town" as in "the white side of town."

6. In Lani Guinier's view, "each voter should enjoy the same opportunity to influence political outcomes. No one is entitled to absolutely equal influence; by the same token, no one is entitled to grossly disproportionate influence or a monopoly on control. The majority should enjoy a majority of the power, but the minority should also enjoy some power too. Thus, proportionate interest representation measures opportunities for fair participation using a baseline of proportional power or proportional influence" (1994, 25).

to the proportionality standard, in an electoral district comprised of two groups of the same size, the two groups should be equally represented.

This standard for judging the equality of political outputs is likely to be relatively unobjectionable. First, a standard of equality that judges outputs based on how they affect individuals as opposed to groups should be appealing given the strong sense of individualism among Americans (Verba and Orren 1985, 6; Feldman and Zaller 1992). Second, most Americans value political equality, especially in terms of inputs, but to some extent outputs as well. "In [American] politics the ideal is democracy and one person, one vote. This ideal condemns gross disparities of political power among individuals and groups, and hence *approaches equality of result*" (Verba and Orren 1985, 8; emphasis added). Third, even those who advocate a more stringent standard of equality would presumably agree that political equality demands at least proportionality.

How can we know if citizens are equal in a proportional sense? We can examine whether minority groups' representation improves where those groups comprise greater proportions of the constituency. In a related way, we can focus on locations where two groups of roughly equal size disagree about the direction of public policy to see which group wins. We adopt both of these approaches below.

For some commentators, the proportionality standard does not go far enough; they argue for a more stringent standard that we refer to as *race-conscious egalitarianism* (Fiss 1976; Colker 1986; MacKinnon 1987; Tribe 1988; Sunstein 1994; Harris 2000; Issacharoff and Karlan 2003; Smith 2003). This view, sometimes associated with the "antisubordination principle," argues that contemporary American society includes some "specially disadvantaged groups," including African Americans and Latinos, among others (e.g., Fiss 1976, 155). These groups have long occupied "the lowest rung" of the social ladder and "they are America's perpetual underclass" according to Yale law professor Owen Fiss, a leading proponent of this view (1976, 150). These writers contend that laws should work to protect and advance the status of these disadvantaged groups. For example, Fiss has argued that government policies should aim not simply for the equal treatment of individual citizens, but for the facilitation of equal status among groups (176). To this end, Fiss and others contend, laws that harm disadvantaged groups, even unintentionally, violate the Fourteenth Amendment's Equal Protection Clause and should be deemed unconstitutional. Fiss contends that "any state action that systematically creates, aggravates, or perpetuates the subjugation of blacks . . . would constitute a violation of equal protection" (2004, 10).

This view explicitly conceives of equality in group terms, rejecting what Fiss calls "a highly individualized conception of rights" (1976, 127), a conception at the heart of the proportionality standard. For example, Rogers Smith (2003) implicitly rejects Justice Clarence Thomas's claim that in the Equal Protection Clause "lies the principle that the government must treat citizens as individuals, and not as members of racial, ethnic, or religious groups" (1).[7] Smith contends "it seems most appropriate to focus on whether government is succeeding in providing basic substantive protections to all groups as well as individuals in American society"(1–2).[8]

To advocates of race-conscious egalitarianism such as Smith and Iris Marion Young (2002), equal protection of individuals is not enough simply because the average individual who happens to be African American or Latino has not enjoyed the economic, social, and political status of the average white individual and currently is still in a disadvantaged status. Proportional decision making is thus not enough to guarantee political equality because proportionality keeps minority views subject to the majority's will. To this end, status-disadvantaged groups often should receive benefits from government decisions that are out of proportion to their size. All the more so, argue Smith and Young, because the American political and legal systems have in large measure created these groups' disadvantaged status. From this perspective, since whites have perpetuated racial categories to their group's advantage, creating an underclass that is a numerical minority, it is unfair for whites today to fall back on majority rule at every turn as the method of aggregating preferences.

Therefore, race-conscious egalitarianism demands more than merely proportional representation. In this view groups (perhaps with the qualifications that they be of some minimum size and have experienced historical discrimination) should be "more than proportionally" likely to see their preferences realized in the decisions of government. If African Americans, Latinos, and whites are to be political equals, according to this stance, the preferences of the minority groups must bear special weight. So, if a racial or ethnic minority group comprises 10% of a district, advocates of this view might argue that the group should be treated as if it comprised 20% or 30% of the district. As the size of the group grows, producing more than

7. *Missouri v. Jenkins*, 515 US 70, 120-21 (1995) (J. Thomas, concurring).
8. As Justice Lewis Powell recognized, "The concept of 'representation' necessarily applies to groups: groups of voters elect representatives, individual voters do not" (*Davis v. Bandemer*, 478 U.S. 109, 167 [1986]).

proportional outcomes leads ineluctably to outcomes in which groups are treated equally. In sum, minorities might merit equal treatment when they comprise some substantial proportion of an electoral district, even if this proportion is smaller than the proportion of whites.

The race-conscious egalitarian view is not simply an abstract principle. Prior to 1976, several federal court decisions found that government policies creating racially disparate impacts violated the Fourteenth Amendment's equal protection requirement.[9] That is, government policies had to provide equal benefits or costs to various racial and ethnic groups. Although the Supreme Court has altered this requirement as a constitutional matter,[10] the Court has indicated that Congress may pass laws banning policies that disproportionately harm minority racial and ethnic groups, and Congress has proceeded to do so. For instance, Title VII of the 1964 Civil Rights Act now allows employment discrimination to be established by proof of discriminatory impact, and the 1982 Amendments to the VRA permit proof of discriminatory impact to establish a violation of that law.[11] So, for example, if an employer uses a hiring criterion that on its face is race-neutral (e.g., a standardized test) but results in no minority employees or even candidates, that employer may be found to have violated Title VII. Or a state law that required proof of identification to vote could be challenged under the VRA on grounds that the implementation of this facially neutral law disproportionately harms African Americans.

Furthermore, arguments for the adoption of a race-conscious egalitarian standard of equality have not been confined to a legal setting. When legal scholars argue that laws disadvantaging minorities should be deemed unconstitutional on equal protection grounds, they are not only backing a change in behavior by the courts, they are implicitly advocating a change

---

9. See, for example, Primus (2003); *Castro v. Beecher*, 459 F.2d 725, 732–33 (1st. Cir. 1972); *Chance v. Bd. Of Exam'rs*, 458 F.2d 1167, 1176–77 (2d. Cir. 1972).

10. In *Washington v. Davis*, 426 U.S. 229 (1976), the Supreme Court ruled that absent evidence of discriminatory intent, facially neutral governmental actions that disadvantage racial minorities are not subject to special judicial scrutiny to determine their constitutionality. However, prominent legal scholars continue to argue for this standard. For example, Tribe (1988, 1516–19) argues that "[m]inorities can also be injured when the government is 'only' indifferent to their suffering or 'merely' blind to how prior official discrimination contributed to it and how current official acts will perpetuate it." Issacharoff and Karlan claim that in *Washington v. Davis* the Court exhibited a "cramped notion of equality" (2003, 3).

11. See *Griggs v. Duke Power Co.*, 401 U.S. 424 (1971) and *Thornburg v. Gingles*, 478 U.S. 30 (1986).

in legislative behavior. That is, if legislatures ceased passing laws exacerbating the subordination of disadvantaged groups, courts would not need to rule these laws unconstitutional. Indeed, scholars have explicitly contended that the antisubordination principle (sometimes called the anticaste or group-disadvantaging principle) speaks to legislative outcomes. For instance, in his seminal article on antisubordination, Fiss (1976, 153) argued that "the judiciary is attempting to rectify the injustice of the political process as a method of adjudicating competing claims." Iris Marion Young (2002, 9) similarly stressed that "courts cannot be the main arenas in which to combat continuing status inequality. . . . [Fiss] calls upon us to notice and theorize status inequality, argue against it to our fellow citizens, and try to change it. Legislative action may be at least as useful as litigation in doing that." Issacharoff and Karlan (2003, 17) take this even further, arguing that the Court's rejection of the antisubordination principle has left it to the legislature to pick up the slack: "[O]nly civic and legislative commitment to the group-disadvantaging principle's capacious understanding of equality has kept it from being eclipsed altogether by the Supreme Court's narrow focus on individual interests." Finally, in defining his "anticaste" principle, Cass Sunstein (1994, 2436, 2440) points out that "[w]e can understand this principle as emphasizing legislative rather than judicial duties," and further that "[i]f the legal culture is to return to the roots of the constitutional commitment and to a better understanding of equality, the legislative branch should take the lead."

What might the race-conscious egalitarian standard look like in practice? On any single vote, the only way for two groups to be equally represented would be for groups to share the same preferences or for one of the roll-call alternatives to lie directly "between" the positions two groups have staked out. However, across multiple votes, elected officials can respond on some votes to the preferences of one group and on other votes to the preferences of another group. Doing so in a way that reflects minorities' preferences substantially more often than is proportional to their group size would satisfy this standard of equality.

The race-conscious egalitarian view surely is the most stringent standard of equality, one with which many may disagree or desire to restrict.[12]

---

12. Consider the extreme form of this argument, which would say that five hundred Native Americans or twenty Laotians in a given congressional district should have substantial say in the formation of policy. Some have argued that application of the egalitarian standard is more compelling with respect to groups that have been historically

For example, even Lani Guinier (1994, 14), the Clinton nominee to head the Justice Department's Civil Rights Division who was labeled by her opponents as the "quota queen," rejects strict race-conscious egalitarianism in favor of something akin to proportional outcomes, arguing that "the purpose [of Guinier's proposed electoral reforms] is not to guarantee 'equal legislative outcomes'; equal opportunity to influence legislative outcomes regardless of race is more like it." Race-conscious egalitarianism is not the present constitutional law of the land, and some may deem that it gives undue influence to minority groups. Nevertheless, it is a standard of equality that has been advocated by noted scholars and applied by the courts and by legislatures in a number of situations involving racial and ethnic groups.

In the context of the relative representation of African Americans, Latinos, and whites, we will test whether American politics meets the yardstick of race-conscious egalitarianism by assessing whether, *as groups*, African Americans and Latinos find that their preferences are *more than proportionally* represented in the decisions of government compared to those of whites, even when whites outnumber African Americans or Latinos in an electoral district. We sometimes focus on whether groups are equally represented because it is a clear benchmark against which to judge the relative representation of these groups. Thus, if minority groups are not equally represented, they are unequal under a very strict race-conscious egalitarian standard of political equality. When feasible, we then loosen this standard to a "more than proportional" comparison, examining whether minority groups are represented as well as whites when the minority groups constitute at least 25% of a state or district population. If so, we conclude that these groups are more than proportionally represented.

A third standard of political equality, *pluralism*, argues that intensely held preferences ought to be specially represented, even when those preferences are in the minority.[13] The "fundamental axiom" of pluralism is that "[i]nstead of a single center of sovereign power there must be multiple

---

disadvantaged by state-sanctioned discrimination (Anaya 1997). For, "while ethnic or cultural groups may not be intrinsically superior to other types of groups (such as associations of skiers or Porsche drivers), they may in some sense be more important" (222). We could add to this the requirement that a group must constitute a minimal proportion of an electoral district to merit equal representation.

13. The opposite view, which Kendall and Carey (1968, 10) term "populistic democracy," contends that if a minority has intense preferences, "[s]o much the worse for the minority. If it feels so strongly about the matter, let it get out and win a majority over to its side."

centers of power, none of which is or can be wholly sovereign. Although the only legitimate sovereign is the people, in the perspective of American pluralism even the people ought never to be an absolute sovereign; consequently no part of the people, such as a majority, ought to be absolutely sovereign" (Dahl 1967, 24). From the pluralist perspective, the political system is divided into numerous policy domains and "who governs" varies in each domain (Polsby 1980). Pluralists therefore generally feel that "the political system [is] open to multiple interests if these interests feel strongly enough about an issue to mobilize pressure" (Manley 1983, 369). That is, intense minorities can exert significant influence in issue domains of unique importance to them. Thus, pluralism is in part an answer to what Dahl called "the intensity problem," which arises when a majority that does not care about an issue opposes a minority that cares deeply about it. Dahl (1956, 90) dramatically claimed that "Madison might argue that government should be designed to inhibit a relatively apathetic majority from cramming its policy down the throats of a relatively intense minority." One reason that we might want to solve the intensity problem is that, according to some, no democracy is viable that fails to take it into account (Kendall and Carey 1968, 10). Another reason is fundamental fairness. According to Mayo (1960, 178), "to count each person . . . equally is absurd: some people feel more strongly about certain issues than others. Would it not fly in the face of common sense and elemental fair play to argue that 50% plus one of the lukewarm should overrule 50% minus one consisting of passionate dissenters?"

Oddly enough, an early proponent of a form of pluralism sought to use this principle to suppress the rights of racial minorities. In his *A Disquisition on Government*, once Congressman, Secretary of War and State, and Vice President John C. Calhoun argued for an interpretation of the constitution that included "concurrent majorities." Writing before the Civil War, Calhoun proposed that a majority from any geographic region (including especially the American South) should have the constitutional power to veto acts of the federal government. Specifically, to avoid a "majority faction," one should "tak[e] a sense of each interest or portion of the community which may be *unequally and injuriously affected* by the action of the government . . . and . . . require the consent of each interest either to put or to keep the government into action" (Calhoun 1953, 20; emphasis added). Only by using this mechanism will "every interest . . . be truly and fully represented" (21).

Pluralism has been a "dominant theory or paradigm of power among American social scientists" (Manley 1983, 368). However, its normative

status is not unquestioned. Some fear that pluralism may be inadequate to protect disadvantaged minority groups. For instance, Schattschneider (1960, 34–35) famously claimed that "the flaw in the pluralist heaven is that the heavenly chorus sings with a strong upper-class accent," meaning that the socially advantaged have much greater influence in the actual workings of government. More generally, "not all groups in the pluralist United States are equal" (Manley 1983, 376). This less sanguine view of pluralism would anticipate that perhaps even on the issues they care more about than whites, minorities may still be unequally represented. Critics of pluralism might also protest that it does not go far enough, arguing that minority groups ought to be more than proportionally represented on a broad range of issues, not just on their "pet issues."

Given pluralism's prominent place in political thought, we pay attention to differences in relative representation across issue domains. In our analyses of minority groups' representation, if minorities are more than proportionally represented on issues that minorities care more about than whites do, we conclude that this standard of political equality is satisfied. Stated another way, if the standard of race-conscious egalitarianism is met in domains that are more important to African Americans or Latinos than to whites, we take this as evidence that the pluralist standard of equality is met.

In the end, we leave for normative scholars the task of sorting out how well numerical minorities, especially racial and ethnic minorities, *should* be represented. Our purpose here is not to advocate one of these standards over another. We simply aim to determine in subsequent chapters whether any of these standards of equality is met with respect to African Americans, Latinos, and whites in the making of public policies, and how various conditions affect these groups' equality relative to these standards.

WHO GOVERNS?

Our focus on groups' relative representation naturally leads us to join a long line of investigations into a core question of politics: Which groups in society enjoy the greatest say in the government's decisions (e.g., Dahl 1961; Polsby 1980; Lowi 1969; Lindblom 1977)? A series of studies have shown that citizens as a whole are effectively represented—that when citizens' support for a policy changes, government tends to respond (e.g., Page and Shapiro 1983; Bartels 1991; Jacobs 1993; Erikson, Wright, and McIver 1993; Erikson, Mackuen, and Stimson 2002; Monroe 1979 and 1998; Wlezien 2004; but see

Page and Bouton 2006).[14] However, citizens do not always agree with one another about what policies they wish their government to pursue. What kind of responsiveness does government provide when groups of citizens disagree with one another about what policy is best? As Dahl (1961) so concisely put it, "Who governs?"

Political thinkers and practitioners have been particularly concerned with protecting the interests of numerical minorities when citizens disagree. Indeed, one of Madison's chief justifications for the proposed constitution was that it would protect against majority tyranny: he claimed in Federalist No. 10 that "[t]o secure the public good and private rights against the danger of [a majority] faction . . . is then the great object to which our inquiries are directed" (Madison, Hamilton, and Jay 1987, 125). Almost two centuries later, Dahl (1967, 10) asked, "[H]ow can larger groups . . . be prevented from exploiting and tyrannizing smaller groups? . . . [W]ill there not be constant dissention, unrest, and even subversion by discontented minorities who find their aims thwarted by more populous groups?"

Most studies that have examined various groups' relative representation have been concerned with what Madison in Federalist No. 10 called minority, rather than majority, tyranny. Specifically, many have asked whether high-income groups exert undue influence on government. Early studies charged that in Washington and at the local level "moneyed interests" have the greatest impact on government decisions (Schattschneider 1960; see also Dahl 1961; Lowi 1969; Lindblom 1977; Polsby 1980). More recent research has found that the wealthiest Americans are much better represented than the poorest Americans in senators' decisions and government policies (Bartels 2008; Gilens 2005; see also Hill and Leighley 1992). For instance, the American Political Science Association Task Force on Social Inequality recently documented the unequal representation of income groups via differential rates of participation, disparate responsiveness by government officials, and unequal policy outcomes (Jacobs and Skocpol 2005). These studies make an important contribution to our understanding of inequalities based on income, one of the important dividing lines in political representation that exists in the United States.

Madison was less concerned about minority than majority tyranny, however, for, as he said in Federalist No. 10, "[I]f a faction consists of less than a majority, relief is supplied by the republican principle, which allows a majority to defeat its sinister views by a regular vote" (Madison, Hamilton, and

---

14. For a review of this literature, see Manza, Cook, and Page 2002.

Jay 1987, 125). Fewer studies have asked whether *majorities* wield too much political influence in the United States. Comparing the representation of African Americans, Latinos, and whites is a natural starting point for such an analysis, given the centrality of race in American politics (Hutchings and Valentino 2004) and the persistent disadvantages that African Americans and Latinos have faced in attempting to gain political equality as numerical minorities. Yet, there are large gaps in our knowledge of which racial or ethnic groups govern. We know relatively little about when and by how much minority groups are disadvantaged or advantaged compared to whites in procuring national policies they favor.

WHICH GROUPS GOVERN?

Scholars have documented the many obstacles to political equality that racial and ethnic minorities confront, such as their numerical minority status in most electoral districts, their disproportionate voting power based on patterns of party support (Bartels 1998), linguistic and citizenship barriers (De la Garza 2004), their generally lower rates of political participation and engagement (Verba, Schlozman, and Brady 1995), the infrequency with which these groups are targeted for mobilization (Rosenstone and Hansen 1993), and the dilution of their voting strength based on districting and electoral rules (Guinier 1994; Lijphart 1997), to name just a few. This state of affairs has led observers to worry that "blacks continue to be underrepresented in federal, state, and local government" (Guinier 1994, 8); there also is a widespread perception among leaders in the private and public sectors that African Americans occupy one of the lowest rungs of the political influence ladder (e.g., Verba and Orren 1985, 188–89).[15] Similarly, others have concluded that there is "little or no direct or indirect substantive representation of Latinos" (Hero and Tolbert 1995, 648; but see Manzano and Norrander 2007).

However, the studies of African American and Latino representation from which we have learned so much have tended to assume that whites are better represented than minority groups and proceeded to examine under what conditions African Americans and Latinos are better represented in absolute terms. Most studies of minority representation assess how the concentration of African Americans or Latinos in electoral districts shapes

15. There is some evidence that public officials have become more responsive to African Americans in recent decades (e.g., Keech 1968; Bullock 1981).

various legislative outcomes, including Democrats' electoral success (Grofman, Griffin, and Glazer 1992), and legislators' activities in office, typically their roll-call behavior (Combs, Hibbing, and Welch 1984; Grofman, Griffin, and Glazer 1992; Cameron, Epstein, and O'Halloran 1996; Lublin 1997; Canon 1999). These studies find that as the African American population in a district grows, representatives vote first more conservatively and then (with further growth) more liberally, although these patterns differ by region, district urbanicity, and legislators' party affiliations and race or ethnicity (Combs, Hibbing, and Welch 1984; Grofman, Griffin, and Glazer 1992; Cameron, Epstein, and O'Halloran 1996; Canon 1999).[16] Others have focused on public policy outcomes. For instance, state policies such as welfare spending are not more likely, and perhaps even less likely, to benefit minorities as their share of the state population increases (Wright 1977; Hero 1998; Johnson 2001).

From our perspective, these studies of minority groups' representation are absolutely vital, showing when and how minority groups' *absolute* levels of representation rise. However, significant factors limit what we know about minority groups' representation *relative* to that of whites. Minority representation studies nearly always compare the representation of African Americans or Latinos in some districts (e.g., districts with few minority constituents) to the representation of African Americans or Latinos in other districts (e.g., districts with many minority constituents).[17] These investigations do not tell us whether or by how much African Americans or Latinos are under-represented compared to whites. Thus, they cannot say much about the political equality, or relative representation, of different groups. We must remember that African Americans and Latinos do not constitute monolithic political communities. There is significant variation in African Americans' and especially Latinos' political opinions (e.g., Gilliam 1996; Leal 2002; Tate 2003a; Gay 2004). As Gilliam (1996, 76–77) puts it, "too much research on racial and ethnic minorities proceeds

16. In a similar vein, Bullock (1981) found that the advent of African American voting rights in the South after the 1965 Voting Rights Act produced a noticeable change in the tendency of southern representatives to support liberal positions and the roll-call alternatives supported by the Leadership Conference on Civil Rights (LCCR).

17. Exceptions include Hajnal, Gerber, and Louch (2002), who found that racial minorities were not much less likely than whites to prevail in the state initiative process, although they did tend to do less well on ballot proposals specifically dealing with racial policies, and Schumaker and Getter (1977), who report a bias toward the spending preferences of whites.

on the assumption of [attitudinal] homogeneity." Latinos' preferences are even more diverse, in part due to the different national origins of Latinos (Leal 2002). Thus, more liberal representatives hailing from districts with large minority populations may not be more representative of their African American or Latino constituents.

To summarize, at this point in time, we do not know how large differences in representation are or whether these differences vary across issue domains. Moreover, we do not know how much these differences in representation are affected by such factors as the racial and ethnic composition of electoral districts, the race or ethnicity of elected officials, or political activity such as voting by minorities. We know, for example, that descriptively represented African Americans (those represented by members of their own group) are better represented than nondescriptively represented African Americans (Canon 1999; Lublin 1997). What we aim to determine is whether even descriptively represented minorities (or minorities who vote) remain underrepresented compared to whites, whether they become equally represented under these circumstances, or whether these conditions turn the tables on whites, leaving them less represented. Our research design, which focuses explicitly on the relative representation of groups, permits us to address these kinds of questions.

THEORETICAL EXPECTATIONS

From a theoretical perspective, why might some groups be better represented than others? When might the relative representation of groups change? We begin by assuming that elected officials desire reelection (Mayhew 1974). As many have pointed out, elected officials may have several goals, including serving the public, enacting certain public policies, and increasing their influence or prestige within their particular institution (e.g., Fenno 1973). However, meeting these goals requires maintaining elected office. Thus, reelection, although not necessarily the only goal, is a primary goal. Furthermore, in the particular context of citizen influence on government action, reelection is the main goal citizens can affect. As Fiorina (1974, 31) puts it, "[R]ealistically or cynically as the case may be, we believe that constituents' preferences are reflected in a representative's voting (if at all) primarily through his [or her] concern for his [or her] electoral survival."

If reelection is a primary goal, when making decisions elected officials will consider, perhaps among other things, how different actions will affect their reelection prospects. In the context of race and ethnicity in the United

States, elected officials are often forced to choose which groups to please. For example, if most whites are in favor of a policy and most Latinos are opposed, an elected official must please one group and disappoint the other.[18] Of course, when different groups agree, an official can please them both. However, as plenty of opinion surveys demonstrate, African Americans, Latinos, and whites often disagree (e.g., Kinder and Sanders 1996; Uhlaner and Garcia 2002). We show this in detail in the next chapter. In the face of divided groups, we assume that the official seeking reelection will choose to please the group that will, in his or her mind, be most helpful in achieving that goal.

Several factors shape a group's ability to affect the probability of reelection. Group size is an obvious factor. All else being equal, especially turnout rates, larger groups can have more influence on reelection than can smaller groups. Second, differences in the salience of the issues at hand will shape the electoral consequences of actions. Various theoretical models of representative behavior have formally demonstrated the incentives for siding with a passionate minority over a passive majority (e.g., Downs 1957; Fiorina 1974). Consider an issue that Latinos are especially concerned with and whites care very little about. Pleasing whites, even if they are in the majority, will not generate much electoral benefit, while pleasing Latinos may reap electoral rewards. Empirical studies have shown that groups are more likely to pay attention to information in the media and election campaigns on issues they care more about and to make choices between candidates based on these salient issues (Iyengar 1990; Hutchings 2001 and 2003). Therefore, the group that cares more about the issue may have greater influence on officials' reelection prospects. Consequently, officials may seek to please the passionate minority group when acting in this particular issue domain.[19]

Third, voting itself plays a role. Voters obviously affect election outcomes more than nonvoters do. Of course, office holders do not want to arouse a previously inactive opposition, but as Bartels (1998, 45) reminds us, "[V]ote-maximizing politicians must care more, other things being equal, about the views of regular voters than about the views of people who seldom or never get to the polls." Empirical studies have added evidence

---

18. A third, more realistic, possibility, at least when a decision allows for alternatives, is to select a position that lies between those of the two racial groups. However, this risks offending both groups. In addition, the compromise, unless exactly in "the middle," will still favor one group over the other.

19. The proliferation of interest organizations that monitor elected officials' behavior in an issue domain and convey it to citizens in distilled form also facilitates this process.

to these contentions (e.g., Martin 2003; Griffin and Newman 2005; but see Ellis, Ura, and Ashley-Robinson 2006). So, the prevalence of voting within a group and the relative prevalence of voting across groups may affect the sensitivity of elected officials to the group's interests.

There are certainly other factors that affect the electoral success of government officials. However, these three factors are most obviously relevant to the relative importance of minority groups in reelection-minded officials' decision making. If we take these three factors into account, we might expect to observe several empirical regularities. First, simply as a result of group size (not to mention greater resources), the views of whites will often prevail in government action. Nationally, whites comprise the majority of the population, which is also true in all but two states (where whites are a plurality) and a handful of congressional districts. Therefore, our baseline expectation is that when whites and minority groups disagree, whites' preferences will win out.

We might also expect that where African Americans or Latinos make up a larger share of an electoral district, they might be represented as well as whites are. However, this may be too simple a story. If the size of the minority population affects the similarity or dissimilarity of whites' and minorities' preferences, the effect of district racial and ethnic composition on minorities' representation may not be perfectly linear. As it turns out, the gap between African American and white opinion does vary with the size of the African American population in congressional districts. According to the 2000 National Annenberg Election Survey (NAES), whites in districts with significant African American populations are somewhat more liberal than whites who reside in districts with very few African Americans, mostly because these tend to be more urban districts. For example, in districts where African Americans make up fewer than 10% of the constituency, 22% of whites identify themselves as liberal or very liberal. In districts with more than 40% African American constituents, 26% of whites called themselves liberal or very liberal. In contrast, African Americans become first more conservative, and then, with still further growth in their proportion of the population, they become more liberal, so that African Americans residing in districts with the largest proportion of African Americans are predicted to be only slightly more liberal than African Americans who live among few whites (see fig. 2.1). The important point is that empirical studies have found that as the African American population in a district grows, representatives vote first more conservatively and then (with further growth) more liberally. Other factors, too, may cause the relationship

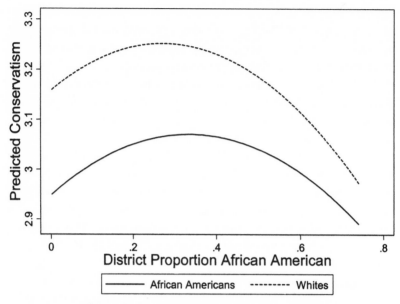

FIGURE 2.1. White and African American conservatism and district racial composition (2000 National Annenberg Election Survey).

between group size and group strength to be conditional (e.g., Combs, Hibbing, and Welch 1984; Grofman, Griffin, and Glazer 1992; Cameron, Epstein, and O'Halloran 1996; Canon 1999).

Even where whites make up the majority, the other factors may on occasion overcome the power of numbers. In terms of salience, we would expect that if whites and African Americans or Latinos care equally about an issue (or whites care more), then whites will carry the day because of greater numbers. However, if Latinos or African Americans care more than whites about an issue, the balance of representation may begin to even out. Thus, we would expect that on issues that African Americans or Latinos care about more than do whites, these groups' representation will be more on par with that of whites. As we will see in chapter 3, African Americans as a group tend to be more concerned than whites about policies related to welfare, health care, and crime, while Latinos tend to be more concerned than whites about welfare, education, crime, and health care.

Finally, we might expect that increased turnout among minority groups would boost their representation relative to that of whites. After all, studies have found that voting generally has its rewards (e.g., Campbell 2003; Martin 2003; Griffin and Newman 2005). Historically and up to the present

day, minorities have voted at rates that do not match those of whites. So, boosting turnout only among minorities may improve these groups' relative representation. However, as we will see in chapter 8, some votes might bring more rewards than others. If so, increasing turnout evenly among all groups, including whites, may not yield equality of representation among these groups.

CONTRIBUTIONS

Armed with these theoretical expectations, we have designed our study to answer important questions about the political equality of minority groups in American politics. First, we take stock of the extent to which whites are better represented than African Americans and Latinos. This shifts the analysis of minority representation, traditionally concerned with the representation of one particular group in isolation, more explicitly toward questions of political equality.

This is significant because people appear to care deeply about their standing relative to others. As Robert Dahl (2006) puts it,

> [H]uman beings are naturally endowed with a sensitivity to the unequal distribution of rewards to others whom they view as comparable to themselves in relevant ways. Whether ... we describe this sensitivity by the aseptic term *inequity aversion*, or use earthier language like *jealousy* or *envy*, what a human being sees as unfairness or injustice will often arouse strong emotions. Given the opportunity, these emotions will then express themselves in actions, which may range from an immediate verbal expression— "It's not fair"—to behavior intended to bring about a fairer distribution, whether by peaceful persuasion or violence. (39)

Members of minority groups are no strangers to these sentiments, which Dahl argues manifest a universal concern for equal distribution of anything of value. In fact, minority group members may even care more about their relative standing since, historically, it has generally not been as favorable as that of whites. Recall from chapter 1 that the NAACP's first objective, according to its mission statement, is to ensure "the political, educational, social and economic equality of all citizens." These goals are explicitly relative—comparing African Americans' political, educational, social, and economic status to that of whites. Moreover, every two years from 1984 to 2000 (except 1998) the American National Election Studies have asked Americans

whether they agreed with the statement, "The country would be better off if we worried less about how equal people are." Over this period, 52% of whites agreed or strongly agreed with this statement, while 46% of Latinos and just 38% of African Americans did so. In addition, experimental results from the "ultimatum game," in which one player first proposes a split of a sum of money and a second player decides whether to accept the proposal or for both players to receive nothing, suggest that African Americans care deeply about inequality (Eckel and Grossman 2001). For instance, one study found that African American "proposers" averaged a $2.11 offer when splitting $5.00, while non–African Americans' average offer was $1.79, suggesting that African Americans generally offered a more even split than did others. Even more tellingly, African Americans were much more likely to reject unfair proposals: African Americans rejected nearly four times as many $1.50 offers as did non–African Americans (47% to 13%). Nearly three in four African Americans rejected $1.00 offers, compared to less than half of non–African Americans. Given a choice between the status quo and an alternative state of the world in which they are better off in absolute terms but worse off in relative terms, a preponderance of African Americans (but not whites) are much more likely to opt for the status quo.[20]

Students of democracy are also concerned with both absolute and relative representation. Dahl (2006, ix) contends that "the existence of political equality is a fundamental premise of democracy." Of course, we want to know when any group's absolute representation increases or decreases. This tells us about the government's responsiveness to public opinion, a cornerstone of democratic politics. However, democratic concern for equality also highlights the importance of knowing if and when some groups are better represented than others. As we have noted, many extant studies examine the former question. Our study examines the latter.

Second, in a related way, we explore whether and why groups are sometimes politically equal. Where earlier studies demonstrate that the racial and ethnic composition of districts or descriptive representation tend to improve African Americans' or Latinos' representation, we ask whether these gains lead to political equality, or if these gains are so small relative

---

20. Other experimental games show that racial minorities are more averse than whites to the *risk* of inequality—that minorities prefer a modest, equal improvement in the welfare of all the participants in the game to the risk that all participants may receive either a more generous, equal benefit or a more generous (in the aggregate) but unequal benefit (Hong and Bohnet 2004).

to the size of the inequality that they leave African Americans and Latinos unequally represented compared to whites. This enables us to see whether there are some conditions under which minority citizens are currently equally represented compared to whites. Highlighting the relative representation effects of factors like descriptive representation and issue salience also suggests reforms that might lead toward greater political equality.

Third, we ask if *any* of the three standards of political equality we have articulated are met. We provide empirical evidence to assess whether minority group representation is more than proportional, as advocates of race-conscious egalitarianism would require. We also determine whether minorities are equally represented as individuals, as a proportional standard of equality demands. For example, we measure citizens' opinions directly and explore how district racial and ethnic composition amplifies or dampens the connection between these opinions and representatives' voting decisions. We also compare the representation of individuals where groups are of roughly equal size. Finally, we ask whether minorities are more than proportionally represented on issues that they care more about than whites, consistent with a pluralist view of democracy. Our articulation of multiple standards of equality advances our understanding of minority representation by allowing us to identify more precisely the circumstances under which minorities are politically equal.

Fourth, we contribute to the study of political equality by focusing on the equality of national government *outputs*. Such a focus is relatively novel. As Sidney Verba observes, "[T]he literature on the receipt of messages and the [equal] response to them is not as well developed as that on the [equality of the] messages sent" (2003, 666). Moreover, studying outputs is important. As Polsby (1980, 484) emphasizes, "[R]esearchers should study the outcomes of actual decisions . . . and not conclude prematurely that the combination of intentions and resources inflexibly predetermines outcomes." To be sure, several studies of racial differences in policy responsiveness examine state policymaking (Hero 1998; Manzano and Norrander 2007). Many of the policies that have important effects on African Americans' lives, such as policies concerning spending on education and welfare eligibility, are made at the state level (e.g., Hero 1998). Our focus on national policies is important because the federal government is increasingly viewed by minorities as an important vehicle for advancing their public interests (Dawson 1994). Relatedly, many national policies have a large impact on minorities' lives, even if some federal programs are ad-

ministered by state governments. Last, studying groups' representation at the national level permits us to measure African Americans' and Latinos' opinions directly, rather than using demographic proxies of opinion as prior studies have done.

Finally, we take into account both citizens' income and their race/ethnicity. By examining race and ethnicity together with income, we advance the study of political equality beyond its typical focus on income alone (e.g., Bartels 2008; Gilens 2005; Jacobs and Skocpol 2005; Lardner and Smith 2005). One reason that several studies examine the relative representation of income groups but few explore racial and ethnic groups in this way may be the presumed equivalence of race/ethnicity and income. These often go hand in hand. For instance, where we have emphasized the racial composition of September 11th and Katrina victims, others have focused on the lofty incomes of many September 11th victims, and the deep poverty "exposed" by the Katrina disaster. After all, 14% of the September 11th victims earned more than $200,000 per year. Meanwhile, according to Census-based calculations by the Center on Budget and Policy Priorities, approximately one in five residents in the counties declared federal disaster areas in Louisiana, Mississippi, and Alabama after Katrina were living in poverty before the hurricane struck.[21]

Although race and income are undeniably related, race is hardly a perfect predictor of income. For instance, Radcliff and Saiz (1995, 776) argue that class "hardly captures the distinctive differences between whites and blacks." Indeed, the gap between the median incomes of whites and African Americans appears to have shrunk over time. Using Census data, figure 2.2 plots the difference in the median incomes of whites and African Americans and whites and Latinos over time. According to the figure, the gap between African Americans' and whites' median incomes has declined approximately 50% since 1960. There is still a considerable difference between the incomes of whites and African Americans, but this disparity has declined substantially. One reason for this is the well-documented emergence of a sizeable African American middle class in recent decades (see, e.g., Dawson 1994). On the other hand, figure 2.2 shows that the income gap between non-Latino whites and Latinos has increased in recent years. One possible (but contentious) reason for this trend is the large-scale legal and

---

21. See the Center on Budget and Policy Priorities Web site: http://www.cbpp.org/9-19-05pov.htm.

FIGURE 2.2. Group differences in income, 1948–2003 (U.S. Census).

undocumented immigration of low-income Latinos to the United States over the past twenty years.[22]

In sum, while racial and ethnic differences in income are significant, race is an imperfect predictor of income and increasingly so for African Americans. Although income plays a significant role in shaping politics in the United States, it is important that studies of income differences in political representation be supplemented with studies of racial and ethnic differences in representation. To be sure that our race- and ethnicity-based findings are not merely masking income-based inequalities, wherever possible we control for income in our analyses. In the end, we show that both race/ethnicity and class are related to political inequality.

Having defined the critical concepts and outlined our expectations, we are now ready to focus on the political preferences and priorities of Latinos, African Americans, and whites. The next chapter demonstrates the extent

22. Increases in legal immigration stem from the 1986 Immigration and Control Act, which offered amnesty to undocumented aliens, and the Immigration Act of 1990, which increased annual immigration quotas. The U.S. Citizenship and Immigration Services (USCIS) also estimates that 150,000 undocumented aliens per year enter the United States from Mexico, and that more than 3.5 million citizens of Mexico and Central and South American countries reside in the United States.

to which these three groups make different demands of government and care about different issues. Identifying differences in policy preferences and priorities enables us to define more substantively the issue domains in which we expect to see greater or lesser degrees of inequality in political outcomes, as measured against the three standards of equality described in this chapter.

PART TWO

Differences in Representation

In this part of the book, we establish a baseline answer to the "Who governs?" question. For one group to be better represented than another, the groups first must hold different preferences about the actions they wish government to take. Otherwise, even if the decisions of government are only intended to reflect the preferences of one of the groups, substantively both groups would enjoy the same responsiveness from government. Moreover, it would be impossible for us to know in this case to which group government was being responsive. Thus, our first task is to establish that African Americans, Latinos, and whites have different policy preferences and different policy priorities. In part 3, these analyses will guide our expectations concerning policy domains where minorities might better represented because of issue salience.

We then get to the heart of the matter, asking whether groups' preferences for policy change are equally represented in the policy outputs of government. We also test whether African Americans, Latinos, and whites are equally represented in the decisions of members of Congress, judged against various standards of equality.

THREE

Differences in Political Preferences and Priorities

Race has divided American society and politics from the beginning. Keen political observers have long feared that racial divisions were unbridgeable and would ultimately rend the republic at its core. Tocqueville considered race relations "the most formidable of all the ills that threaten the future of the Union" and believed emancipation would lead to a race war (Kinder and Sanders 1996, 11). Thomas Jefferson was even less hopeful, finding a harmonious racial society inconceivable. Rather, he predicted in *Notes on the State of Virginia* (1955, 138) that emancipation of slaves and the establishment of a biracial society would lead to "convulsions which will probably never end but in the extermination of one or the other race." Even Abraham Lincoln considered the establishment of black colonies in the Caribbean or Central America the best solution to racial tensions. As he argued in a debate with Stephen Douglas, blacks' and whites' physical differences were so great that they "forever forbid the two races living together upon the footing of perfect equality" (1953, 3:16).

Even after the Emancipation Proclamation, the passage of the Thirteenth, Fourteenth, and Fifteenth Amendments, and the Civil Rights Movement, race continues to divide American society and politics. In the late 1960s, as race riots raged, Otto Kerner, governor of Illinois, and his National Commission on Civil Disorders warned that the United States was "moving toward two societies, one black, one white—separate and unequal" (National Advisory Commission on Civil Disorders 1968, 1). More recently, Stephen Carter claimed that "[r]ace, more than any other organizing category . . . continues to drive our nation into frenzies that lead to unparalleled viciousness" (1994, xvii–xviii). These divisions are a defining feature of American politics. In fact, Kinder and Sanders (1996, 27) conclude from years of opinion surveys that the differences in policy preferences between

African Americans and whites is "a divide without peer." Over the past decades, the dividing lines have changed from simple black and white char-
acterizations to include several growing racial and ethnic groups, most
notably Latinos. As we will see, both in terms of broad political perspectives
and on specific issues, the views of African Americans, Latinos, and whites
are quite distinctive.

In this chapter, we introduce the data we use to measure individuals' political preferences and then describe the differences in the political preferences and priorities of African Americans, Latinos, and whites in several
issue areas. We find that the differences in groups' preferences vary greatly
from issue to issue. Moreover, while there are many similarities between
African Americans' and Latinos' preferences relative to those of whites, we
see that it is important to analyze these groups separately. Beyond differences in policy preferences, we note that the minority groups have distinctive policy priorities as well. Not only do African Americans, Latinos, and
whites want the government to do different things, the issues these groups
care most about differ. These preference and priority differences lay the
groundwork for the remaining chapters in part 2. Chapter 4 compares the
groups' preferences with the policies of government and chapter 5 compares the decisions of individual government actors.

DATA SOURCES

Our chief source of opinion data is the 2000 National Annenberg Election
Survey (NAES), of which we use portions that include a total of 57,197 respondents.[1] These surveys include more than 5,000 African American and
5,000 Latino respondents, a sample that few mass-level political surveys
can match. The sheer size of the NAES enables us to overcome some of the
technical hurdles to examining critical substantive questions. For example,
the large sample allows us to estimate the preferences of the three groups in
many states. Most surveys simply do not include enough respondents in a
substantial number of states to allow reliable state-level analyses. Additionally, unlike approaches using other surveys (Erikson, Wright, and McIver

1. To generate our data set, we combine the NAES national cross-section data, which
were obtained between December 1999 and January 2001, the NAES Super Tuesday
cross-section, and the NAES Second Tuesday cross-section. For the sampling protocol
of the NAES, see Romer et al. (2004).

1993; Brace et al. 2002), the NAES does not need to be aggregated over a long period of time (just over a year) to generate state-level estimates. Pooling over longer periods raises concerns about aggregating data that may not be stable over time.

We also rely on other data sources for measures of political preferences among the three groups. In particular, the General Social Survey (GSS) conducted by the National Opinion Research Center (NORC) regularly asks respondents about their preferences for national government spending in various areas. We examine these spending preferences for the period 1973–2002. In addition, we rely on data from the National Election Studies (NES) to compare the groups' policy priorities and for several other purposes. These surveys were conducted from September to November of even-numbered years, 1974–2002.[2]

DIFFERENCES IN IDEOLOGY

We begin broadly, by comparing the general ideological orientations of the three groups, asking how liberal or conservative they tend to be. In the nation as a whole, these groups hold distinctive ideological views. The NAES asked respondents to place themselves on a five-point ideology scale ranging from very liberal (recoded 1) to very conservative (recoded 5).[3] A straightforward way to compare the groups' ideological orientations is to examine the distribution of self-placements for each group. As figure 3.1 shows, whites are the most conservative of the three groups, with an average ideology of 3.19, while African Americans are the most liberal group with a mean of 3.01, and Latinos are roughly in between with a mean of 3.10. In each case, the differences between whites and minorities are statistically significant. In terms of the distribution across the five categories, although approximately equal proportions of each group claim to be very conservative, whites are much more likely than African Americans to be conservative, and somewhat more likely than Latinos to be conservative. Meanwhile, a greater proportion of African Americans identify themselves as very liberal, liberal, and moderate than either of the other two groups. To convey the magnitude of

2. We also use NES data to measure racial groups' spending preferences in dealing with crime, as no comparable item was included in the NAES.
3. The wording of the ideological orientation question was, "Generally speaking, would you describe your political views as very conservative, conservative, moderate, liberal or very liberal?"

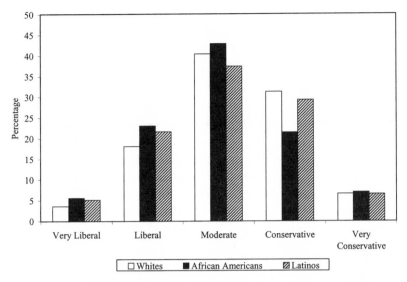

FIGURE 3.1. Ideological orientation, African Americans, Latinos, and whites (2000 National Annenberg Election Survey).

these differences, we note that the difference between the mean ideology of whites and African Americans (.18) is about three times the size of the difference between the average ideology of NAES respondents with incomes between $15,000 and $25,000, the 25th percentile in the income distribution, and NAES respondents with incomes between $50,000 and $75,000, the 75th percentile in the income distribution. Finally, we note that using the NAES five-point ideology scale rather than the seven-point scale used in other surveys may minimize the reality of group differences in ideology.[4]

We also note that the variance in all three groups' ideologies is similar (with minorities actually exhibiting slightly more variation than whites).[5]

4. For instance, 2002 NES data indicate that more than four times as many African Americans as whites identify themselves as "extremely liberal," and nearly twice as many African Americans as whites identify themselves as "liberal." Pooling NES data from 1990 to 2002 to compare whites and Latinos reveals that even using a seven-point ideological scale, Latinos are modestly more liberal than whites. For instance, about 60% of Latinos identify themselves as either extremely liberal, liberal, slightly liberal, liberal, or moderate, compared to about 55% of whites. Unfortunately, the much smaller sample size of the NES does not permit us to use this measure in our analyses, but the greater liberalism of African Americans in the NES suggests that our results may somewhat understate racial differences in representation.
5. The standard deviation of white ideology is 0.93, while the standard deviations of African American and Latino ideology are 0.97 and 0.98, respectively.

While there is certainly some truth to the conventional wisdom that African Americans are more politically cohesive than whites, overwhelmingly supporting the Democratic Party and its candidates (Frymer 1999), there clearly is significant variation among African Americans' (and Latinos) ideological orientations (see also Dawson 1994; Gilliam 1996; Canon 1999; Uhlaner and Garcia 2002; Tate 2003a). Similarly, more Latinos support Democrats than Republicans, but these tendencies clearly do not indicate uniformly liberal ideologies among Latinos. This point has substantive and technical significance. Substantively, if African Americans or Latinos as a group hold a diversity of ideological orientations, simply electing liberal officials (usually Democrats) may not lead to improved representation for all or even most members of minority groups. In addition, it is generally easier to represent a more homogeneous group compared to a group with heterogeneous preferences simply because it is impossible to please everyone (or even a sizeable majority) in a diverse group. Thus, diversity in all three groups poses a representation challenge for any elected representative. More technically, significant ideological variation is important because without sufficient variation within a group's preferences, it is difficult to observe some types of representation as commonly measured by scholars of Congress (e.g., Miller and Stokes 1963; Achen 1978; Bartels 1991; Ansolabehere, Snyder, and Stewart 2001).

It is possible that these ideological differences are driven by large differences in group preferences in just a few states. However, when we look at the state level, we continue to find widespread and significant differences. We must first confront the difficulty that there are relatively few African Americans and Latinos in many states. Fortunately, the NAES provides a sample with at least 50 African Americans and an average of more than 200 African Americans sampled in 26 states, and at least 48 Latinos and an average of more than 250 Latinos in 21 states. These samples provide reasonably valid and reliable estimates of state-level opinions for the three groups, although predictably, the measures were somewhat less reliable for the minority groups.[6] As we proceed with our analysis, we pay particular

6. Under standard definitions of reliability (see Jones and Norrander 1996), state-level mean white attitudes were highly reliable, while African Americans' and Latinos' state-level ideological orientations were less reliable. The reliability coefficient ranges from 0 to 1. Jones and Norrander classify values over .7 as "highly reliable," between .6 and .7 "moderately reliable," and below .6 as "unreliable" (302). The reliability coefficient for white ideology was .97; for African American and Latino ideology, it was .53 and .44, respectively. These state-level ideology measures are highly correlated with the percentage of the 2000 presidential vote George Bush received in the state minus

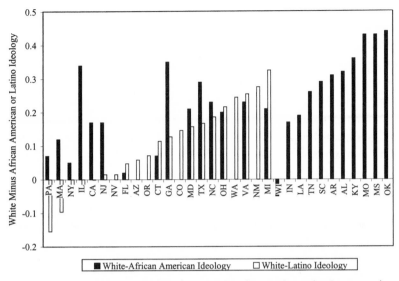

FIGURE 3.2. Bias in state ideology (2000 National Annenberg Election Survey).

attention to the relatively less precise measures of minority group opinion and compensate accordingly.

For now, the important point is that, among NAES respondents, there are significant differences at the state level between whites and African Americans and between whites and Latinos.[7] Figure 3.2 presents the difference between African Americans' and whites' ideology in each state (see black columns) along with the difference between Latinos' and whites' ideology in the relevant states (see white columns). Positive values in figure 3.2 indicate

---

the percentage Al Gore received (r = .93), and Erikson Wright, and McIver's (1993) state ideology measure (r = .94). As an additional validity check, we correlated our measures of white ideology and African American ideology with Erikson, Wright, and McIver's (subsequently, EWM) pooled CBS/*New York Times* data (1978–93). The two measures of white ideology were highly correlated (both .94), while the two measures of African American ideology were somewhat less highly correlated (.58). This may be attributable to the changing attitudinal composition of the African American population (e.g., Dawson 1994; Tate 2003a), given that our data begins more than two decades after EWM's data begins. Furthermore, the geography of state white, African American, and Latino ideology also comports with intuition. For instance, African American ideology is more conservative in the South (FL, LA, NC) and more liberal in the Northeast (MA, NJ, NY) and on the Pacific Coast (CA). Latino ideology is more conservative in Florida and Texas than it is in California.

7. For more on racial differences in state-level preferences, see Norrander (2005).

that the mean white opinion in a state is more conservative than the mean African American or Latino opinion. As a group, African Americans are significantly more liberal than whites in their general orientation toward politics, and in most states this difference is most likely not due to chance alone.[8] In contrast, the difference between Latinos' and whites' ideologies within states is generally quite a bit smaller.[9] Like African Americans, Latinos are more liberal in the majority of states where Latinos and whites exhibit different ideologies. However, in several Northeastern states whites are more conservative than African Americans yet more liberal than Latinos (NY, MA, PA). In about half the states we examine, the difference between white and Latino opinion is statistically significant.[10]

The noticeable variation in the difference between whites' and African Americans' ideologies and whites' and Latinos' ideologies across states begs for explanation. For instance, differences in white and African American ideology appear to be larger in the South than elsewhere. Why states vary in the difference between whites' and minorities' attitudes is an interesting and important question, and insofar as we know, unanswered. However, the principal goal of this study is to examine whether variation in these differences in attitudes relates to the manner in which elected officials vote on public policies, and so for our purposes it is sufficient to demonstrate that these differences exist. There is plenty of ideological disagreement between whites and African Americans and between whites and Latinos within states, and thus the possibility of disparate representation across the full range of issues decided by statewide elected officials.

It is important to note a potential pitfall of our use of ideological orientation to measure minorities' general preferences across many policies. Ideological orientation is generally believed to relate less strongly to some political characteristics such as party identification among Latinos and African Americans as compared to whites (Uhlaner and Garcia 2002, 98;

8. $p < .10$ in 20 of 26 states (two-tailed test). We also compared white and African American ideology using Erikson, Wright, and McIver's pooled CBS/*New York Times* measures of ideology (1976–93), which were measured on a three-point scale. We found that among the 33 states that contained more than 50 African Americans in the EWM data, 27 states show a significant difference between white and African American ideology ($p < .10$).

9. This is not solely driven by Cubans, who tend to be more conservative (Uhlaner and Garcia 2002). Excluding Cubans does not significantly alter the mean for Latino opinion, mostly because there are few Cubans in the NAES sample (191).

10. That is, in 10 of 21 states $p < .10$, two-tailed test. The states with significant differences are CO, GA, MI, NC, NM, OH, PA, TX, VA, and WA.

McClain and Stewart 2002). However, ideological orientation relates similarly to many of the *issue positions* of whites, African Americans (Tate 2003a), and Latinos (Uhlaner, Gray, and Garcia 2000; Uhlaner and Garcia 2002). According to Tate (1993, 31–32), while a substantial proportion of African Americans do not offer an ideological orientation when queried, so that liberal-conservative ideology may not be a useful construct for this group, African Americans who *do* identify themselves as liberal or conservative tend to converge on a common set of reference points for this self-assessment. Namely, like whites who identify themselves as liberal, African Americans who identify themselves as liberal favor equality and social reform, including a commitment to investment in social programs. Similarly, scholars have concluded that ideology "is useful in understanding Latino opinions," even if its usefulness is limited (Uhlaner and Garcia 2002, 99). However, the concern that ideology may be a poorer measure of preferences for minorities is one of several reasons to go beyond general ideological orientations and compare the groups' preferences on specific issues.

AFRICAN AMERICANS' AND WHITES' PREFERENCES ON SPECIFIC ISSUES

Even at the level of specific issues, these three groups exhibit different preferences. We first compare African Americans' and whites' preferences on specific issues; then we compare Latinos' and whites' preferences. Many scholars have examined the specific issue preferences of African Americans and whites, and in many issue areas, these preferences diverge considerably (Tate 1993; Kinder and Sanders 1996; Canon 1999; Kinder and Winter 2001). These groups' mean attitudes differ dramatically on issues directly related to race, such as affirmative action, job discrimination, and civil rights, and somewhat less so on "implicitly racial" issues like education, health care, and welfare spending (Kinder and Sanders 1996; Lublin 1997; Canon 1999). These differences in attitudes may arise from African Americans' "distinctive, and difficult" place in the nation's history (Canon 1999, 21), from "group animosities and solidarities" (Kinder and Sanders 1996, 7; Kinder and Sears 1981), from differences in political values and principles (Sniderman and Piazza 1993; Kinder and Winter 2001), and from the ways elites frame issues (Kinder and Sanders 1996). We need not concern ourselves with the source of these differences in political preferences—it is useful for our analysis simply to know that they are widely agreed to exist. On the other hand, African Americans' and whites' attitudes are believed to differ much less on issues that have

little racial content, such as foreign affairs, immigration, and social issues such as abortion and school prayer (Kinder and Sanders 1996; Canon 1999).

We examine differences in preferences for federal government spending on various types of programs. These include implicitly racial issues such as welfare, education, health care, and crime, as well as potentially race-related issues such as the environment and defense.[11] To make our comparisons, we generally use the 2000 NAES, but for one issue, we draw on comparable NES data.[12] Respondents were asked if the federal government should spend "more, the same, less, or none" in these domains. Using this data, we estimated an ordinary least squares (OLS) model with race (0 white, 1 African American) predicting preferences for increased spending on social security, education, health care insurance, Medicare, aid to mothers with small children, crime, defense, and the environment.[13] From these estimates, we calculated the predicted level of support for increasing spending. If a group's predicted response equals four on this measure, all members of the group favored more spending; if three, the average member of the group favored no change in spending, if two, the average member favored less spending, and if one, no spending at all.

On six of eight issues, we found that African Americans were more likely than whites to prefer more spending (see fig. 3.3; compare the solid lines).

11. Several recent studies have documented instances of "environmental racism": situations that generate racial differences in environmental quality (Camacho 1998; Adamson, Evans, and Stein 2001). Because 21% of U.S. military volunteers are African American, defense spending may have special consequences for minority groups due to their overrepresentation in the armed forces (Fears 2003).

12. The NAES question wording was as follows: "Social Security benefits—should the federal government spend more money, on this, the same as now, less, or no money at all?" Responses are coded from 1 ("no money at all") to 4 ("more money"). The remaining lead-ins were worded as follows: "Providing financial assistance to public elementary and secondary schools"; "Providing health care for people who do not already have it"; "Providing health care for elderly people, usually called Medicare"; "Providing assistance to poor mothers with young children"; "Maintaining a strong military defense"; and "Protecting the environment and natural resources." The environmental item asked if the government should expend more or less effort rather than resources. We use the NES surveys from 1984, 1992, 1994, 1996, 2000, and 2002 to measure preferences for dealing with crime. These use a three-point scale, asking respondents whether spending should be increased, kept the same, or decreased/cut out entirely. For comparability with the NAES items, we coded these 4, 3, and 2 respectively.

13. Ordered probit models yield very similar results, but are more difficult to display graphically.

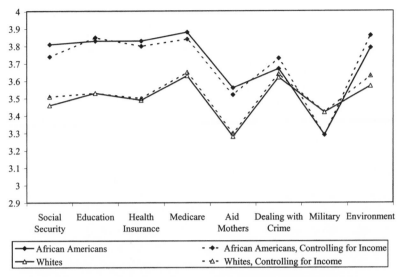

FIGURE 3.3. Predicted support for increasing spending in eight policy areas, whites and African Americans (2000 National Annenberg Election Survey).

The only issues we examined for which whites and African Americans showed similar support for spending were military spending and spending to deal with crime, with whites a little more supportive of spending on the former and African Americans a little more supportive on the latter. In terms of absolute rather than relative levels of support, the average African American was quite near to supporting an increase in spending in five of the eight issue areas, with somewhat less enthusiasm for spending to deal with crime, even less but still substantial support for welfare, and relatively little support for military spending. By comparison, the average white respondent was quite ambivalent about increasing spending in seven of the eight issue areas, with a group mean near 3.5, while the average white favored no increase in spending to help mothers with young children.

We also examined a separate, implicitly racial NAES item related to federal government effort rather than spending per se: whether the respondent believed that the government should or should not try to reduce income differences between rich and poor Americans. We found that 69% of African Americans thought that this should be a goal of government, while only 46% of whites thought so.

Notably, where differences in political attitudes exist, they do not appear to be reducible to differences in income. Indeed, one study found that

the estimated size of the racial gap in opinion between whites and African Americans on explicitly racial policies such as fair employment, federal spending on programs that assist African Americans, and the preferential hiring of African Americans was not reduced at all after accounting for family income, level of educational attainment, and occupational status (Kinder and Sanders 1996, 299; see also Kinder and Winter 2001). In the NAES, we similarly found that African Americans' greater liberalism regarding the government's proper level of involvement in preventing job discrimination against African Americans as well as whether the Confederate flag should be removed from the South Carolina state capitol building were robust to a control for income.[14]

When we control for income in the models of spending preferences, the racial divide remains vast, as the dashed lines in figure 3.3 indicate. The differences in preferences among lower-income whites and African Americans were only slightly attenuated, so racial differences in spending preferences are not simply proxying differences in income groups' preferences. The same is true for preferences about government attempts to reduce income inequality. Among whites and African Americans earning less than $35,000 per year, 74% of African Americans agreed that this should be a goal of government, compared to 57% of whites. In sum, even on many implicitly racial issues such as federal spending on welfare, health insurance, and education, African Americans and whites who share the same income express rather distinctive preferences, creating the possibility for unequal representation on these issues.

These patterns of spending preferences are also found in the GSS and Roper surveys that we use in later analyses. Beginning in 1972, in most years the GSS has queried citizens about their preferences for government spending in nine issue areas useful for our analysis: national defense, the environment, education, crime prevention, health care, foreign aid, welfare, aid to cities, and the space program. Respondents were asked, "We are faced with many problems in this country, none of which can be solved easily or inexpensively. I'm going to name some of these problems, and for each one I'd like you to tell me whether you think we're spending too much money on it,

---

14. In an ordered probit model of the job-discrimination item, the parameter estimate for an African American indicator was 1.31 in a bivariate model. Controlling for income, the estimate for the African American indicator fell just to 1.25. In a probit model of the Confederate flag item, the parameter estimate for an African American indicator was 0.78 in a bivariate model, and actually rose to 0.90 in a model controlling for income.

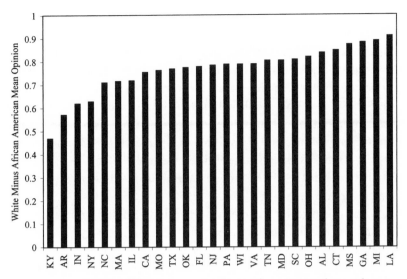

FIGURE 3.4. State-level bias on race-related issues (2000 National Annenberg Election Survey).

too little money, or about the right amount."[15] Unfortunately, the GSS did not go to great effort to distinguish Latino respondents from the "other" category until 2000, so we rely exclusively on the Roper surveys in our analyses of Latinos. In the GSS/Roper surveys, African Americans continue to favor increased spending more than do whites. Latinos are again closer to whites, but tend to favor increased spending to a greater degree than do whites.

These national-level differences in specific issue preferences extend to the states as well. We generated a state-level measure of opinion on these kinds of racial and implicitly racial issues for whites and African Americans. Using principal components factor analysis, we combined responses to two NAES items concerning race-related issues: whether the federal government should do more to end job discrimination against African Americans, and whether poverty is a serious national problem.[16] Figure

15. This statement was followed by these phrases: "space exploration program," "halting the rising crime rate," "improving and protecting the environment," "improving and protecting the nation's health," "solving the problems of the big cities," "improving the nation's education system," "the military, armaments, and defense," "foreign aid," and "welfare."

16. The exact item wordings follow: "Trying to stop job discrimination against blacks—should the federal government do more about this, the same as now, less, or

3.4 presents the racial differences in citizens' "racial ideologies" across the twenty-six states for which we have already observed differences in whites' and African Americans' overall ideological orientations. Again, positive scores indicate that whites are more conservative than African Americans.

In every state, the mean white opinion on these issues is more conservative than the mean African American opinion, and in all twenty-six states the difference in means is statistically significant ($p < .01$; two-tailed test). There is also some variation in the racial bias of opinion on these issues, with several southern states (LA, GA, MS, AL) exhibiting some of the greatest differences between whites and African Americans, and several northeastern states (MA, NY) exhibiting some of the smallest differences.

LATINOS' AND WHITES' PREFERENCES ON SPECIFIC ISSUES

Next, we compare the preferences of Latinos and whites on specific issues. Before doing so, however, we confront the reality that "Latino opinion" is something of a misnomer, because the Mexican, Puerto Rican, Cuban, and other Latino populations that comprise this group often differ markedly in their attitudes (e.g., De la Garza et al. 1992; Leal 2002). Rather than an obstacle to measuring differences in political representation, however, this as an analytical advantage. If we wish to observe whether senators are responsive to variation in Latino attitudes across the country, that is, whether states with conservative Latinos have more conservative senators than states with more liberal Latinos, there must be variation in Latino attitudes. Moreover, there is considerable variation in whites' and African Americans' preferences, yet we do not hesitate to define these as politically relevant groups.

There appear to be "more differences than similarities in the opinions of Anglos and Latinos" (Leal 2002, 33; see also Uhlaner and Garcia 2002). In general, prior studies find that Latinos are somewhat more liberal than whites on a variety of policies, including bilingual education and affirmative action (Leal 2002; De la Garza et al. 1992; Uhlaner and Garcia 2002). We

---

nothing at all?"; and "The amount of poverty in the United States—is this an extremely serious problem, serious, not too serious, or not serious at all?" This analysis retained one principal factor (eigenvalue = 1.54), with factor loadings of 0.56 and 0.57 for the two items. We then generated a factor score for each NAES respondent (both white and African American) answering both items, and used the state white and African American means of these scores to measure racial groups' state-level preferences on race and race-related issues.

extend these investigations to the same issue domains in which we compared whites' and African Americans' preferences above.

To compare the gap in white/Latino opinion on specific issues to that in
white/African American opinion and to determine the extent to which differences in white/Latino opinion are explained by differences in income, we
return to questions about government spending in the eight issue domains
used above, this time comparing whites and Latinos. As figure 3.5 shows,
Latinos are quite a bit more favorable than whites toward increased spending for education and welfare aid to mothers with dependent children (compare solid lines). There are other issue differences, but the gaps between
the two groups are not as great as we observed between whites and African
Americans in figure 3.3. Also, in contrast to what we observed in figure 3.3,
Latinos and whites have a somewhat greater difference in preferences on
spending to deal with crime. Finally, income appears to account for somewhat more of the gap in white/Latino opinion than the gap in white/Afri-
can American opinion (see dashed lines). Still, there are clear differences in
white and Latino opinion, even within income groups.

As we did above, we also examined whether white or Latino respondents
were more likely to believe that the government should try to reduce income differences between rich and poor Americans. We found that 68% of
Latinos thought that this should be a goal of government, while only 46% of

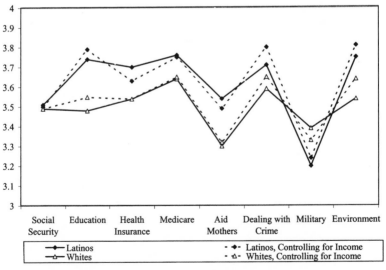

FIGURE 3.5. Predicted support for increasing spending in eight policy areas,
whites and Latinos (2000 National Annenberg Election Survey).

whites thought so; this difference in opinion was modestly smaller among lower-income Latinos and whites (74% to 57%, respectively). Finally, we compared white and Latino opinion in one additional area—immigration. It appears that Latinos are only a little more liberal than whites on immigration policy, with nearly identical proportions of whites and Latinos indicating that the rate of immigration to the United States is an extremely serious problem (27%) and only about 4% more Latinos than whites indicating that immigration is not a problem at all. This is consistent with what prior studies have found (Uhlaner and Garcia 2002).

To sum up, we have seen that in their general ideological orientations, African Americans are more liberal than whites. This is true across the nation as a whole, as well as within at least half of the nation's states. These differences extend to preferences for government action on specific issues. African Americans and whites differ most on spending for welfare, health care, education, and the environment, with smaller differences on defense spending. In some issue areas, both whites and African Americans prefer more spending, but as a group African Americans are more in favor of increased spending than whites, while in other areas, only African Americans prefer more spending. Latinos are more liberal in their general ideological outlooks than whites, but less liberal than African Americans. Latinos differ most from whites in their attitudes toward spending on education, spending to reduce income differences, and spending to deal with crime. Finally, minorities' distinctive preferences are not explained away by income differences across groups. These differences in many of the issue positions create the possibility that some groups are better represented in the decisions of government, and that we can uncover evidence of this disparate representation in some issue domains.

DIFFERENCES IN ISSUE PRIORITIES

In the areas where we have observed differences in the issue *positions* of these groups, we will also want to know if there are differences in their issue *priorities*. To answer this question, we must identify issues that are of higher priority for African Americans and Latinos, that is, issues that these groups find more salient than do whites. Note that this task differs from that of identifying the most salient issues for African Americans and Latinos. An issue might be very salient for one of these groups, but if it is also very salient for whites, its *relative* salience for the minority group is quite small.

Not surprisingly, prior studies have shown significant differences in the salience of issues to racial groups. African Americans place a higher priority on civil rights issues than do whites, and members of Congress are thus more responsive to the size of their African American constituency on these issues (Iyengar 1990; Hutchings 1998). In addition, the size of African American constituencies appears to be related to congressional voting on social welfare issues, which suggests that these issues may also be more salient for African Americans than for whites (Hutchings, McClerking, and Charles 2004; Whitby and Krause 2001).

Comparisons of the issue priorities of whites and Latinos have identified three issue areas that are more salient for Latinos: education, economic security, and crime (Martin 2000; Uhlaner and Garcia 2002). It is not hard to imagine why these may be more salient issues for Latinos, given the economic, residential, and educational status of this group. Notably, we have already observed (fig. 3.5) that whites and Latinos differ substantially in their attitudes on spending to improve education, to reduce income differences, and to deal with crime. Whites and Latinos not only have quite different preferences on these issues, but the salience of these issues is relatively greater for Latinos.

We can elucidate these differences more fully. The most common technique scholars have used to identify individuals' issue priorities within a survey context is to ask respondents to name "the most important problem [hereinafter MIP] facing this country" (e.g. Smith 1985a and 1985b; Uhlaner and Garcia 2002). We can also refer to issue-specific measures of issue salience in which respondents are asked to judge the urgency of a single issue without comparing it to others.

We first compared the open-ended responses of whites, African Americans, and Latinos to the MIP item used by the NES from 1974 to 2000. To do so, we calculated the proportion of each group's respondents identifying welfare (or one of its synonyms), education, health care, crime, national defense, or the environment as the nation's most important problem.[17] We then divided the percentage of African American responses by the percentage of white responses in each policy category, and the percentage of Latino responses by the percentage of white responses in each policy category. Finally, we calculated the natural log of these ratios. If an equal proportion

17. We use the following response codes for NES variable number VCF0875b to form the binary indicators: welfare (60, 61, 63, and 90); national defense (700); the environment (150, 151, 153); health care (40); crime (340, 360), and education (20).

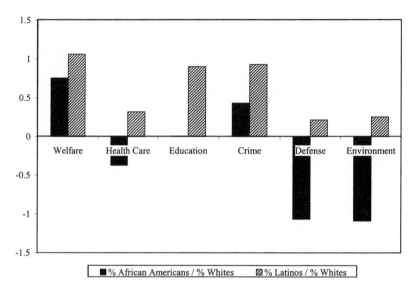

FIGURE 3.6. Relative issue salience across groups (American National Election Studies, 1974–2000).

of whites and African Americans identified an issue as the nation's most important, this measure equals 0. If twice as many African Americans as whites identified an issue as most important, this measure equals 0.69, if half as many –0.69, and so on. The results are summarized in figure 3.6.

Welfare policy has been the nation's most important problem for more than twice as many African Americans as whites, and nearly three times as many Latinos as whites. Latinos were 2.5 times as likely as whites to identify crime as the nation's most important problem, while African Americans were 1.5 times more likely. Latinos were about 2.5 times as likely as whites to mention education as the nation's most important problem, while African Americans and whites were about equally likely to do so. Latinos were somewhat more likely than whites to name health care as the nation's most important problem, while African Americans were a little less likely than whites to do so. However, other surveys find that African Americans are more concerned about health care than are whites. Finally, both national defense and the environment were much less often identified as national problems by African Americans than by whites, while the salience of these issues for Latinos and whites was fairly similar.

In the case of African Americans, these results uncover one clear issue area that is more salient for African Americans—welfare—and two others

where we will see that the evidence is more mixed—health care and crime. These findings generally match the observations of political commentators who focus on the African American community.[18] In the case of Latinos, these findings also largely confirm prior studies: education, economic security, and crime are more salient issues for Latinos than for whites. In addition, Latinos appear to be more concerned than whites about health care. These findings also largely reflect the state of Latinos' priorities today. According to a 2004 survey of Latinos commissioned by the National Council of La Raza (NCLR) and conducted by Zogby International, 34% of Latinos thought that education was the most important issue facing the Latino community, while 22% identified the economy and jobs as the most important issue. Health care was also one of the top five issues identified.

These findings largely match another measure of issue salience. The NAES asks to what extent respondents believe that poverty, the "number of criminals who are not punished enough," and "the number of Americans without health insurance" are extremely serious problems. As figure 3.7 shows, only 29% of whites considered poverty an extremely serious problem, compared to 36% of Latinos and 46% of African Americans, a difference of 7 and 17 percentage points, respectively. A larger proportion of Latinos than whites thought that crime was an extremely serious problem, while (in some contrast to what we observed in fig. 3.6) about equal proportions of whites and African Americans viewed crime as an extremely serious problem. Finally, a far larger proportion of African Americans (55%) than whites (36%) thought that the number of individuals without health insurance was an extremely serious problem. In the NAES, a greater proportion of Latinos than whites were concerned about health insurance. Latinos' focus on health care costs is also reflected in the NCLR survey, with 72% of those surveyed indicating that obtaining health insurance was a "big problem" for Hispanics in their area. Ultimately, we focus on three issues as being at least potentially more salient for African Americans than whites: welfare, crime, and health care. Likewise, we consider these three issues, along with education, as distinctively salient to Latinos.

Next, we develop a measure of the overall importance of issues that incorporates both the relative importance of issues to each group and the ab-

18. According to Ronald Walters, in February 2004 five issues were most important for African Americans: jobs and economic well-being, including welfare reform; criminal justice; education; health care; and the war in Iraq. See his comments on the MSNBC Web site: http://msnbc.msn.com/id/4137295/.

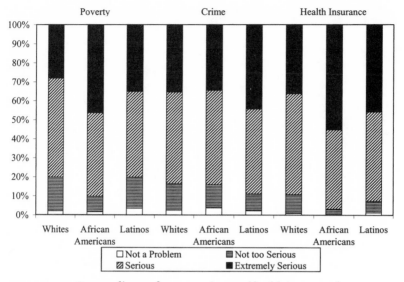

FIGURE 3.7. Group salience of poverty, crime, and health insurance (2000 National Annenberg Election Survey).

solute importance of issues for each group. Our previous focus on relative importance was intended to establish a set of expectations regarding which issues might properly be evaluated under the pluralist standard of equality, which stresses that minority groups should enjoy more than proportional representation on issues that are more salient for them than they are for whites. Because we should not simply ignore the absolute importance of issues for groups, we developed an "impact score" that reflects both the relative and absolute importance of issues to groups. This "impact score" takes the percentage of all NES respondents in a minority group who identified an issue as most important and multiplies it by the ratio of this percentage to the percentage of whites who did the same (see fig. 3.8). This score shows that welfare and crime have the largest overall impact on African Americans, while welfare, health care, education, and crime have the greatest impact on Latinos in an overall sense. These impacts mirror what we observe in figures 3.6 and 3.7, but provide an important robustness check.

CONCLUSION

In summary, African Americans and whites differ over what government should do. They hold different ideological orientations and disagree about

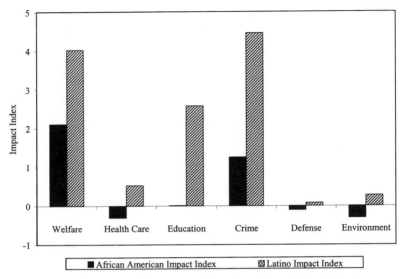

FIGURE 3.8. Impact scores for group salience (American National Election Studies, 1974–2000).

a host of racially related policies, including welfare, education, health care, and the environment. We also have established that Latinos and whites hold different ideological orientations and disagree about many policies, including welfare, education, health care, and crime expenditures. Moreover, we have seen that welfare, crime, and health care may be more salient to African Americans than whites, while education, income security, health care, and crime are more salient issues for Latinos than for whites. Finally, these differences in political preferences are not simply a reflection of differences in income. In fact, differences in political preferences are usually just as large even when we compare individuals within groups who have similar incomes.

As we have observed time and again, Latinos, African Americans, and whites view the political world very differently. By and large, these groups want government to do different things and to focus its energies on different issues. These differences in political preferences create the possibility that government will follow some groups' agendas and ignore others. When one group prefers more spending in an area and another prefers less, which group's views carry the day? Testing whether the potential for political inequality between groups is realized in the policies of government is the task of the next chapter.

FOUR

Differences in Policy Representation

In 2003, the poverty rate for whites was 8%, while the rate for African Americans and Latinos was approximately three times higher: 24% and 23%, respectively. Approximately 10% of white children lived in poverty, compared to 33% of African American children and 40% of Latino children. In the same year, 11% of whites did not have medical insurance. The proportion of African Americans without health insurance was nearly double that of whites (20%),[1] and the proportion of uninsured Latinos was about triple that of whites (33%).[2] According to the National Assessment of Educational Progress (NAEP) in 2000, 92% of whites ages 18–24 had completed high school, while only 84% of African Americans and 64% of Latinos had done so. Seventeen-year-old African Americans' scores on the NAEP reading scale were 10% lower than whites' scores, while Latinos' scores were 9% lower. On the NAEP math scale, African Americans scored 10% lower and Latinos 7% lower than whites.[3]

From economic security to health care and education, racial and ethnic minorities in the United States fare far worse than whites. These disparities have many sources, but in its policy choices government can either attempt to ameliorate or blindly exacerbate them. Each year the federal government passes a budget and decides how much effort (if any) to commit to reducing

---

1. In December 2004, the *American Journal of Public Health* reported that 886,000 more African Americans died between 1991 and 2000 than would have died had equal health care been available.

2. Income and health insurance data are reported by the U.S. Census. See DeNavas-Walt, Proctor, and Mills 2004. For the U.S. Census Bureau data, see the bureau's Web site: http://www.census.gov/hhes/www/income.html.

3. See "Status and Trends in the Education of Blacks" on the Web site of the National Center for Education Statistics: http://nces.ed.gov/pubs2003/2003034.pdf.

income inequality through its income tax and entitlement programs, how much effort (if any) to devote to producing race-neutral health outcomes by subsidizing health insurance, and whether to direct additional resources toward minority educational programs. If it were up to members of minority groups, many government policies would be different. For instance, each year the Congressional Black Caucus releases an "Alternative Federal Budget" that it believes would better reflect the issue concerns and priorities of the African American community.[4] Moreover, as we saw in the last chapter, African American and Latino citizens' preferences for government spending often differ dramatically from whites' preferences.

In this chapter, we ask which groups "govern" the ultimate output of government actions—public policies. This chapter is devoted to answering three questions. First, do whites' preferences predict federal policies better than the preferences of minorities? Second, how much better a predictor are whites' preferences? Third, if whites are more often policy "winners," is this simply a function of whites' generally higher income levels and levels of political involvement?

"COLLECTIVE" AND "DYADIC" REPRESENTATION

We begin our investigation of the extent of each group's representation by looking at one specific type of representation, "collective" representation, which considers "representation in terms of *institutions* collectively representing a people" (Weissberg 1978, 535; emphasis in original). That is, we examine the degree to which the outputs of the policymaking process as a whole reflect citizens' preferences. In later chapters, we explore the link between individual senators and members of the House of Representatives and their particular constituents. This relationship between individual members and their constituents, commonly referred to as "dyadic" representation, tends to be the focus of studies of policy representation. However, collective representation is an important place to start for a number of reasons. First, studying the connections between minority preferences and actual government policy is vital because the link between public opinion and the final decisions of government holds a fundamental place in democratic theory. As V.O. Key stated, "Unless mass views have some place in the shaping of policy, all the talk about democracy is nonsense" (Key 1961, 7).

---

4. For an example, see the Web site of the U.S. House: http://www.house.gov/scott/legislative/issues/CBC%20ALT%20BUDGET%20FY2007.html.

Public policies are at the heart of whether government ultimately responds to the preferences of citizens or does not. Policies, much more than the roll-call votes or other activities of members of Congress (MCs), affect the well-being of citizens—their education, health care, housing, and economic security, among other things. According to Verba (2003, 666), "Political equality in its fullest sense would be equal policy output."

Second, as Robert Weissberg notes, "whether or not a particular legislator follows his or her constituency is an important question, but this question is not necessarily the most appropriate one if we ask, 'do representatives represent?'" (1978, 547). There may be important differences in the extent to which constituents are represented in the collective and dyadic senses. On one hand, some constituents may be better represented by their particular members of Congress than they are by the House of Representatives or the Senate as a whole. Liberals in Massachusetts or conservatives in Arizona may find their policy preferences perfectly represented by the liberal Senator Edward Kennedy (D-MA) or the conservative Senator John Kyl (R-AZ). However, the decisions made by the Senate as a whole and ultimately the policies forged collectively by the Senate, House, and president, may be far from what these constituents prefer.

On the other hand, Weissberg (1978) shows that constituents are generally better represented by Congress as a whole than they are by their individual members. This is because it is difficult for any individual to represent almost seven hundred thousand constituents in a congressional district even if he or she wanted to. However, it is likely that of the 435 members of the House, one or more of them hold views and engage in activities that match relatively closely those of each of the seven hundred thousand constituents in a particular district. This may be especially true for African American or Latino MCs, some of whom explicitly seek to represent members of their group who are not in their home district. For example, Tate (2003a, 126) notes that "when Adam Clayton Powell of New York was one of two Blacks serving in Washington, he dealt with problems from Blacks all over the country, and not just those who had elected him, his Harlem constituents." She also argues that "the Congressional Black Caucus would declare its mission as national" as opposed to the local concerns of each particular member's district (Tate 2003a, 126–27). In the end, then, evidence that individual representatives act more in line with the preferences of their white constituents than their minority constituents may not mean that minority constituents are less well off in terms of collective policy outputs. A liberal Latino constituent represented by a

conservative MC is poorly represented in dyadic terms, but this does not guarantee poor representation in collective terms.

As we noted in chapter 2, there are plenty of reasons to expect that whites are advantaged in the policy process, including their numerical superiority, greater resources, and greater involvement in public affairs. Our aim here is to test whether whites actually do find their preferences for policy realized more often than do African Americans or Latinos. However much we might anticipate that whites are advantaged in the policy process, this does not obviate the need for us to document the *extent* of whites' advantage. Using measures of the public's spending preferences from 1972 to 2002 and actual federal budget outlays from fiscal years 1972–2003, we evaluate whether whites are more likely than African Americans and Latinos to have their preferences realized in policy outcomes.

DEMAND FOR GOVERNMENT SPENDING AND GOVERNMENTAL RESPONSE

In our first investigation of relative political representation, we examine whether African Americans' and Latinos' preferences for change or stability in policy are translated into actual policy change or maintenance to the same degree that whites' preferences are. Examining the extent of policy responsiveness requires clear indicators of government policy and clear measures of public preferences about policy. These are not available for all government policies. Survey organizations do not typically ask the public its preferences on many of the technical details of government policies. Furthermore, policies often do not lend themselves to easy mapping onto survey items. For instance, it is difficult to say how much "more" gun control the Brady Bill established, and how much "more" environmental regulation the Clean Air Act produced.

Federal spending decisions meet the needs of this type of analysis. Since 1972, survey organizations have regularly asked rather specific questions about the public's desire for more, less, or the same amount of federal spending in various policy domains each year. These are specific questions about the preferred course of policy. In addition, the federal government must make decisions about how much to spend in various domains every year via the budget process. Thus, we can analyze specific public opinion questions and policy decisions at regular intervals. Furthermore, because both the survey questions and spending decisions pertain to specific issue domains, we can examine the link between preferences and policy across several issues.

Our specific measure of policy outputs is annual federal expenditures as recorded in the U.S. budget (fiscal years 1972–2003) in billions of dollars.[5] In this chapter, we analyze outlays in six policy domains: national defense, the environment, education, foreign aid, aid to big cities, and the space program. These policy areas were selected primarily because citizens have regularly been surveyed about their spending preferences in these domains. These are also domains that are *not* more salient for African Americans than whites (as we saw in chapter 3), and we wish first to compare racial groups' representation in domains that are either equally salient for the groups or more salient for whites than minorities.[6] We compare the policy representation of whites and African Americans on welfare, health care, and crime policy—the domains in which their preferences differ and where the issue appears more salient for African Americans—in chapter 6. For the same reason, we do not compare whites' and Latinos' representation on education, crime, health care, and welfare policy in this chapter.[7]

Our measures of public spending preferences are drawn from surveys the GSS and the Roper Organization conducted, which we introduced and discussed in chapter 3. Our data for African Americans' preferences are primarily drawn from the GSS (1972–1994, 1996, 1998, 2000, and 2002), supplemented with three years of data from the Roper survey in years in which the GSS was not conducted (1979, 1981, and 1992) and before the Roper series was discontinued in 1994. In contrast, all our data for comparing the

---

5. See Office of Management and Budget 2004. See also the White House Web site: http://www.whitehouse.gov/omb/budget/fy2005/pdf/hist.pdf.

6. We did not discuss preferences for spending on foreign aid, space exploration, or big cities in chapter 3 because these were not queried in the NAES. In the GSS, the three groups held different spending preferences in these areas. There were no differences across the groups in terms of the salience of these issues. In fact, in each case less than 0.1% of NES respondents identified one of these issues as most important between 1974 and 1986, and no one mentioned any of these issues after that. These issues are not differentially salient for racial and ethnic groups, nor are they salient for any of the groups in an absolute sense.

7. To determine if budget line items should be assigned to an issue domain, we closely followed Wlezien (2004). Education spending included spending on elementary, secondary, and vocational education, higher education, and research and general educational aids; foreign aid included international development and humanitarian assistance, as well as international security assistance; aid to cities included community-development spending and area and regional development; welfare spending included housing assistance, food and nutrition assistance, and other income security. The remaining domains included all spending itemized in the budget function/subfunction.

representation of whites and Latinos is drawn from the Roper series, because the GSS did not include a specific survey question to identify Latino respondents until 2000. These measures of Latino opinion begin in 1979, after the Roper series began to query respondents about whether they were "Hispanic," and conclude in 1994.[8]

By mapping the opinion data onto the expenditure data, we identify whether individuals were on the "winning" side of federal budget decisions in a series of policy domains in the year the individual was surveyed.[9] Specifically, if a respondent desired more (less) spending in an issue area and federal outlays increased (decreased) more than 5% in constant dollars, then we call that respondent a "winner" in that issue area. For that same issue and year, we call respondents who desired no change in spending "losers." Finally, we affectionately call respondents who preferred less (more) spending "big losers."[10] We consider citizens who desired no increase in spending in a policy domain winners if the percentage change in outlays in the following fiscal year was between a 5% increase or decrease.[11]

WHITES, AFRICAN AMERICANS, AND "POLICY WINNING"

We begin by assessing whether African Americans are less likely than whites to be on the "winning side" of policy decisions. We simply tabulate the proportion of whites and African Americans who are winners, losers, and big losers in each policy domain. The results of these tabulations indicate that in some issue areas African Americans are less likely than whites to be policy winners (see fig. 4.1). In three of the six policy domains—defense, aid to big cities, and space exploration—African Americans are clearly less likely to be winners than whites. Moreover, African Americans were much more likely than whites to be big losers on spending for defense, aid to big

8. We opted to pool the smaller GSS and Roper survey samples over time rather than using the larger NAES sample because the pooling approach allows us to gain a sense of whether racial minorities have *generally* been policy winners or losers in a domain averaged over a number of years, whereas the NAES only permits us to form comparisons between racial groups for fiscal year 2001, for which the budget may or may not be indicative of spending decisions in prior and subsequent years.

9. For a similar approach see Hajnal, Gerber, and Louch (2002).

10. One difficulty in using this approach arises when spending does not change. In those years, the measure of policy "winning" does not have the same range, because there are no "big losers."

11. We experimented with various cutoff points for defining policy winners and losers. The 5% cutoff we use here tends to generate more conservative results.

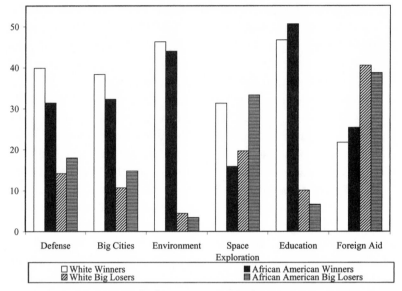

FIGURE 4.1. Percentage of policy winners and big losers, whites and African Americans, 1972–2002 (Office of Management and Budget 2004; General Social Surveys, 1972–1994, 1996, 1998, 2002; Roper polls, 1979, 1981, 1992).

cities, and space exploration. In one area, the environment, whites have a narrower advantage. In two areas, education and foreign aid, African Americans are a little more likely than whites to be winners.

Whites were quite a bit more likely to be winners in outlays for defense— nearly 40% of whites were winners in this domain, compared to around 31% of African Americans. A sizeable proportion (18%) of African Americans were "big losers" on defense spending, compared to 14% of whites. In general, these individuals preferred less spending on defense when defense spending increased significantly. On spending for big cities and space exploration, white winners outpaced African American winners somewhat less. Where 38% of whites were winners on aid to big cities, 32% of African Americans were winners. Moreover, a greater proportion of African Americans (15%) than whites (11%) were big losers in this domain. Most dramatically, about one in three whites were winners on space exploration, but only about 16% of African Americans were winners. Moreover, one in three African Americans were "big losers"—most of whom wanted less spending when outlays rose over 5%. Not only were "big losers" double the number of winners for African Americans, but the percentage of African American "big losers" was

14 points greater than the percentage of white "big losers." Of the domains we examined, African Americans' preferences are reflected least well in the domain of space exploration, both in absolute terms (the raw percentage of African American winners compared to other domains) and in relative terms (the difference in African American winners compared to white winners).

On the environment, whites hold a smaller advantage over African Americans—46% of whites were winners, while about 44% of African Americans were winners. In chapter 5, we probe this small difference further, asking whether whites and African Americans are equally proximate to their representatives using votes identified by the League of Conservation Voters as key roll calls. As we will see, whites' preferences tend to be much better reflected in Congressional roll-call voting on the environment.

Finally, there are two domains where African Americans are somewhat more likely to be policy winners: spending on education and foreign aid. Three factors may account for African Americans' unexpected advantage regarding education. First, these results may suggest that it is a more important domain for this group than our figures in chapter 3 reflect. For instance, a recent book-length study of African American and Latino representation in four northeastern cities focused on these groups' representation in two policy domains: education and public safety (Burns 2006). Its justification for doing so was that "these issue areas strongly affect traditionally excluded groups" (8). Moreover, as noted above, political scientist Ronald Walters recently identified education as one of the five most important issues for the African American community.[12]

Second, it may be that office holders respond to the priorities of minority groups in general, rather than group by group. Since many of the issues Latinos and African Americans care about more than whites do are the same (e.g., welfare, crime, health care), office holders may assume that any issue especially salient to Latinos is also especially salient to African Americans. As we saw in chapter 3, education is more often salient to Latinos compared to whites, but not to African Americans, at least according to our data. Officeholders may be assuming that education is also especially salient to African Americans.

Note that the first two factors that may account for this unexpected finding suggest that education is either actually more salient for African Americans than whites (even though our data do not show this) or that officeholders perceive it to be distinctively salient to African Americans. A

12. See, http://msnbc.msn.com/id/4137295/.

third account accepts that education is not more salient to African Americans compared to whites and that officeholders realize this. However, African Americans may benefit from Latinos' more intense preferences on education issues. We will see in chapter 6 that on issues distinctively salient for minority groups, those groups tend to be equally represented—or even better represented—compared to whites. In fact, we will see that Latinos tend to win almost as much as whites do on education spending. African Americans may benefit from this because African Americans' preferences for spending on education are far closer to those of Latinos than to those of whites. Therefore, if Latinos are winners on education spending, many African Americans will also be winners.

Finally, a slightly larger percentage of African Americans than whites were winners on foreign aid: 25% to 22%. However, neither whites nor African Americans do particularly well when it comes to foreign aid. We found fewer winners on foreign aid than on any other issue we examined. In fact, about 40% of each group were big losers on foreign aid. So, the one domain in which African Americans are somewhat more likely than whites to be winners is also the domain in which African Americans are least likely to be winners at all. For the most part, both African Americans and whites wanted less or the same amount of spending when outlays remained the same or rose significantly. This pattern is presumably a product of Americans' tendency to vastly overestimate the amount that the United States spends on foreign aid each year (Gilens 2001).

WHITES, LATINOS, AND "POLICY WINNING"

Next, we assess whether Latinos are less likely than whites to be winners with regard to policy decisions. There are reasons to believe that Latinos may fare better than African Americans relative to whites, and other reasons to believe that they may fare worse. On the one hand, we saw in chapter 3 that, compared to the preferences of African Americans, Latinos' preferences generally are less different from those of whites. This relative similarity dampens differences in the frequency of winning between whites and Latinos. On the other hand, Latinos are confronted by unique obstacles to political representation that African Americans do not face. The most important of these is that many Latinos are not citizens and thus cannot legally vote. In addition, English is not the first language for many Latinos. These factors limit Latinos' electoral clout and their likelihood of communicating their preferences to elected officials, which are two important routes to political representation.

Our approach to comparing whites' and Latinos' rates of winning parallels that which we have just seen for whites and African Americans, with two departures. First, we rely exclusively on the Roper data for these analyses because the GSS did not clearly identify Latino respondents for most of the period under study. Second, in addition to reserving the analysis of welfare, health care, and crime spending, we reserve discussion of spending on *education* for chapter 6 because this issue is more salient for Latinos than for whites. Respondents are coded as Latino if they identified themselves as "Hispanic" in the Roper surveys, and they are coded as white if they were self-identified whites who did not also identify themselves as Hispanic. Because the sample sizes of Latinos are smaller than those of African Americans in our comparisons of whites' and African Americans' rates of winning, we are less confident in these results. Despite the need for caution, the results prove enlightening.

When we tabulate policy "winners" among whites and Latinos, we again find that in some domains Latinos are less likely to be policy winners (see fig. 4.2). Latinos are quite a bit less likely than whites to see their preferences realized in policy on national defense and environmental regulation, and somewhat less likely to be policy winners on foreign aid. On the other hand, Latinos are roughly equally likely to be policy winners on aid to big cities and space exploration.[13]

Looking at the specific results, we see some of the patterns we saw when comparing African Americans and whites. In the three domains where a greater percentage of whites than Latinos were winners, the gap was between 3 and 7 points. White winners outpaced Latino winners by just under 7 points on defense spending (36.3% to 29.7%), by 5 points on environmental spending (45% to 40%), and by 3 points on foreign aid (34% to 31%). These differences are generally smaller than the differences between whites and African Americans that we observed in figure 4.1. Also in contrast to African Americans, the percentage of Latino "big losers" substantially exceeds the percentage of white "big losers" in just one domain, aid to big cities. In summary, Latinos were less likely than whites to be winners in three of

---

13. The predicted probabilities for whites are a bit different than those in figure 4.1. This is likely due to different data sources (GSS versus Roper) and different time periods of study. For our primary purpose of assessing the relative representation of different groups, the relative probability of winning between whites and Latinos (or whites and African Americans), rather than the absolute probability of winning, is the critical measure.

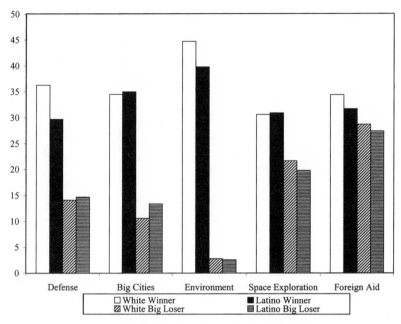

FIGURE 4.2. Percentage of policy winners and big losers, whites and Latinos, 1979–1994 (Office of Management and Budget 2004; Roper polls, 1979–1994).

five domains and were more likely to be big losers in a fourth domain (aid to big cities).

INCOME AND POLICY WINNING

Returning now to the comparison of whites and African Americans, recall that in the four domains in which whites win more often, the percentage of white winners outpaced the percentage of African American winners by 2 to 10 points. Each of these differences (except environmental spending) is statistically significant at the .05 level. Substantively, does this 2–10-point gap constitute a "big" difference, one we should be concerned about? One way to judge this is to compare the difference in the probability of winning for two demographic groups where we would anticipate that one group should be much more politically influential than the other. There has long been a belief and concern that groups with higher incomes exert greater influence in politics than those with lower incomes (e.g., Schattschneider 1960; Gilens 2005; Bartels 2008). In order to compare the racial differences in policy representation that we have found to income differences in representation, in

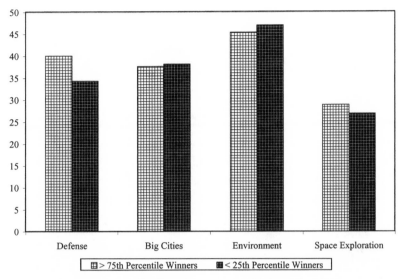

FIGURE 4.3. Percentage of policy winners among high- and low-income respondents (Office of Management and Budget 2004; General Social Surveys, 1972–1994, 1996, 1998, 2002).

the same four domains we compared predicted probabilities of being policy winners between GSS respondents whose income in constant dollars was above the seventy-fifth percentile of the income distribution and respondents who were located below the twenty-fifth percentile of the income distribution (see fig. 4.3).[14]

Although the higher income group (white checked columns) was sometimes more successful in getting its preferred outcome, this was not always the case. For outlays on the environment and big cities, higher-income respondents were not systematically more likely to be policy winners at all. While higher-income respondents were more likely to be policy winners in two domains—defense and space exploration—in these domains the racial differences in the likelihood of winning we have uncovered were equal to or greater than the income differences. In general, the "policy winning gap" between African Americans and whites is greater than that between the wealthy and the poor.

14. We employ only the GSS data because the Roper data report income using a different scale, one that is not comparable over time. We do not report big losers for presentational reasons, but note that lower-income earners were somewhat more likely to be big losers on defense, crime, and space exploration spending.

Our analysis of race and policy representation thus far only indicates general differences between African Americans and whites, without taking income into account. We know that African Americans tend to earn lower incomes than whites, and, as we have just seen, lower-income earners tend to be less well represented in some domains (see also Gilens 2005; Bartels 2008). To get a sense of the direct effect of race on an individual's probability of being a policy winner, in the four domains where we have observed that whites are more likely than African Americans to be policy winners, we tabulated the proportion of each racial group that was a policy winner among respondents with high (greater than the 75th percentile), middle (less than the 75th percentile and greater than the 25th percentile), and low (less than the 25th percentile) incomes, where incomes were measured in constant dollars. These tabulations indicate the extent to which race and related factors such as relative voting power (Bartels 1998) are directly related to the probability of being a policy winner, over and above the effect of race on income.

The results of these tabulations suggest that both income and race play roles in winning and losing (see fig. 4.4). All four of the policy domains include evidence that whites were more likely to be winners even within income groups. For example, figure 4.1 showed that 40% of whites were winners on spending for defense, but only 31% of African Americans were winners. This difference remained about the same when controlling for income. Looking only at high-income earners, the gap is the same: 41% of whites to 32% of African Americans (see fig. 4.4a). The same is basically true among middle-income earners, as 38% of whites were winners, compared to 30% of African Americans (see fig. 4.4b). Among low-income earners, the gap decreased, but even here a gap remained, with 35% of whites winners, compared to 31% of African Americans (see fig. 4.4b). Other policy domains exhibit a similar pattern. Although income is related to policy winning, race continues to be powerfully linked to winning and losing. African Americans' incomes help little at all to explain why members of this group are less likely to be policy winners.[15]

ARE POLICY WINNERS JUST MORE ATTENTIVE CITIZENS?

Our evidence that whites win more often than minorities may simply be spurious in a way we have ignored thus far. Government policy decisions

15. We did not conduct a similar analysis of Latinos and whites because the Roper polls we use to analyze whites and Latinos do not measure income in constant dollars.

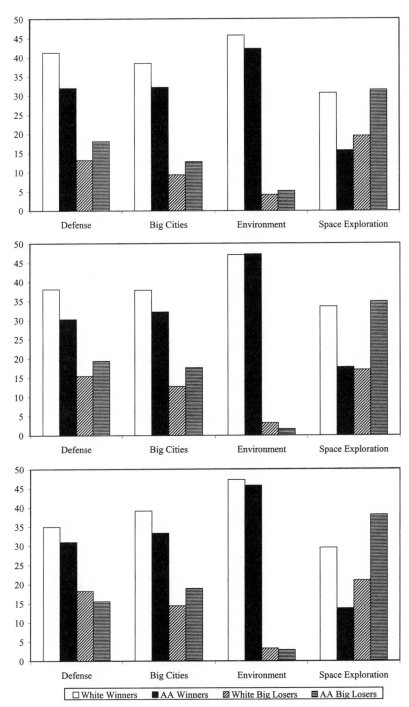

FIGURE 4.4. Percentage of policy winners and big losers, by income. (Top)
High-income whites and African Americans; (middle) middle-income whites and
African Americans; (bottom) low-income whites and African Americans. (Office of
Management and Budget 2004; General Social Surveys, 1972–1994, 1996, 1998, 2002).

may be directly responsive to developments that expose policy shortcomings, and citizen opinion may be responsive to these events in similar ways, creating a spurious correspondence between citizen opinion and policy change. For example, after a major environmental disaster, such as the Exxon Valdez oil spill, public preferences for spending on the environment may increase. This disaster may also convince public officials to increase spending regardless of any change they observe in public preferences. Moreover, if whites are more likely than African Americans and Latinos to be interested in and pay attention to such events, this potentially spurious relationship between opinion and policy will be greater for whites. If this occurs, the disparities in winning we have uncovered may be due to a combination of the effect of actual events on policymaking and differences among respondents in attention to the real world.

Ideally, we would like to incorporate citizens' level of political attention or knowledge to account for this. Unfortunately, neither the GSS nor the Roper polls regularly queried their respondents about their interest in and knowledge of political affairs or world events. To test for spuriousness in our findings that whites are more likely to be policy winners for spending on defense, aid to big cities, the environment, and space exploration, we repeated our tabulations in figure 4.1 for the subset of white and African American respondents who reported *not voting* in the most recent presidential election. The logic here is that nonvoters tend to be less interested in and attentive to politics, and so presumably less likely to revise their spending preferences on the basis of world events (Bennett and Resnick 1990; Verba, Schlozman, and Brady 1995). If we find that even among the subset of GSS respondents who are nonvoters whites are more likely to be policy winners, we will gain confidence that racial differences in attention to public affairs are not driving our results. Unfortunately, this approach excludes all of the Roper respondents because those surveys did not query about respondents' turnout. The unhappy consequence of this is we cannot perform this robustness check for Latinos because we rely exclusively on the Roper data for those analyses.

As figure 4.5 shows, even among less politically interested citizens (i.e., nonvoters), whites remain more likely to be policy winners compared to African Americans. In all four issue domains in which whites were advantaged, African American nonvoters are systematically less likely to be policy winners compared to white nonvoters. Moreover, comparing these results to those in figure 4.1 reveals that the magnitude of the difference between nonvoting whites and African Americans in being policy winners appears generally to rival that between all whites and African Americans.

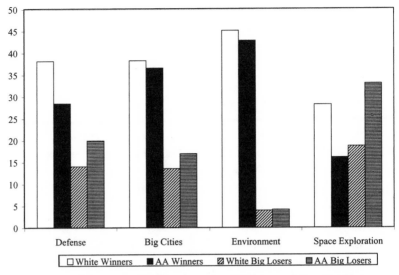

FIGURE 4.5. Percentage of policy winners and big losers, white and African American nonvoters (Office of Management and Budget 2004; General Social Surveys, 1972–1994, 1996, 1998, 2002).

Finally, in unreported tests controlling for related factors such as education, income, age, gender, and ideological orientation, African American nonvoters remain less likely than white nonvoters to be policy winners in the same domains.

IMPLICATIONS

To this point, we have demonstrated that African Americans and Latinos are often less likely than whites to be policy winners. Because these comparisons have not taken into account the racial and ethnic composition of the national population, they are best characterized as evaluations of race-conscious egalitarianism—testing whether racial and ethnic groups are equally represented *as groups*. According to a strict application of this standard of equality, African Americans and Latinos appear somewhat unequal. The average white American is, more often than not, more likely to see his or her preferences realized in government action than is the average African American or Latino.

Our analysis of differences in rates of policy winning adds to existing research in two important ways. First, studies comparing the representation

of different groups in policy have tended to study different income groups (Gilens 2005). We show the importance of supplementing studies of income differences in policy representation with studies of racial and ethnic differences in representation. Both race/ethnicity and income are related to political representation. Studies of political representation should take into account the racial, ethnic, and income differences in representation that we have demonstrated.

Second, our finding that African Americans, and (somewhat less so) Latinos generally win less than do whites also has important political implications. Since the legislative branches are elected bodies and whites far outnumber minorities, we might anticipate that elected bodies will produce outcomes that favor whites. However, other institutions in the policy-making process may "correct" such unequal representation. For instance, Frymer (2003, 483) has documented the intervention of the judicial branch to protect the interests of racial minorities "when elected officials won't." Our findings indicate that in these domains any disparities in representation in the legislative branches generally are not offset by the other bodies of government. While this may happen in some areas, our analyses in this chapter show that not all disparities in representation created by the electoral system are corrected in the policy process.

Our approach in this chapter provides an important view of the relative representation of racial and ethnic groups. However, this is only one view. The picture we see from the perspective of collective rather than dyadic representation does not show us everything about the relative representation of these groups. Our search for clear indicators of policy preferences, policy outputs, and a close connection between them has led us to focus on preferences for federal spending and subsequent federal outlays. The analytical advantages of this approach necessarily limit our investigation by excluding issues that do not clearly relate to spending. Important and controversial issues like abortion, civil rights, gun control, immigration, and same-sex marriage have unclear budgetary implications. It is unclear whether a citizen who prefers that same-sex marriages be legalized would prefer more, less, or the same amount of spending related to same-sex marriages, for example.

In addition, our measures of preferences only allow citizens to indicate whether they want more or less spending (or the same amount). They do not allow them to express how much more or less. Therefore, our ability to assess the connection between preferences and government response is limited. For example, if an African American citizen wants spending on big cities to double and spending increases by only 6 percent, our method

considers this citizen a winner. However, this citizen's preference is clearly not perfectly met.

In a related way, even if a citizen wanted more spending on education, and federal outlays on education actually did increase, we do not know if the citizen is happy with the way the government spent the money. A citizen who wanted more bilingual education programs probably would be unhappy if the government increased funding for basic research on physics at universities. Finally, since the government as a whole reaches a single decision that affects everyone, it is impossible to examine how representation might differ under varying circumstances that we know will affect representation, like descriptive representation or the size of minority populations, which vary across districts but not over the nation at any given time.

Although our approach here does not tell us everything, the approaches taken in the next chapters help to fill out our picture of relative representation of African Americans, Latinos, and whites by focusing on the blind spots of this chapter's approach. This chapter takes the first step in our investigation. As we have seen, there are significant disparities in policy representation regarding government budget decisions. Whites appear to enjoy better representation than African Americans and Latinos regarding policy in many of the issue domains that are not more salient for minorities. In domains where there are differences in the frequency of winning, these differences are often much larger than the difference in winning rates between wealthy and less wealthy citizens. Moreover, differences in policy winning do not appear to be an artifact of whites' greater attentiveness to political affairs.

In the next chapters we unpack this general finding to discover some of the sources of unequal representation. In chapter 5 we widen our scope by turning to dyadic representation, exploring the connections between individual legislators and their constituents. Unfortunately for minority groups, the story is unlikely to improve since "collective representation will never be worse than dyadic representation" (Weissberg 1978, 547). We begin in the next chapter by examining whether the three groups are unequally represented by their elected representatives' behavior. We know that such a step is necessary because, as we have seen, government policy often better reflects whites' preferences than those of African Americans and Latinos.

FIVE

Differences in Legislative Representation

In the Federalist No. 52, James Madison argued that the proposed Congress, and in particular the House of Representatives, "should have an immediate dependence on, and an intimate sympathy with, the people" (Madison, Hamilton, and Jay 1987, 323–4). However, not all "the people" feel an "intimate sympathy" with their representatives. There are significant differences in racial and ethnic groups' perceptions that elected officials are responsive to their group, as figure 5.1 shows. In the 2002 National Election Studies, conducted during the time period we analyze, 43% of the nation's African Americans and 32% of the nation's Latinos agreed that "[p]ublic officials don't care much what people like me think," while just 27% of whites held this view. In that same year, 39% of African Americans and 34% of Latinos agreed that "[p]eople like me don't have any say in what the government does," compared to just 24% of whites. Finally, 44% of African Americans and 39% of Latinos disapproved of Congress's performance, compared to 36% of whites. In this chapter, we evaluate whether these perceptions reflect reality, examining the extent to which the nation's legislative bodies are equally attentive to the preferences of all "the people."

In the last chapter, we focused on collective representation, the connection between citizens across the country and the policies the government as a whole produces. In this chapter, we explore the connection between individual members of Congress (MCs) and their particular constituents, or dyadic representation.[1] This shift offers several benefits. First, it enables us

---

1. For other studies of dyadic representation, see Miller and Stokes 1963; Achen 1978; Erikson 1978; Ansolabehere, Snyder, and Stewart 2001; Bartels 1991 and 2008.

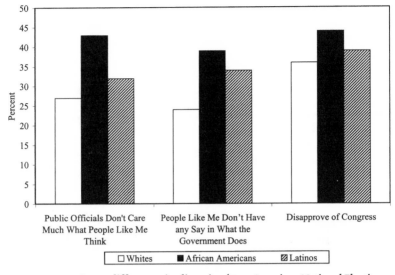

FIGURE 5.1. Group differences in alienation (2002 American National Election Study).

to use methods that complement the previous chapter's policy analysis by avoiding the limitations of that type of analysis. Second, studying representation within the nation's legislatures permits us to assess one important mechanism by which minorities' preferences become disadvantaged in the policy process: legislative roll-call voting. Chapter 4 described differences in policy representation but did not tell us much about how these disparities come about. The nation's legislatures offer a natural first place to look for the origins of differences in policy representation. Members of Congress are elected under plurality electoral rules by districts that are often home to far more whites than African Americans and Latinos. Once in office, they make decisions by simple majority or, in the case of the Senate, modest supermajority rule. These are just two features of Congress that would seem to work to the disadvantage of minority groups.

Third, by looking at both collective and dyadic representation, we explore different facets of representation, an inherently multifaceted phenomenon. If elections, the hallmark of democratic politics, help establish and maintain the connection between the governed and the government, we should see a connection between elected officials and those who elect them. We as citizens may have little influence over a member of Congress

from another state, but we can at least vote against our own member in the next election. Ultimately, if we find similar results by looking at different facets of representation and using complementary empirical methods, we will have more confidence in our findings and have a more comprehensive picture of relative representation among these groups.

Finally, this approach allows us to explore a matter that is critical to our study: the ways in which variation in state or district conditions such as the racial or ethnic composition of states affects the decisions of federal officials. This enables us to evaluate the performance of the political system against an additional standard of political equality. Our analyses in the previous chapter compared the groups' frequency of policy winning against a strict standard of race-conscious egalitarianism—that groups should have a relatively equal likelihood of being on the winning side of outcomes—but could go no further. Studying groups' legislative representation permits us to assess the performance of the political system against a *proportional* standard of political equality. Moving from chapter 4's national-level analysis to state- and congressional district-level analysis enables us to examine relative representation in a number of different settings, simply because some districts have very few African Americans or Latinos, while in other districts African Americans or Latinos make up a substantial proportion and sometimes even a majority of the constituency. Thus, we can see whether minorities are equally represented in legislators' voting decisions when they comprise a larger share of an electoral district. We structure the present chapter around these two standards of equality, first comparing groups' legislative representation against race-conscious egalitarianism, and then against a proportional standard of equality. We leave our discussion of the pluralist standard of political equality for the next chapter.

Our assessment of the groups' representation against each of these standards of equality adopts two measures of legislative representation— the *responsiveness* and *proximity* of legislators relative to racial and ethnic groups. Since representation is a complex phenomenon, scholars must examine different facets of representation. Following the lead of Miller and Stokes (1963), many works examine the extent to which representatives' roll-call votes relate to the average opinion in their district (Achen 1978; Erikson, Wright, and McIver 1993; see also Erikson 1978; McCrone and Kuklinski 1979; Bullock and Brady 1983). Among these opinion/roll-call studies, one approach evaluates legislators' *responsiveness* as a group to district opinion, estimating the extent to which liberal legislators represent liberal

constituencies and conservative legislators represent conservative constituencies (e.g., Achen 1978; Ansolabehere, Snyder, and Stewart 2001; Erikson and Wright 2000). Other studies examine the aggregate "distance" between individual legislators' actions and all their constituents' preferences, a concept Achen termed *proximity* (Powell 1982; Wright 1978). According to Achen (1978), these concepts of responsiveness and proximity capture different, important features of representation—whether, respectively, "the representative system adapts to citizen preferences," and "everyone's voice [is] counted equally" (490, 481).

For reasons that will become clear, adopting these measures of representation naturally leads us to investigations of both national legislative institutions, the U.S. Senate and the U.S. House of Representatives. The Senate and the House each offer unique analytical advantages for assessing the extent of the three groups' relative representation. Although many have studied representation in the Senate generally (e.g., Wright 1989; Erikson 1990; Wood and Hinton Andersson 1998; Fowler 2005), most studies of minority representation examine the House, meaning we know far less about differences in representation in the Senate. Yet the Senate may be especially unresponsive to minorities' interests, since African Americans and Latinos typically constitute less than 20 percent of state populations and thus there are no majority-African American or Latino states where African Americans' or Latinos' interests may be especially well represented. Historically, there also have been very few African American or Latino senators. In contrast, analyzing the House of Representatives enables us to assess how larger concentrations of minority constituents and the race or ethnicity of MCs affect groups' substantive representation (we analyze the impact of MCs' race and ethnicity in chapter 7).

RACE-CONSCIOUS EGALITARIANISM

To evaluate the groups' legislative representation against the standard of race-conscious egalitarianism, we follow most studies by focusing on the relationship between citizens' preferences and their elected representatives' voting behavior.[2] As we relate citizens' preferences to their representatives' decisions, if groups are politically equal by a strict, race-conscious

2. Of course, roll-call voting constitutes only one way for MCs to represent their constituents. For discussions of other representational activities MCs can engage in, see Canon (1999) and Tate (2003a).

egalitarian standard, then minorities' preferences and whites' preferences aggregated within electoral districts will be equally effective in predicting their representatives' decisions. Second, if the groups are politically equal under this standard, then individual members of racial and ethnic groups will be on average equidistant from their representatives. At the very least, under this standard of equality, representation should be equal across groups when minorities constitute some substantial share of the population, making minorities' representation more than proportional.

Race-Conscious Egalitarianism and Responsiveness | The most common approach to studying representation assesses legislators' *responsiveness* to constituent opinion. We start by following in this tradition, analyzing senators' roll-call votes as a function of their African American, Latino, and white constituents' preferences. This specific approach overcomes three of the limits of the previous chapter's policy analysis. First, it allows us to explore issues we could not explore in that analysis (i.e., we can move beyond federal spending decisions). Second, we explore citizens' general ideological perspectives, which enables us to take magnitude into account much more than does the policy approach. In the spending policy analysis, constituents could only express a preference for more, less, or about the same amount of spending, not how much more or less spending they would prefer. In the present approach, constituencies can be more than just "liberal" or "conservative." They can be extremely liberal or moderately liberal. This approach also allows MCs to vary widely (and continuously) in the degree to which they are liberal or conservative. Third, the substance of the roll-call votes is much more clear than is true for simply "more" or "less" spending. For example, we analyze one roll-call vote related to boosting unemployment benefits. We compare this to whites' and minorities' preferences regarding federal attempts to reduce income differences between rich and poor Americans. Both the roll-call vote and the preference measure are more specific than the rather general preference for more/less/the same spending and the general budgetary response of more spending.

Before we examine specific roll-call votes though, we begin by analyzing senators' votes across a full range of issues. To measure overarching patterns in senators' roll-call voting in the 107th Congress (2001–2002), we use a summary measure known as W-NOMINATE coordinates. These coordinates are generally agreed to reflect a legislator's mean roll-call behavior on a liberal-conservative social welfare spectrum ranging continuously

from –1 to +1, with larger values indicating more conservative roll-call voting patterns.[3]

The responsiveness approach requires district-level measures of citizens' preferences. In forming these measures, prior studies of representation tend to treat citizens as an undifferentiated group; however this design can be adapted to study responsiveness to groups *within* electoral districts. For example, Bartels (2008) used a variant of this approach to determine that senators respond disproportionately to constituents with higher incomes. As a practical matter, though, the data requirements of the responsiveness approach often are difficult to meet when studying groups within geographic constituencies.

Fortunately, the NAES provides relatively representative and reliable state-level measures of the three groups' ideological orientations. As noted above, these data include 26 states with at least 50 African Americans and 21 states with at least 48 Latinos.[4] In addition to the size of the sample (more than 57,000 respondents), which far exceeds that of most surveys, the NAES sampling method offers another advantage for creating state-level measures of opinion. The NAES used a Random Digit Dialing (RDD) procedure, rather than a stratified clustered sample (as used by the National Election Studies).[5] The RDD design more closely approximates the ideal of making everyone in

3. W-NOMINATE coordinates are generated by placing legislators and the midpoint between non-unanimous roll-call alternatives in a two-dimensional ideological space, making the assumption that legislators always vote for the nearest alternative, and then iteratively relocating legislators and roll-call midpoints until the number of roll-call "errors" is minimized (see Lewis and Poole 2004 for a more complete description). These coordinates correlate highly with alternative, summary measures of legislator roll-call behavior like interest group ratings and Heckman-Snyder scores (Burden, Caldeira, and Groseclose 2000). This version of the W-NOMINATE scores is appropriate because it measures behavior in a single legislative term, independent of other terms served. Analyses of congressional roll-call voting have regularly used various versions of W-NOMINATE scores as dependent variables (e.g., Ansolabehere, Snyder, and Stewart 2001; Bartels 2008).

4. The states we use in our comparisons of whites and African Americans include AL, AR, CA, CT, FL, GA, IL, IN, KY, LA, MA, MD, MI, MO, MS, NJ, NY, NC, OH, OK, PA, SC, TN, TX, VA, and WI. The states we use in our comparisons of whites and Latinos include AZ, CA, CO, CT, FL, GA, IL, MA, MI, MO, NC, NJ, NM, NV, NY, OH, OR, PA, TX, VA, and WA.

5. The stratified sampling method is typically designed to draw a sample that is representative of the nation, but not states (see Brace et al. 2002). For example, a survey may sample several respondents in a major population center like Detroit, but not in other areas in that state. Such a sample would not necessarily be representative of all of Michigan.

a state equally likely to be sampled, thereby generating more representative state-level samples. In fact, the NAES state samples match census data fairly closely, suggesting that these samples are quite representative.[6]

In addition to being representative, as we noted in chapter 3 (see note 6), under standard definitions of reliability state-level mean white ideological orientations were highly reliable; African Americans' and Latinos' state-level ideological orientations were less reliable. To compensate for the lower reliability of the measures for African Americans and Latinos, when we anticipate that African Americans and Latinos are likely to be underrepresented, we use an errors-in-variables estimator to account for measurement error. This boosts the estimated relationship between African Americans' and Latinos' opinions and senators' decisions, thereby minimizing the amount of unequal responsiveness we will find. This "stacks the deck" in favor of equal representation across groups. If we continue to find inequality under these conditions, we will be all the more confident in our conclusions. To summarize, we calculated the mean opinions of whites and African Americans in 26 states, and the mean opinions of whites and Latinos in 21 states yielding *African American Ideology*, *Latino Ideology*, and two measures of *White Ideology*. The roll-call and opinion measures are coded with conservative alternatives higher, so positive estimates for white and African American/Latino opinion indicate positive responsiveness.

To determine the responsiveness of senators' votes to the preferences of African Americans, Latinos, and whites, we model each senator's votes as a function of his or her mean white and mean African American or Latino constituents' opinions. If senators' votes respond more to whites' preferences, the estimated relationship for whites' preferences will be greater than that for African Americans' or Latinos' preferences. If senators are not responsive to a particular group's preferences at all, the estimated parameter for that group will be zero. These models are not intended to explain senators' votes, but to describe the correspondence between senators' votes and constituents' preferences. Other factors surely affect senators' votes,

6. To evaluate the representativeness of the NAES state-level samples, we compared the demographics of the NAES data to the reported state demographics in the 2000 U.S. Census. We found that in the twenty-six states on which we focus our analyses of African Americans, the proportions of the population that is African American in the NAES and in the census correlate at .98. The state median income correlates with the (collapsed) NAES income self-placement scale at .85. The percentage of state residents who live in urban settings and have college degrees in the NAES and the census correlate at .88 and .87, respectively.

but our present task is simply to test whether the end product of those other factors, actual votes, better reflect their white or African American/Latino constituents' preferences.[7]

We first estimate a simple model of w-NOMINATE scores as a function of just white ideology or African American ideology, along with MCs' party affiliations (see the left side of table 5.1). Comparing the first two columns in table 5.1, we observe that white ideology is a better predictor of senators' w-NOMINATE scores than is African American ideology (compare coefficients of 1.09 for whites and 0.67 for African Americans).[8] This no longer appears to be true after we account for the lower reliability of our African American ideology measure using an errors-in-variables estimator in the third model (see column 3, where the African American ideology parameter is 1.28).[9] However, in some states, especially in the South, both whites and African Americans are more conservative than their counterparts in other states, so white ideology is related to African American ideology.[10] African American ideology might be spuriously related to senators' roll-call voting based on its correlation with white ideology. To control for this, we included both white and African American ideology in a single model (see column 4). White ideology once again becomes a better predictor of senators' voting behavior, relative to African American ideology.[11] In fact, the estimate for

7. For an example of this general approach as applied to the representation of business interests, public opinion, and other factors on foreign policy, see Jacobs and Page 2005; see also Bartels 2008.

8. Out of concern that the two observations for each state exhibit correlation in the independent variables, we also estimated separate models of each state's junior and senior senators. In these models, once again senators are responsive to variation in white but not African American ideology.

9. We also estimated this model using senators' second-dimension w-NOMINATE scores as the dependent variables. In some historical periods, these second-dimension scores appear to measure legislators' voting behavior on racial issues (Poole and Rosenthal 1997). We found that neither white nor African American ideology predicted senators' second-dimension scores in the 107th Senate.

10. The correlation coefficient between them is .50.

11. We also randomly sampled among whites to create measures of white and African American ideology that were based on the same state sample sizes. Estimating the model reported in table 5.1, column 3 using these measures yielded a coefficient for white ideology that was somewhat smaller and statistically significant ($p < .01$), while the coefficient for African American ideology remained insignificant. To guard against the possibility that white and African American ideology are collinear, we also regressed senators' w-NOMINATE scores on the *difference* between white and African American ideology, finding that as whites become more conservative relative

TABLE 5.1. GROUP DIFFERENCES IN RESPONSIVENESS, 107TH SENATE W-NOMINATE SCORES

	Whites and African Americans					Whites and Latinos				
	(1)	(2)	(3)	(4)	(5)	(6)	(7)	(8)	(9)	(10)
Estimator	OLS	OLS	Errors in Vars	OLS	Errors in Vars	OLS	OLS	Errors in Vars	OLS	Errors in Vars
White Ideology r	—	—	—	—	.97	—	—	—	—	.95
African American/ Latino Ideology r	—	—	.53	—	.53	—	—	.44	—	.44
White ideology	1.09* [.22]	—	—	1.06** [.26]	1.09* [.47]	1.27** [.29]	—	—	1.16** [.30]	1.05** [.38]
African American ideology	—	.67* [.28]	1.28* [.50]	.06 [.28]	.09 [.83]	—	—	—	—	—
Latino ideology	—	—	—	—	—	—	.67* [.32]	1.67* [.74]	.36 [.29]	.98 [.79]
Republican MC	1.15** [.06]	1.29** [.06]	1.28** [.06]	1.16** [.06]	1.15** [.07]	1.18** [.06]	1.25** [.07]	1.19** [.07]	1.17** [.06]	1.14** [.07]
Constant	-4.11** [.69]	-2.67** [.84]	-4.50** [1.51]	-4.21** [.82]	-4.38 [1.40]	-4.66** [.90]	-2.73** [.98]	-5.77* [2.25]	-5.44** [1.09]	-6.96** [1.88]

Sources: 2000 National Annenberg Election Survey; Lewis and Poole 2004.

Notes: Dependent variable: Senators' W-NOMINATE scores. "Errors in Vars" denotes errors-in-variables regression.

* $p < .05$; ** $p < .01$; standard errors in brackets.

African American ideology drops sharply and becomes statistically insignificant. Accounting for measurement error in the final model of whites and African Americans does not alter the results significantly (see column 5). In sum, these models indicate that, across the full spectrum of issues captured in the w-NOMINATE scores, senators are much less responsive to African Americans' preferences.[12] Indeed, after we account for whites' preferences, senators appear not to be responsive to the preferences of African Americans *at all*, which violates any standard of political equality.

Turning to a comparison of senators' responsiveness to whites and Latinos, we find a similar pattern of results (see the right side of table 5.1). We first observe that when we include these measures in the model independently, and before we account for measurement error, senators are more responsive to whites' preferences than Latinos' preferences (compare the parameter estimate of 1.27 for white ideology in column 6 to the estimate of 0.67 for Latinos in column 7). Once again, when we correct for measurement error in Latinos' preferences but not in whites' preferences, senators appear to be more responsive to Latinos than whites (see column 8). Since Latino ideology is modestly correlated with white ideology, the relationship between Latino ideology and senators' roll-call votes may be spurious.[13] When we include both groups in the model in column 9, the 1.16 estimate for whites far exceeds that for Latinos, and the 0.36 estimate for Latinos in column 9 is hard to distinguish from zero. Finally, when we correct for measurement error in both whites' and Latinos' preferences, the estimates for the groups are similar in magnitude, but only whites' preferences systematically predict senators' voting decisions at anywhere near traditional levels of statistical significance (see column 10).

To illustrate the substantive magnitude of the relationship between constituents' ideologies and their senators' votes, we simulated the predicted w-NOMINATE score of senators representing states at the 25th and 75th percentiles of the white and African American and white and

---

to African Americans within states, senators across the country become more conservative in their roll-call behavior ($p < .05$).

12. As a robustness check, we also estimated these models using Erikson, Wright, and McIver's pooled CBS/*New York Times* data (1976–93). In this data, the reliability of white ideology is .98, while the reliability of African American ideology is .83. Regressing senators' w-NOMINATE scores on Erikson, Wright, and McIver's measures of state ideology, we again find that the parameter estimate for white ideology is much greater than the estimate for African American ideology.

13. The correlation coefficient between them is .34.

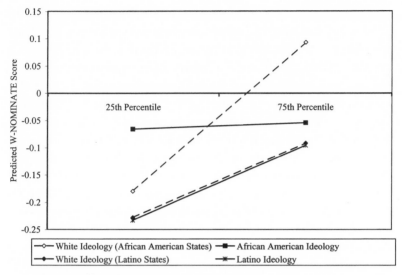

FIGURE 5.2. Effect of group ideology on predicted senator W-NOMINATE score, 107th Congress (2000 National Annenberg Election Survey; Lewis and Poole 2004).

Latino ideology distributions (see fig. 5.2).[14] The differences between these changes in predicted values indicate the degree to which senators' votes respond better to whites' opinions than to African Americans' and Latinos' opinions. Across the twenty-six states in which we compare responsiveness to whites and African Americans, the magnitude of responsiveness is dramatically greater for whites than for African Americans. These simulations reveal that a conservative shift in white ideology is predicted to lead to an increase of .27 points on the –1 to +1 W-NOMINATE scale (see fig. 5.2, dashed line with open diamonds). This is a significant change, one that is about one-third the effect of senators' party affiliations on these scores estimated in table 5.1. By comparison, a similar, conservative shift in African American ideology would barely have a positive effect on senators' conservatism. Senators are estimated to shift in a conservative direction by a mere .01 points.[15] Across the twenty-one states in which we compare senators'

14. These figures rely on the estimates in columns 5 and 10 in table 5.1.
15. Note that the ranges of white (0.56) and African American (0.48) ideology are similar. Note also that we are interested in the relative correspondence of whites' and African Americans' preferences more than the level of either marginal effect on its own. We could calculate this just as easily using a smaller shift in opinion. Marginal effects were simulated using the software program CLARIFY (See Tomz, Wittenberg, and King 2003).

responsiveness to whites and Latinos, senators do not appear to be more responsive to the changing preferences of whites than Latinos (see dashed line with closed diamonds and solid line with asterisks in fig. 5.2). However, recall that the predicted values for Latinos are based on an estimated effect that is so imprecise that we cannot distinguish it from zero.

While these results suggest that senators respond more to their white constituents than their African American and Latino constituents, an alternative interpretation is that they reflect senators' attentiveness to their constituents who share their party affiliation (i.e., co-partisans; e.g., see Powell 1982; Bullock and Brady 1983). Since MCs are especially responsive to the co-partisans in their state or district (e.g., Fiorina 1974; Bullock and Brady 1983; Hurley and Hill 2003), and the group of whites may be comprised disproportionately of co-partisans by virtue of the composition of state populations, our results may just reflect senators' disproportionate responsiveness to co-partisans rather than to whites per se. We explored this possibility by asking whether whites represented by a senator who shares their party affiliation are advantaged over African Americans/Latinos represented by a senator from their party, modeling senators' w-NOMINATE scores as a function of the mean ideology of their white co-partisan constituents and their African American/Latino co-partisan constituents' ideology. Although we do not present the results so as not to stray too far from our main point (we present similar results from the House below), we found that even among each senator's co-partisans, whites are much better represented. In fact, like African Americans at large, senators as a group do not respond to their African American constituents at all, even when they identify with their senators' party. The results for Latinos paralleled those for African Americans. On the basis of this analysis, we can be fairly sure our results in table 5.1 are not spurious.[16]

---

16. A second, alternative interpretation of these results is that senators' roll-call voting may have a much greater influence on the ideologies of whites than on those of African Americans. This would be consistent in some respects with evidence that elite behavior can affect constituent opinion (e.g., Gerber and Jackson 1992; Hill and Hurley 1999; Hurley and Hill 2003). However, while several studies show that individual citizens' attitudes on specific issues may be influenced by their elected officials' roll-call voting, we have not located a study showing that citizens' aggregated ideological orientations are subject to such influence. It seems more likely that a senator's vote on a minimum-wage bill, for instance, would influence their constituents' opinions on the minimum wage than that the same vote, or a series of votes, would alter constituents' identifications as liberals, moderates, or conservatives. We deal more with this alternative interpretation in later analyses.

Race-Conscious Egalitarianism and Proximity in the House of Representatives | According to the responsiveness model, senators are not meeting the race-conscious egalitarian standard. However, the responsiveness approach does not allow us to observe every aspect of representation we might be interested in. In addition to knowing whether MCs are *more* liberal in states with more liberal constituencies, we would like to know whether liberal constituents are represented by *equally* liberal MCs. However, responsiveness does not guarantee a close match between individual constituents and their MCs. It is possible that senators are responsive to state-level variation in constituents' ideology, but roll-call behavior may not actually reflect constituent preferences in the sense of being "close" to what constituents want (Powell 1982). Consider the following hypothetical situation, in which districts and legislators are deciding an issue on a 0–10 scale, with 10 being the most conservative option (see fig. 5.3). District constituent preferences range from 5 to 9 (the diamond-shaped points), all fairly conservative. Their representatives' actions (the square-shaped points) range from 0 to 5, all significantly more liberal than their districts would prefer. However, as districts become more conservative, their representatives vote more conservatively in a one-to-one linear fashion. Although there is perfect responsiveness in this situation, we may consider this less than perfect representation.

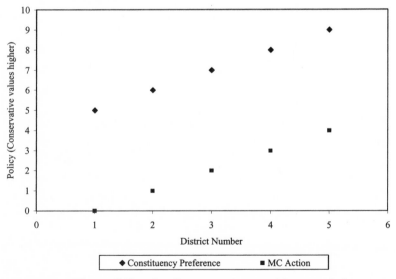

FIGURE 5.3. The possibility of perfect responsiveness without proximity.

To be sure we are finding meaningful differences in political equality and to explore a new facet of representation, we consider an alternative measure of equality: proximity (Achen 1978; see also Miller 1964; Powell 1982; Wright 1978). Proximity measures also allow us to examine members of the House of Representatives, so that we can now compare results across policy outcomes (as in the previous chapter) and across both chambers of Congress.[17]

Proximity measures allow us to ask whether, on average, African Americans' and Latinos' preferences are "closer to" or "farther from" their House representatives' decisions than are white constituents' preferences. This proximity is important in its own right because the extent of opinion correspondence between constituents and MCs influences constituents' evaluations of MCs' performance (Wright 1978; Powell 1989; Binder, Maltzman, and Sigelman 1998), and these evaluations are one indicator of how well individuals feel they are being represented (Tate 2003a).

Analysis of proximity offers several analytical advantages. As is true for responsiveness, the proximity approach enables us to compensate for the limits of the policy analysis, allowing us to examine a wider set of issues, taking the magnitude of preferences and actions into account, and providing a clearer connection between preferences for specific policies and specific action. In addition, this approach directly measures the "closeness" of citizens to their MCs, which we just saw is not taken into account in the responsiveness approach. Finally, in later chapters we tap into another advantage of this approach: since we are looking at proximity between constituents and their individual representatives, we can use this approach to examine the effects of descriptive representation.

Despite their advantages, measures of proximity raise an important methodological challenge. Specifically, they require indicators of constituent preferences and MC behavior that are on the same scale. The lack of a common scale for legislators and their constituents has confounded legislative scholars for decades (Miller 1964; Achen 1978; Wright 1978; Kuklinski 1978; Powell 1982; Burden 2004). For example, there are plenty of survey measures of constituents' preferences on a 7-point scale, but most measures of MC behavior involve some type of roll-call score on scales of –1 to +1 or 0 to 100. The earliest approach to resolving this scaling problem, and one still

17. Methodologically, we have little choice but to move to proximity measures in the House; the NAES does not provide reliable estimates of minority group opinion at the district level simply because there are many districts with very few minorities sampled.

advocated today, was simply to transform the scales measuring MCs' decisions and constituents' attitudes to the same range (Miller 1964; Achen 1978; Burden 2004). Another tactic was to transform MCs' decisions to a somewhat narrower range than the opinions of constituents since relatively few ideologically extreme legislators get elected (Powell 1982 and 1989).[18] Yet another method was to standardize both measures (Wright 1978). One reason for this proliferation of distance measures is that each measure has been subject to criticism of one form or another.[19] Rather than adjudicating between the merits and demerits of these measures, we use as many of them as possible in our analysis to increase our confidence in the results. We also develop another proximity measure, which we describe below.

One advantage to our focus on relative representation is that it eases the burdens of measurement. We recognize that proximity measures are somewhat flawed. However, they are likely *equally flawed* across racial/ethnic groups and MC race and ethnicity. Therefore, if we observe, for example, that the distance between African Americans and their MCs differs from that of whites, we can be fairly confident that the two groups' *relative* proximity differs, which is our chief concern.[20] Even so, we probe the robustness of our findings that rely on measures of proximity.

As a measure of MCs' voting behavior over a wide range of issues, we again use W-NOMINATE coordinates, focusing on the 107th Congress for most of our analyses. We focus on non–descriptively representative MCs (e.g., non–African Americans representing African Americans), leaving our analysis

18. More precisely, Powell used "knowledgeable" contributors' placements of incumbents to map legislators' interest-group scores onto an ideological scale (1989). The result of this mapping was that incumbents ranged from 2.0 to 6.1 on the 7-point scale (278).

19. For instance, Powell (1982, 663) questioned the underlying assumption of many of these measures that the means and variances of incumbents' and citizens' positions are equal.

20. One concern is that the ideology measure may have greater error for minority respondents because many African Americans and Latinos are economically liberal but socially conservative (e.g., McClain and Stewart 2002). If African Americans' ideology is measured with greater error, they may appear farther from their MCs than they really are. However, it seems highly unlikely that there is greater error in the ideology measure for African Americans *only* when they are represented by whites, and less error for African Americans represented by African Americans. Therefore, if we find in a later chapter that African Americans are more distant than whites when both groups are represented by whites, and both groups are equally distant when represented by African Americans, greater error in the measure of African Americans' opinions would need to be specific to legislator race to generate misleading inferences.

of the effect of descriptive representation on minority groups' political representation for a subsequent chapter.[21] As our measure of citizens' ideological locations, we again use citizens' NAES ideological self-placements. For our first measure of proximity, following Miller (1964), Achen (1978), and Burden (2004) (hereinafter MAB) we rescaled the W-NOMINATE scores to match the 1–5 range of the NAES ideology item.[22] Next, following Powell (1982) we rescaled the roll-call scores to a more narrow range.[23] Third, like Wright (1978), we standardized the W-NOMINATE scores and the NAES ideology item.[24] We also introduce a new measure of proximity that takes advantage of citizens' placement of House incumbents on a 7-point ideology scale in the National Elections Studies (NES) in order to group incumbents into the same "bins" in which respondents are asked to place themselves.[25] We reiterate that we are not advocating one measure of distance over the others. We recognize that each has its benefits and drawbacks, so we merely look for common results across all four measures. When we find commonalities, we are more confident in the conclusions we draw from the results.

21. The race/ethnicity of MCs was obtained from the Congressional Research Service Report, "Black Members of the United States Congress, 1789–2001" (Amer 2004), and for Latinos, from *Hispanic Americans in Congress, 1822–1995*, prepared by the Library of Congress, which maintains an updated list of Latino MCs on its Web site at http://www.loc.gov/rr/hispanic/congress/.

22. The formula we use to convert W-NOMINATE scores to the ideological self-placement scale is $(\text{W-NOMINATE} * 2) + 3$.

23. The formula we use to convert narrowed W-NOMINATE scores to the ideological self-placement scale is $(\text{W-NOMINATE} * 1.5) + 3$. Powell's technique narrowed the scale 10% on each end; our technique narrows the scale 14% on each end.

24. Specifically, we use the mean and variance of strong partisans' ideologies to standardize the distribution of all respondents, while standardizing the distribution of legislators to a mean of zero and a standard deviation of one.

25. We thank Jim Snyder for this suggestion. Using NES data, we pooled partisan, college-educated citizens' placements of their MC during the years 1996–2002, a period during which the ideological composition of Congress was relatively stable. We then use the distribution of citizens' MC placements on the 7-point ideological scale to generate cut points for the distribution of MC W-NOMINATE scores for the 104th–108th Houses. Few citizens placed MCs at the extremes of the scale, so we collapsed the extreme values in the scale with their neighboring values, resulting in a 5-point scale. Using the tabulated percentages of MCs that citizens placed in each bin, we then selected cut lines for the W-NOMINATE distribution in each of the Congresses we analyzed such that the percentage of MCs at each point is equal to the percentage of citizen MC placements at that point. These MC placements tell us, from citizens' perspective, the percentage of MCs who should be placed in each of the "bins" in which NES respondents place themselves. We then compare MCs' binned locations to NES respondents' ideological self-placements, also collapsing these self-placements to a 5-point scale.

For all these distance measures, we calculate relative proximity across the groups by determining the absolute distance between MCs' decisions and each of their NAES respondents. We then average the distances for each group and perform a difference-of-means test to assess whether the average distances between MCs and each group are equivalent. First, we ask whether whites' preferences are systematically closer to the decisions of their MCs than are the preferences of African Americans and Latinos. Figure 5.4 presents two sets of analyses, one comparing the proximity of African Americans to their representatives with the proximity of whites to their representatives and another comparing the proximity of Latinos to their representatives with the proximity of whites to their representatives. The black columns in figure 5.4 represent the average proximity of African Americans to their MCs minus the average proximity of whites to their MCs. We call this the "proximity gap." A positive difference in the figure indicates that African Americans or Latinos are farther on average from their MCs than are whites. For example, using the MAB measure of distance, whites are 0.98 points away from their MCs on average, while African Americans are 1.06 points away from their MCs on average. Subtracting

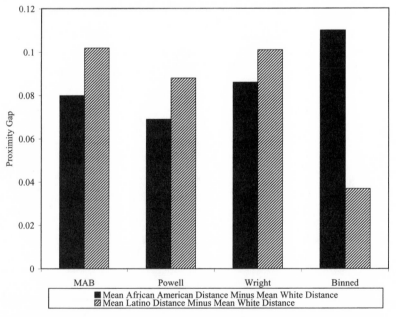

FIGURE 5.4. Nondescriptive MCs and the proximity gap, 107th House. (2000 National Annenberg Election Survey; Lewis and Poole 2004).

these distances shows that African Americans are 0.08 points farther from their MCs, which is the proximity gap graphed in the first black column in figure 5.4. The columns with diagonal lines represent a parallel analysis comparing the mean proximity of Latinos to their MCs with the mean proximity of whites to their MCs. We interpret no difference between the groups' mean distance as evidence of political equality.

When we compare the distance of African Americans and whites, we see that African Americans are more distant than whites on all four distance measures (three of four measures at the 0.01 level, the binned measure at the 0.05 level; see black columns). While the difference in distance differs by measure, African Americans generally are between 0.07 and 0.11 "farther" from their representatives on the ideological scale. To put this in context, we calculated the proximity gap for various groups in American society, groups that are often thought to be politically unequal. Figure 5.5 presents this proximity gap, showing that, for example, women are on average about 0.02 points farther than men from their MCs when both groups are represented by male MCs. The figure also shows that college graduates are about 0.04 points closer than high school graduates to their MCs (all MCs). Similar to what we saw in the previous chapter, high-income earners (> 90th percentile) are about 0.07 points closer to their MCs than are low-income earners (< 25th percentile). Older Americans are about 0.08 points closer to their

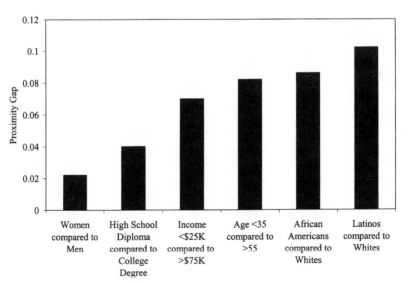

FIGURE 5.5. Size of the proximity gap, various groups (2000 National Annenberg Election Survey; Lewis and Poole 2004).

MCs than are younger Americans. Thus, the proximity gap between African Americans and whites represented by non–African American MCs is on par with or even greater than that associated with many of the significant demographic divides that observers have noted in American politics (Bartels 2008 [income]; Campbell 2003 [age]; Griffin, Newman, and Wolbrecht 2006 [gender]). Not only do these gaps provide a point of comparison for the gaps between racial and ethnic groups, but finding that the wealthy and the educated are better represented than the poor and the uneducated, which is in line with prior studies (Gilens 2005; Bartels 2008), helps to validate the proximity approach.

Turning to a comparison of whites and Latinos represented by whites and African Americans (columns with diagonals in fig. 5.4), according to all four measures, on average Latinos are farther from their MCs (three of the four measures at $p < .01$). According to some measures the proximity gap between Latinos and whites represented by non-Latino MCs appears to exceed the gap between African Americans and whites.

In light of the diversity of Latino opinion by national origin and (relatedly) by region, we also examined the relative representation of Latino subgroups, finding some important variation. Latinos of Puerto Rican and especially Mexican origin are farther than whites from their MCs (0.04 and 0.13 points farther, respectively).[26] In contrast, Latinos of Cuban descent are actually 0.16 points closer than whites on average, though we hesitate to draw inferences based on the small Cuban sample (119 respondents). To the extent that this finding holds, we suspect that this is attributable to the rather homogenous ideological conservatism of Cuban-Americans, a group that is usually represented by Republicans. Regionally, Latinos in the Pacific Coast and Mountain states and Latinos in the Southeast and South Central states show the largest proximity gap compared to whites (0.09 and 0.10 respectively), while the gap is somewhat smaller in the Northeast (0.06).

A Closer Look at Race-Conscious Egalitarianism | Thus far we have seen that as groups, whites find their preferences better reflected in their MCs' voting records than do African Americans or Latinos. However, as we noted earlier, a more widely accepted test of the race-conscious egalitarian standard is to

---

26. When we control for turnout, income, district racial/ethnic composition, and MC ethnicity and party affiliation, the only substantial change in the results is that Latinos of Puerto Rican origin are no longer significantly further than whites from their MCs.

ask whether minorities are just as close as whites to their MCs when these groups constitute a large proportion but not a majority of the constituency. As we discussed in chapter 2, advocates of the race-conscious egalitarian standard would usually require that minorities' likelihood of being on the winning side of outcomes would be "more than proportional" rather than fully equal. Thus, minorities should not necessarily be represented as well as whites when minorities make up some small share of a constituency, but in districts with substantial minority populations, perhaps greater than 25% or even 40%, more than proportional representation begins to approach a requirement of equal representation.

Figure 5.6 compares the relative proximity of minorities and whites across districts with different racial and ethnic compositions, using the Wright measure of ideological proximity. The figure points to two significant findings. First, African Americans remain farther than whites from their MCs even in districts where African Americans make up more than 25%, 40%, or even 50% of a constituency. In fact, if we pool the districts where African Americans make up more than 40% of the constituency, the proximity gap (0.07 points) is about the same as it is in the nation as a whole; however, because there is relatively little data, we cannot be very certain that the mean distances are in this case actually different from each other ($p = .19$).

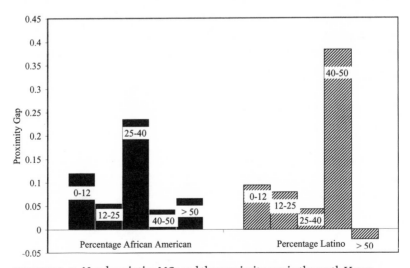

FIGURE 5.6. Nondescriptive MCs and the proximity gap in the 107th House, by district percentage African American or Latino (2000 National Annenberg Election Survey; Lewis and Poole 2004).

Second, the figure provides some evidence of what some scholars have called "white backlash" against African Americans in districts where they constitute a significant minority of the population (e.g., Key 1949; Blalock 1967; Bullock and Rodgers 1976; Giles and Buckner 1993; but see Lublin 1997). These studies argue that in districts in which African Americans pose an electoral "threat" to whites, whites become politically mobilized, and candidates and elected officials tend to cater to the majority whites' preferences. The figure shows that the proximity gap between African Americans and whites is greatest in districts where African Americans constitute between 25% and 40% of the population, reaching 0.24 points, more than three times the gap between whites and African Americans in the country as a whole.

The results for Latinos are even more telling. Again we see evidence of backlash, as the proximity gap is enormous in districts where Latinos make up a large minority of the constituency. In districts where Latinos comprise 40–50% of the population, Latinos are more than 0.38 points farther than whites from their MCs.[27] If we pool the data across multiple categories, in districts where Latinos comprise at least a quarter of the population, Latinos fare worse than they do in all districts (a 0.14 point gap vs. a 0.10 gap nationally; see fig. 5.4). In districts where Latinos make up at least 40% of the constituency, the proximity gap (0.22 points) is more than twice as large as it is in the nation as a whole. To restate the most significant point for our present purposes, figure 5.6 suggests that minorities are not more than proportionally represented—because even when they make up a near-majority of a district's population, they are not equally represented—and thus that the race-conscious egalitarian standard of equality is not satisfied. We discuss the results for districts that are majority African American or Latino below.

---

27. Although we cannot be certain, one reason why "backlash" occurs most in districts where African Americans comprise between 25% and 40% of the population and where Latinos comprise a higher percentage (between 40% and 50%) relates to Latinos' lower rates of citizenship. If the Latino population makes up 40% of a district's population, some in this group will be ineligible to vote, so the voting-eligible population is actually in the 25–40% range. However, this hypothesis requires whites to be sophisticated enough to estimate the size of the voting-eligible Latino population, as opposed to the entire Latino population. This may be an unreasonable assumption. Another potential reason is more baldly racial in nature—whites may simply consider African Americans more "threatening" than Latinos. At this point, we have no evidence to support either hypothesis.

Before we move on, we note that our key finding—that African Americans and Latinos tend to be farther than whites from their MCs—is robust in a number of ways. First, we know that politics is often different in the South, especially when it comes to conflict between whites and African Americans (Key 1949). Racial politics in the South have been more intense and divisive than in other regions. Therefore, we examined whether African Americans are farther away from their MCs than whites in both the South and other areas of the nation. The results show that they are, although African Americans are generally worse off in the South. One reason that they may be worse off in the South is that African Americans' and whites' attitudes are more divergent in this region than in other parts of the country.[28] If MCs generally side with whites, then the farther African Americans are from whites, the worse off they will be. In addition, given that African Americans generally make up a larger percentage of congressional districts in the South than elsewhere, these results are an early warning that the proportional standard of political equality may not be met for African Americans. We examine this question more directly below.

Second, using a regression framework, we controlled for three factors that are likely related to political equality: the racial or ethnic composition of districts (the percentage of each district composed of African Americans or Latinos), constituents' household income, and self-reported turnout in the 1996 election. Even when controlling for these factors, African Americans and Latinos remained significantly farther from their white MCs than were white constituents.

Third, perhaps whites are nearer than African Americans and Latinos to their white MCs because whites are more likely to identify with the same party as their MCs and co-partisans are generally thought to be better represented (Bullock and Brady 1983). However, we found that even among co-partisans, African American and Latino constituents were significantly farther from their MCs than were whites (see table 5.2). African American co-partisans were an estimated 0.20 points farther than whites from their MCs (see column 1). This gap shrank a bit when we included controls for income and turnout, but remained significant (see column 2). Latino co-partisans were about 0.24 points farther than whites from their MCs, a gap that shrank only marginally when we added controls (see columns 3 and 4).[29]

28. The difference in the mean ideology (1–5-point scale) of whites and African Americans outside the South is 0.19; in the South, the difference is 0.24.

29. Note that these proximity gaps are actually greater among co-partisans than they are for all constituents (0.20 for co-partisan African Americans, compared to around

TABLE 5.2. MODELS OF DISTANCE FROM WHITE MCs AMONG
CO-PARTISAN CITIZENS AND CITIZENS REPRESENTED BY
FRESHMEN MCs

	Co-partisan citizens				Citizens represented by freshmen MCs			
African American	.199** [.018]	.142** [.025]	—	—	.135** [.444]	.166** [.060]	—	—
Latino	—	—	.236** [.763]	.195** [.025]	—	—	.075* [.041]	.025 [.057]
Household income	—	-.022** [.003]	—	-.020** [.003]	—	.008 [.007]	—	.008 [.007]
Turnout	—	-.058** [.016]	—	-.072** [.016]	—	-.064* [.035]	—	-.093** [.033]
Constant	.763** [.005]	.930** [.021]	.763** [.005]	.933** [.021]	1.01** [.011]	1.13** [.046]	1.108** [.011]	1.144** [.043]
N	17,505	9,436	17,995	9,670	5,824	2,964	6,157	3,113

Sources: 2000 National Annenberg Election Survey; Lewis and Poole 2004.
Note: Dependent variable: Senators' W-NOMINATE scores, 107th Senate.
$* p < .05; ** p < .01$; standard errors in brackets.

Fourth, if white constituents change their views to match those of their representatives more than other groups do, our evidence could again be misleading. It could be that whites' preferences are more responsive to the voting behavior of their MCs than are those of African Americans or Latinos when both groups are represented by whites. To limit the possibility of endogeneity, we analyzed the subset of NAES respondents who were represented by a freshman MC in the 107th Congress. This means we used constituent opinion measured before MCs cast a single roll-call vote to model votes from MCs' first two years in the chamber. This design purges the model of reciprocal effects because MCs' first-term votes cannot affect their constituents' ideologies prior to their election. We found that even among citizens who were represented by a freshman member of the House in the 107th Congress,

---

0.10 for all African Americans; see fig. 5.4). This does not mean that Democratic MCs are farther than Republican MCs from African American or Latino constituents. As we note below, Democrats are much closer than Republicans to their minority constituents. Instead, this result suggests that whites benefit even more than African Americans or Latinos from electing co-partisans.

African Americans and (less so) Latinos were politically unequal compared to whites when both groups were represented by whites (see table 5.2).

Fifth, some have suggested that MCs may vote more conservatively or liberally on average than their constituents would like (e.g., Bafumi and Herron 2007). That is, members' votes may generally be more conservative than the w-NOMINATE scores we use would indicate. Therefore, we examined whether shifting MCs as a group in a conservative (or liberal) direction would alter the nature of our conclusions (see fig. 5.7). If we uniformly shift the ideological location of all MCs 0.5 units to the right on the –1 to +1 scale, the results are virtually unchanged for African Americans compared to those we report—they remained further than whites from MCs in general as well as when the African American proportion of the district exceeded 12%, 25%, and even 40% (all $p < .05$, results not shown). For Latinos, shifting MCs to the right improves their relative representation, both in general and when Latinos make up a larger proportion of districts. For instance, across all districts Latinos are on average 0.07 points further than whites from their MCs ($p < .01$), whereas this group averaged 0.11 points further prior to the rightward shift. Although this is a better situation for Latinos, note that Latinos continue to be significantly farther from their MCs than are whites.

When we shift MCs to the left, the pattern for the groups is reversed—the picture becomes rosier for African Americans, relative to whites, but at least

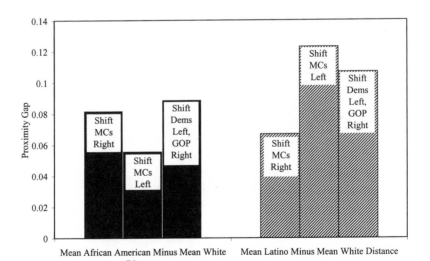

FIGURE 5.7. The proximity gap if Congress is more conservative, liberal, or varied (2000 National Annenberg Election Survey; Lewis and Poole 2004).

as bad if not worse for Latinos compared to whites. Specifically, we find that all African Americans are about 0.055 points farther than whites from their MCs, that there is a smaller backlash in districts with somewhat large African American populations, and that African Americans are no further than whites from their MCs once the African American population tops 40%. All Latinos are 0.12 points further than whites from their MCs, a gap that stays the same as the proportion of the district that is Latino increases to at least 12%, and then grows as this proportion increases to 25% (0.16), and 40% (0.21).

We also shifted Democratic MCs to the left and Republican MCs to the right. Upon doing so, we found that the proximity gap between whites and all African Americans remained about the same as it was prior to any manipulation of MCs' ideological locations (0.086), and this gap widened as the African American population increased, until the population exceeded 40%, at which point the two groups were equally distant from their MCs. Meanwhile the proximity gap between whites and all Latinos was similar to what we originally found (0.11), and this gap again grows as the Latino proportion of the district increases to more than 25% (0.16) or 40% (0.25). In sum, whether MCs as a group are actually more liberal or conservative than our measure suggests, or whether this differs by MC party, African Americans and Latinos remain further than whites from their MCs; systematic shifts in the location of MCs only affect the degree to which groups are unequally represented.

Next, it may be that it is difficult for MCs to represent many African Americans and Latinos well simply because they are more likely to reside in districts that are difficult to represent. If a district is heterogeneous, meaning the constituents in that district hold a wide variety of opinions, it will be impossible for any MC to represent this diversity when representation is conceived as proximity. In contrast, in a district in which the overwhelming majority of constituents is liberal or conservative, it is easier for an MC to represent most constituents well. To see whether this might be driving our results, we modeled constituents' distance from their MCs, controlling for district heterogeneity, household income, and MC party. To measure heterogeneity, following Sullivan (1973) and using data from the census, we calculate the fractionalization of the district's constituency based on race, income, and educational attainment.[30] Just as we anticipated, we find that

---

30. We calculate this by summing the squared proportions of residents in each category of a characteristic, dividing this sum by the total number of characteristics, and subtracting this value from 1. In calculating this measure, we use five racial subdivisions, three income subdivisions (to increase variation), and seven education subdivisions.

district heterogeneity increases the distance of MCs from their constituents (see table 5.3). In addition, and more important for our purposes, we find that African Americans and Latinos are significantly farther than whites from their MCs even after controlling for district heterogeneity.

Our final look at proximity gaps to evaluate race-conscious egalitarianism in the House looks at whites' and African Americans' proximity to their MCs on a specific issue—environmental protection—rather than overall ideology. We examine environmental protection in relation only to whites and African Americans because, as we saw in chapter 3, these groups' opinions differ on it (see fig. 3.3), an independent interest group has identified significant roll-call votes in this issue domain, and the issue is more salient for whites than African Americans (see figs. 3.6 and 3.8). As a result of this last point, our theoretical expectation is that whites would be advantaged in this specific domain. However, as we saw in the last chapter, whites were only slightly more often winners on environmental spending decisions compared to African Americans. Here, we extend the analysis of environmental policies beyond budgetary considerations to other votes on environmental issues. Finally, these comparisons afford

TABLE 5.3. GROUP DIFFERENCES IN PROXIMITY, CONTROLLING FOR DISTRICT HETEROGENEITY

	Whites and African Americans	**Whites and Latinos**
African American	0.063**	
	[.014]	
Latino		0.074**
		[0.014]
District heterogeneity	0.326**	0.453**
	[0.073]	[0.068]
Household income	−0.011**	−0.011**
	[0.002]	[0.002]
MC Republican	0.066**	0.045**
	[0.007]	[0.007]
Constant	0.901**	0.849**
	0.040	[0.038]
N	46,714	50,008

Sources: 2000 National Annenberg Election Survey; Lewis and Poole 2004; U.S. Census.
Note: Dependent variable: Distance from MC (Wright measure of distance).
*$p < .05$; **$p < .01$; standard errors in brackets.

us an opportunity to extend the broad-brush ideological analyses of this chapter to a specific issue.

To compare citizens' positions on environmental policy to legislators' actions, we examined key environmental votes identified by the League of Conservation Voters (LCV) in the 107th Congress. We use citizens' expressed opinions regarding environmental policy to assign them LCV scores, after reflecting the scaled 0–100 scores of representatives so that higher scores indicate less support for the LCV position.[31] We then used most of the techniques we have introduced to generate proximity measures.[32] These comparisons, summarized in figure 5.8, reveal that, according to two of the three available measures on this issue, whites are closer to their representatives than are African Americans. These results give us greater confidence that whites are more likely than African Americans to get what they want in the domain of environmental policy. In sum, our finding that African Americans and Latinos are farther from their MCs than are whites is robust to a number of related factors.

Race-Conscious Egalitarianism and Proximity in the Senate | We also apply the proximity approach to the Senate using the Wright measure of distance. Because each of the NAES respondents is represented by two senators, we compare each NAES respondent's ideological preference to both of their senators' voting behavior (again W-NOMINATE in the 107th Congress). These results, reported in figure 5.9, first show that, regardless of the proportion of a state's population that is African American or Latino, minorities are on average farther than whites from their senators. Even when African Americans or Latinos make up at least a quarter of the state population, they remain significantly farther than whites from their senators' voting patterns. Second, the proximity gap appears to be generally larger for African Americans than for Latinos. For example, in states where African Americans make up 12% or less of the population, the gap between whites' and African Americans' proximity to their senators (0.12 points) is twice the gap between whites and

31. The 2000 NAES question wording was, "Protecting the environment and natural resources—should the federal government do more about this, the same as now, less, or nothing at all?" We assigned citizens who indicated they preferred to increase federal effort to protect the environment a score of 0, those who wanted the same level of support a score of 25, those who desired less support 50, and those who desired no support a score of 100.
32. We could not use the binned technique because the NES did not ask citizens to place their representatives on an environmental scale.

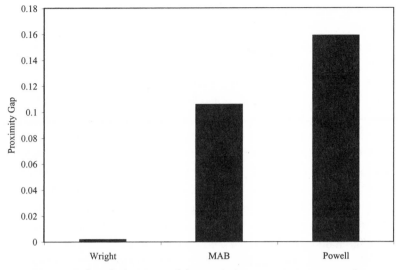

FIGURE 5.8. Nondescriptive MCs and the proximity gap on LCV votes, 107th Congress (2000 National Annenberg Election Survey; Web site of the League of Conservation Voters: http://www.lcv.org/scorecard/past-scorecards/ at 2001 and 2002).

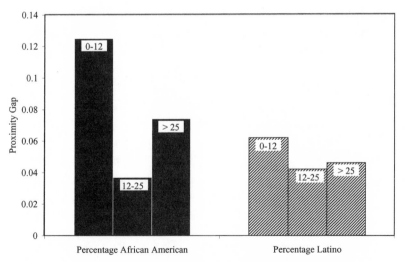

FIGURE 5.9. The proximity gap in the Senate, by state percentage African American or Latino (2000 National Annenberg Election Survey; Lewis and Poole 2004).

Latinos in states with 12% or fewer Latinos (0.06 points). In states where African Americans comprise at least a quarter of the population, the proximity gap is greater than 0.07 points, but the gap between whites and Latinos is just over 0.04 points in states where Latinos make up at least a quarter of the population. Third, the relative representation of African Americans does not steadily improve where they make up a larger share of the state's population, although this is generally true for Latinos.

One additional advantage of exploring proximity in the Senate is that it allows us to do a limited number of comparisons between specific senators and their constituents. That is, the sample sizes enable us to do some within-state comparisons. Our general approach is to measure each respondent's distance from his or her MC and then average across a number of different districts. To probe whether this averaging creates unexpected results, we compare the distance between African Americans in California and the California senators and the distance between whites in California to those same senators. Our data provide a large enough sample of African Americans and Latinos to perform meaningful analyses in California, New York, and Texas (for Latinos only). Figure 5.10 presents the proximity gaps

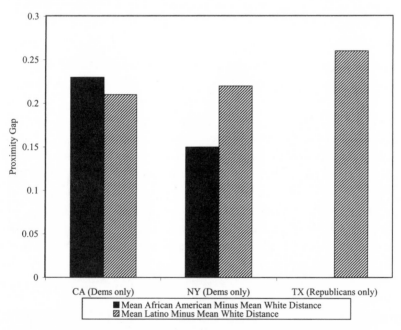

FIGURE 5.10. The within-state proximity gap (2000 National Annenberg Election Survey; Lewis and Poole 2004).

in these states. In each case, the senators were much farther from their co-partisan minority constituents than co-partisan whites. This gives us confidence that our methods of averaging across districts and states are not unduly skewing our results.

To summarize our findings to this point, senators' voting behavior is much more responsive and proximate to whites' preferences than those of African Americans or Latinos. Indeed, the responsiveness approach indicates that once we control for whites' preferences, the attitudes of racial and ethnic minorities appear to have *no impact at all* on the responsiveness of senators' roll-call patterns. Applying a race-conscious egalitarian standard to this finding, we see that minorities are politically unequal, since even relatively small racial and ethnic groups should be represented to some degree. In addition, the proximity gaps between minorities and whites exceed the gaps related to sex, age, education, and income. Moreover, African Americans and Latinos remain farther than whites from their MCs even where these groups make up a significant share (25–40%) of a district, which also points to a failure of the race-conscious egalitarian standard.

PROPORTIONALITY

This chapter's results thus far may seem somewhat unsurprising, given African Americans' and Latinos' generally much smaller share of state and congressional district populations compared to that of whites. Some might argue that if African Americans and Latinos comprise on average 12–14% of state and district populations, each group should exert about that percentage of the total influence on representatives. In this section we test this, examining whether the voting patterns of senators and representatives satisfy the requirements of the proportional standard of political equality. Specifically, we ask if the differences in responsiveness and proximity we report in table 5.1 and figure 5.4 are diminished in states and congressional districts with larger African American and Latino populations. We also see if representatives appear to be more responsive to individual whites than to individual members of minority groups.

Proportionality and Responsiveness | To assess whether African Americans and Latinos are proportionally represented in states with larger African American and Latino populations within a responsiveness framework, we first interact African American and Latino ideology with the percentage of

TABLE 5.4. STATE RACIAL/ETHNIC COMPOSITION AND
RESPONSIVENESS, 107TH SENATE

	Whites and African Americans	Whites and Latinos
African American opinion* state percentage African American	-3.209 [8.115]	—
African American opinion	-0.434 [1.307]	—
State percentage African American	6.768 [24.710]	—
Latino opinion* state percentage Latino	—	-.625 [7.442]
Latino opinion	—	1.198 [1.177]
State percentage Latino	—	2.102 [22.707]
White opinion	4.626** [0.650]	2.946** [.909]
Constant	-13.236** [4.133]	-13.164** [4.194]
N	52	42

Sources: 2000 National Annenberg Election Survey; Lewis and Poole 2004.
Note: Dependent variable: Senators' W-NOMINATE scores.
* $p < .05$; ** $p < .01$; standard errors in brackets.

each state's population comprised of African Americans or Latinos as measured by the U.S. Census. If senators respond to their minority constituents
more when they constitute a larger part of their constituency, this interaction term will be positive and statistically significant. As table 5.4 shows,
the interaction term is negative and fails to reach statistical significance,
meaning senators' relative responsiveness to African Americans and Latinos does not increase in states with larger African American or Latino
populations.[33]

33. Excluding the white ideology term from these models does not alter these results
in any important way. We also used a quadratic, linear in the terms model, but did not
find evidence of a systematic but nonlinear relationship. Finally, we estimated a parallel errors-in-variables model of the fifteen states where African Americans comprise at

The most likely explanation for this, in our view, is that the size of African American and Latino populations in most states is not large enough to boost minorities' likelihood of winning in the Senate. Indeed, prior studies of the House of Representatives find that, where the size of a district's African American population is larger, there is not a liberalizing effect on representative voting until African Americans comprise about 40% of the district, a level only a few states approach (Cameron, Epstein, and O'Halloran 1996; Lublin 1997). According to the 2000 Census, the states with the largest concentrations of African Americans, Mississippi and Louisiana, have populations that are 36% and 33% African American, respectively. In New Mexico, 42% of the residents are Latino, as are about 32% of the residents of California and Texas.[34] One way to test this explanation is to examine the proportionality standard of equality in the House of Representatives, where African Americans and Latinos, independently and in combination, often comprise a much larger share of electoral district populations. We turn to this in the next section.

Some might contend that this evidence is merely inferential, because we have simply found that in districts or states with larger minority populations, minority groups' representation relative to whites does not improve. This does not necessarily imply that individual African Americans or Latinos are less well represented than whites. There would be no need for a minority group to be better represented when its share of the population is larger if it was *ex ante* better represented than its numbers merited. Although our evidence thus far casts considerable doubt on this interpretation, we want to test the proportionality standard in as many ways as possible. Therefore we also assess the proportionality standard by examining the responsiveness of House representatives as a group to a national sample of individuals representing racial and ethnic groups.[35] For instance, to assess the responsiveness of MCs' votes to whites' and African Americans' preferences, we model each MC's W-NOMINATE score as a function of his

---

least 12% of the population. This estimation also showed that only white ideology has a positive effect on senators' general roll-call patterns. From any angle, state racial composition does little to improve responsiveness to minority preferences in the Senate.

34. We also examined an interaction between African American or Latino opinion and the combined percentage of African American and Latino state populations. These interactions were statistically insignificant for both Latinos and African Americans.

35. Our analyses focus on members of the House rather than senators for methodological reasons. Specifically, because the model requires the roll-call data to be replicated for each legislator's constituents, in order to obtain accurate standard errors we need

TABLE 5.5. INDIVIDUAL-LEVEL MODELS OF RESPONSIVENESS

	Whites and African Americans	Whites and Latinos
White ideology	.017** [.003]	.018** [.003]
African American ideology	.007** [.002]	—
Latino ideology	—	.007** [.003]
African American	.016 [.015]	—
Latino	—	.023** [.013]
MC Republican	.866** [.019]	.865** [.019]
N	10,796	10,496

Sources: 2000 National Annenberg Election Survey; Lewis and Poole 2004.
Notes: Dependent variable: MCs' W-NOMINATE scores. The probability that the white ideology and African American ideology estimates are equal is <.01. The probability that the white ideology and Latino ideology estimates are equal is also <.01.
* $p < .05$; ** $p < .01$; standard errors in brackets.

or her individual white and African American constituents' opinions, controlling for each respondent's race or ethnicity.[36]

Table 5.5 reports the results of these models for whites and African Americans and whites and Latinos. To be sure that the larger sample of whites in the NAES is not driving our results, we randomly sample among whites while retaining all of the African American and Latino respondents, so that the number of whites and African Americans (each 5,398) or whites and Latinos (each 5,248) in our models is identical. We find that MCs are

---

to cluster on the electoral district. This effectively reduces the sample size to the number of legislators in the model. By studying the House, we are able to bring much more data to bear on our question.

36. We are grateful to Ben Page for suggesting this approach. The model takes the form $y_j = a + b_1 x_{1ij} + b_2 x_{2ij} + b_3 x_{3ij} + b_4 x_{4j}$, where y_j is the W-NOMINATE score of the MC from district j, a is a constant, x_{1ij} is the opinion of white constituent i in district j, x_{2ij} is the opinion of African American constituent i in district j, x_{3ij} is the race (African American or white) of constituent i in district j, x_{4j} is the party affiliation of the MC from district j, and b_1, b_2, b_3, and b_4 are parameters to be estimated. If representatives' votes

about twice as responsive to individual whites' preferences as to they are to individual African Americans' preferences. The estimated parameters of 0.017 and 0.007 are significantly different from one another at the .05 level. The results are very similar when we compare whites and Latinos. Once again the estimated parameters of 0.018 and 0.007 are significantly different ($p < .05$). We take this as evidence that the average white constituent's preferences are a better predictor of MC votes than are those of the average African American or Latino constituent.

Proportionality and Proximity | In this section, we ask whether minority citizens are "closer" to their elected House representatives when they reside in congressional districts that contain a larger proportion of their racial or ethnic group. One way to test this is to compare the ideological proximity of racial and ethnic groups to their MCs when whites and minorities make up roughly equal shares of the district. In this case, the proportionality standard would demand that the groups be equally proximate. To gauge the degree of representation in these districts, we refer back to figure 5.6. We have already seen there that in districts that are at least 40% African American or Latino but that are not descriptively represented, whites are closer to their MCs than are minorities. So, even when minority populations begin to rival those of whites, minorities appear to remain unequally represented.[37]

---

respond more to whites' preferences, b_1 will be greater than b_2. As with our previous responsiveness models, this model is not intended to explain MCs' votes, but to describe the responsiveness of MCs' votes to constituents' preferences. If the preferences of individual whites correspond more with the behavior of their MCs than do those of individual African Americans, this would provide additional evidence that African Americans are unequal under a proportional standard of equality.

37. We also modeled ideological proximity (using the Wright 1978 measure) as a function of citizens' race, the percentage of census respondents in their district who share their race, the product of these factors, and respondent income. This is a systematic test of the interaction of district racial composition and respondent race on ideological distance that we observed in figure 5.6. In this model, the interaction term falls far short of statistical significance for African Americans. Where African Americans comprise a larger share of congressional districts, individual African Americans' ideological locations *are no more proximate* to their representatives' W-NOMINATE score. This is largely because, as we saw in chapter 2, whites in districts with larger African American populations tend to be more liberal, often because these districts tend to be more metropolitan. Thus, liberal MCs may be representing their white constituents in these districts rather than being especially sensitive to their African American constituents. In contrast, when we examine the relative proximity of Latinos and whites who are not represented by Latinos, we find that Latinos are somewhat nearer to their

A more stringent test of the proportionality standard is to compare the ideological proximity of groups to their MCs in districts where minorities amount to at least 50% of the constituency. In these districts, we would actually expect that if minorities are proportionally represented they should be *closer* than whites to their MCs. Of course, there are very few of these districts that are not represented by African American or Latino MCs, and thus few NAES respondents upon which to base our comparisons. So, the conclusions we draw from these analyses can be no more than preliminary. In these districts, on average, African Americans are 0.07 points further than whites from their MCs, even in districts that are majority African American. In contrast, Latinos are modestly (0.02 points) closer to their MCs than whites when they reside in majority Latino districts, although the difference is not statistically significant.[38]

To summarize our findings on the proportionality standard, we find no evidence that African Americans are equally represented by this standard. The size of the African American population makes senators no more responsive to African American preferences, the average white constituent's preferences are far better predictors of MC roll-call votes than the average African American's preferences, and African Americans in majority districts remain significantly farther than whites from their MCs (at least in districts not represented by African American MCs). In contrast, we found some evidence that Latinos are equally represented in a proportional sense. As we just saw, Latinos residing in majority Latino districts are just as close as whites are to their MCs. This evidence is not overwhelming, so we simply conclude that there is at least some evidence of proportional equality for Latinos.

PARTY DIFFERENCES IN RESPONSIVENESS AND PROXIMITY

Before we conclude this chapter, we probe another of the important contours of the gaps in political representation we have seen so far. Since the Democratic Party has long been the political home of racial minority groups

---

representative where the Latino proportion of the district is larger, but we do not have much confidence in this conclusion ($p = .15$). If we look only at Latinos represented by whites, we find that Latinos are more clearly proximate, relative to whites, when they comprise a larger proportion of an electoral district and are represented by whites (i.e., the p value of the interaction term is <.01).

38. We also found that these patterns hold even when we control for income. In addition, controlling for Latino threat districts, it appears that Latinos generally gain ground on whites in a linear fashion where the size of the Latino constituency is larger.

(e.g., Carmines and Stimson 1989), we might also expect that Democratic MCs would be more responsive to and closer to their minority constituents than are Republican MCs. This could be the result of at least two factors. First, candidates and officeholders who identify with the Democratic Party may simply hold policy views more in line with many African Americans' and Latinos' views. Although there are obviously exceptions, Democratic MCs tend to be more liberal, as do minority constituents. Second, Democratic candidates often rely on minority votes as critical elements of their voting coalition (Canon 1999). As a result, they may work especially hard to act in accordance with the preferences of their minority constituents (Bullock and Brady 1983). We can see whether Democrats really do represent minority preferences better by analyzing Democratic MCs and Republican MCs separately.

Doing this also yields analytical advantages. Some of our results so far ignore the powerful effects of MCs' partisanship on their roll-call decisions because we simply want to describe differences in proximity, whatever their pathway. It may be that the political inequality that we have seen thus far is simply a proxy for partisan effects. Do Democrats respond to minority preferences better than Republicans? In general, yes. When estimating the simple bivariate OLS model in table 5.1 for just Democratic senators, we find that Democratic senators respond to the preferences of African American constituents, as shown by the positive and statistically significant coefficient for African American ideology in table 5.6, column 1. In contrast, the results in column 2 show that Republican senators do not. Similarly, Democrats respond to their Latino constituents' preferences in a bivariate model (see table 5.6, column 5), but Republicans do not (column 6).

Although Democratic senators respond to minority preferences more than do Republican senators, even Democrats respond more to their white constituents than their minority constituents. When including both white and minority preferences in the model, we see that Democrats respond to white constituents' preferences, but not African American constituents' preferences. In fact, the coefficient for responsiveness to white preferences is seven times as large as that for African American preferences (column 3). When comparing Democrats' responsiveness to whites' and Latinos' preferences (column 7), we see that Democrats are responsive to both groups' preferences ($p = .10$ for Latinos), but are more responsive to whites' preferences. There, the responsiveness coefficient for whites' preferences is almost twice that of Latinos' preferences. Thus, in terms of responsiveness in the Senate, Democrats represent minority preferences better than do

TABLE 5.6. PARTY DIFFERENCES IN RELATIVE RESPONSIVENESS

MC party	Whites and African Americans				Whites and Latinos			
	Dem	GOP	Dem	GOP	Dem	GOP	Dem	GOP
White ideology	—	—	1.133** [.345]	.897* [.393]	—	—	1.014** [.332]	1.369* [.615]
African Am. ideology	.856* [.360]	.237 [.460]	.161 [.372]	-.190 [.461]	—	—	—	—
Latino ideology	—	—	—	—	1.015* [.398]	.236 [.530]	.618 [.363]	.093 [.479]
N	28	24	28	24	24	18	24	18

Sources: 2000 National Annenberg Election Survey; Lewis and Poole 2004.
Note: Dependent variable: Senators' w-NOMINATE scores.
*$p < .05$; **$p < .01$; standard errors in brackets.

Republicans, but even Democrats appear to favor their white constituents. We note, however, that a strong word of caution is required here since these models are based on very few observations, fewer than 30 senators each.

When we move to the House of Representatives and measures of proximity, we find some similar results. Figure 5.11 shows the average distance of whites, African Americans, and Latinos from their MCs, using the Wright measure of proximity. Recall that for African Americans, we look only at non–African American MCs, and for Latinos, we look only at non-Latino MCs, saving the discussion of descriptive representation for chapter 7. While Democrats and Republicans are about the same distance from their white constituents, Democrats are closer to their minority constituents than are Republicans. In fact, contrary to what we saw in the Senate, comparing the proximity of whites and African Americans represented by non–African American Democratic House representatives shows that African American constituents on average are actually *closer* to their MCs than are white constituents. In contrast, white constituents are to a much larger degree (four times as much) closer to Republican MCs than are African Americans. African Americans are clearly in a better position in terms of political equality with whites when represented by Democrats in the House.

The story for Latinos is a bit different. Whether represented by Republicans or Democrats, Latinos are on average farther than whites from their House MCs. Both parties seem to give whites an advantage. However, the proximity gap for Latinos is much larger (two times larger) when the MC is Republican. In general, the Democratic Party represents the preferences of minority groups much more than does the Republican Party, although we

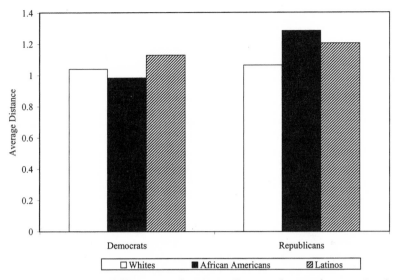

FIGURE 5.11. Party differences in the average distance of groups (2000 National Annenberg Election Survey; Lewis and Poole 2004).

have seen some evidence that minorities still seem to hold less sway than whites in both parties.

SUMMARY

In this chapter we presented a host of findings. We collect and summarize those findings here. In general, in the last two chapters we have seen inequality in the extent to which minority groups' preferences are reflected in the roll-call votes of senators and members of the House, as well as in the policies these votes ultimately produce. Looking across various political actors, issue domains, and analytical methods, we have seen that whites tend to be better represented than African Americans and Latinos. Specifically, where they are not descriptively represented, we have found the following:

- African Americans and Latinos are unequally represented in both the House of Representatives and in the Senate under the "more than proportional" rule of race-conscious egalitarianism.
- African Americans are unequally represented in both the House of Representatives and in the Senate under the less stringent proportional standard

of equality; in districts where African Americans make up a larger share of the district, they do not necessarily fare better.

- Significantly, these inequalities of representation are not simply reducible to income differences across groups.
- Moreover, these inequalities are not traceable solely to the effects of co-partisanship, endogeneity, or greater heterogeneity of opinion in the districts where African Americans and Latinos reside.
- These inequalities are evident whether we adopt a responsiveness or a proximity conceptualization of representation.
- There is some evidence that Latinos and whites are equally represented by the proportionality standard. In majority Latino districts, Latinos' preferences are reflected in MCs roll-call voting records every bit as much as whites' preferences are, even when their MCs are not Latino.
- In relative terms, Democratic MCs represent minority groups much better than do Republicans, although the members of both parties represent minorities worse than whites.

The previous two chapters paint a broad picture of inequality. In part 3, we pay close attention to more specific features of the American political system to see whether the broad strokes we have identified here hold under specific conditions. We explore whether the patterns of inequality described in the last two chapters are etched in stone or vary across different contexts within American politics.

PART THREE

Reducing Political Inequality

We saw in part 2 that African Americans, Latinos and whites are nearly always unequally represented when judged according to a race-conscious egalitarian standard of equality. Furthermore, there is no evidence that African Americans are equally represented when judged against a proportional standard of political equality, and only mixed evidence that Latinos are equally represented under this standard. Moreover, these differences in political representation extend both to policy outcomes and to the congressional voting decisions that lead to these outcomes. We anticipate that many democratic theorists will be troubled by these observations and eager to explore ways to enhance minorities' political equality. This is our next step. In part 3, we explore three prominent means by which these differences in political representation might be alleviated. In doing so, we seek to answer Robert Dahl's fundamental question, "How is it possible to provide and maintain a real equality of representation and power over government?" (1967, 10).

First, we determine if there are particular domains in which minority groups' representation improves relative to whites. If so, these groups may be able to boost their relative representation by communicating to elected officials the significance of additional issues to the group. A second potential way to lessen disparities in political representation is to elect more African American and Latino representatives. A third way is to promote minority political participation. These investigations help us to "sort out why preferences and elite decisions overlap" (Verba 2003, 666), or to explain why some groups are better represented than others. This knowledge is important in and of itself, but also because it contributes to the fashioning of public policies to enhance the equality of representation.

SIX

Pluralism and Political Representation

The time has come when powerless and small groups of people, minority people, can not be shunted away, can not be set aside or pushed aside without explanation.

CESAR CHAVEZ,
Speech at Santa Clara University, October 26, 1972

I have a dream that one day this nation will rise up and live out the true meaning of its creed: "We hold these truths to be self-evident, that all men are created equal."

MARTIN LUTHER KING JR.,
Speech at Civil Rights March on Washington, August 28, 1963

The successes of farm workers in improving their working conditions and wages and of African Americans in upending legal discrimination in the 1960s and 1970s suggest that even groups substantially in the minority can see their preferences realized in the decisions of government. But does this occur only under extraordinary circumstances, when minorities take to the streets or organize mass protests, or does the regular operation of government protect minority rights?

In this chapter, we ask whether specific issue domains constitute pockets of political equality among African Americans, Latinos, and whites. In particular, we ask whether minority constituents and whites are equally represented in issue domains that minorities care about more than whites do. Both theoretical reasoning and empirical regularities suggest that this may be the case. After reviewing the basis of our expectations, we assess whether minorities are equally represented in terms of policy outcomes and legislators' voting behavior on issues distinctively salient

for them. Finally, we discuss the implications of our findings for strategies to reduce disparities in political representation.

As noted in chapter 2, the notion that intensely held preferences *ought* to be specially represented, even when those preferences are in the minority, has a long association with the pluralist view of government. Robert Dahl proposed pluralism as a way to solve what he called "the intensity problem" that arises when intense minorities are opposed by an apathetic majority. Scholars have built on the normative claim that, at least in some cases, intense minorities should prevail with theoretical explanations for how this might occur and empirical investigations of whether it does occur. On the theoretical side, models of representative behavior show that reelection-minded legislators have incentives to act on behalf of a minority group against the majority when the minority group holds disproportionately intense preferences (e.g., Downs 1957; Fiorina 1974). Specifically, Fiorina proved that where the intensity of a minority group's preference is sufficiently large relative to that of the majority, this can offset its numerical weakness, causing a vote-maximizing legislator to side with the minority group. For example, "If a representative estimates that [intensity of preference is at a maximum] for a local sportsmen's club on a gun-control vote and miniscule for everyone else, [vote] maximizing may dictate voting with the hunters despite their small numbers" (55–56). Similarly, Dahl (1967, 130) argued that citizens' political influence is partly a function of "dedication," for "[a] Congressman is likely to be sensitive to a group so intensely committed on a particular issue that they are likely to vote against any candidate who takes the 'wrong' position, as in the case of Negroes [sic] on civil rights and integration." In addition, the proliferation of domain-specific interest organizations that transfer information in that domain from legislators to constituents and back suggests that intense preferences are better communicated and therefore better represented (Wright 1996, 91). Thus, the presence of an active interest organization in a domain may generate better minority representation in this domain. In sum, officials' reelection calculus may help prevent apathetic majorities from trampling the preferences of intense minorities.

On the empirical side, scholars have long held that public opinion is structured around "issue publics," groups of citizens who are especially concerned about a specific issue (Converse 1964; Krosnick 1990). In addition, the record shows that government policies and the decisions of legislators are more responsive to public opinion on issues or specific votes that are more salient for citizens *as a whole* (Miller and Stokes 1963; Page and Shapiro 1983; Krosnick and Telhami 1995; Campbell 2003; Hutchings,

McClerking, and Charles 2004; Wlezien 2004). One reason that government appears more responsive to citizens on salient issues is that on issues they care more about, citizens are more likely to pay attention to information in the media and election campaigns, and to make choices between candidates based on these salient issues (Iyengar 1990; Hutchings 2001 and 2003).[1] For example, African Americans pay greater attention than whites to civil rights issues in the media and in election campaigns, and African Americans more than whites were able to identify their senator's vote on Justice Clarence Thomas's appointment to the Supreme Court (Iyengar 1990; Hutchings 2001). Citizens who care more about an issue may also be more likely to engage in various forms of political participation to articulate that concern, which will improve their representation in that particular area (Visser, Krosnick, and Simmons 2003). Finally, legislators' roll-call patterns are more sensitive to the racial and ethnic composition of their districts on issues more salient for minorities (Lublin 1997; Hutchings 1998; Canon 1999).

We build on these studies by comparing the representation of African Americans and Latinos to whites' representation on issues uniquely salient for minority groups. In doing so, we aim to answer an important empirical question central to democratic theory: "Is there reason to believe that certain identifiable minority groups are permanently . . . disadvantaged by the existing rules for making decisions, and in a way that does not facilitate handling of [Dahl's] intensity problem?" (Kendall and Carey 1968, 24). If we find that African Americans and Latinos are not permanently disadvantaged, that is, if minorities' representation rivals or exceeds that of whites in some areas, we will conclude that under a pluralist standard of political equality, these groups are politically equal. We examine this question from the three vantage points introduced in chapters 4 and 5. We begin with the broad view, comparing constituent opinion and government policy. We then move to the Senate to examine senators' responsiveness and finish in the House of Representatives, where we explore the question via our measures of constituents' proximity to their representatives. These three sets of analyses all point in the same direction, adding up to three waves of evidence suggesting that African Americans and Latinos are politically equal compared to whites under the pluralist standard of equality.

---

1. Relatedly, highly important attitudes are more likely to affect individuals' decision making, perhaps because information about important issues is more cognitively accessible (Schuman and Presser 1981; Krosnick 1988 and 1990; Boninger, Krosnick, and Berent 1995).

ISSUE SALIENCE AND POLICY REPRESENTATION

In chapter 4, we explored collective representation, assessing the connection between groups' preferences and government outlays in a number of issue domains. We found that compared to whites, African Americans and Latinos were less likely to be policy "winners" in most domains we examined. However, we only examined issues that were not disproportionately salient for minorities—issues that were either of equal salience across the groups or were more salient for whites. We intentionally reserved the study of policies that are uniquely salient for African Americans or Latinos for this chapter. Recall from chapter 3 that welfare, and perhaps health care and crime spending, are issues that are more salient for African Americans than whites, and that welfare, crime, health care, and education spending are issues that are much more salient for Latinos than for whites (see figures 3.6, 3.7, and 3.8). In addition to differences in salience, there are also substantial differences of opinion among these groups on these issues (see figures 3.3 and 3.5). In this section, we ask whether government outlays in these domains equally reflect group preferences.

To do so, we proceed in the same fashion as in our analyses of other issues. First, looking at the period from 1973 to 2002, we compare individuals' preferences for more, the same, or less spending with changes in the next year's federal government outlays to determine whether the individual was a policy winner, loser, or big loser in an issue domain. Figure 6.1 presents the percentages of winners and big losers in each domain.

In contrast to our previous finding that whites generally are better represented in federal outlay decisions, we find that on issues uniquely salient for minority groups, those groups are often represented *equally well or even better* than whites. Recall, first, that in the policy domains where we observed that whites are advantaged, whites are generally about 5–9 percentage points more likely than minorities to be policy winners. This will be our benchmark against which to judge the impact of changing policy domains on minorities' political equality. On welfare spending, which is more salient for both minority groups, African Americans and Latinos are both more likely than whites to be winners: 42% of African Americans were welfare winners, compared to 20% of whites. This 22-point difference far exceeds the 5–9-point benchmark. In fact, it exceeds the greatest difference between whites and African American winners we found (16 points for space exploration). In addition, twice the percentage of whites were

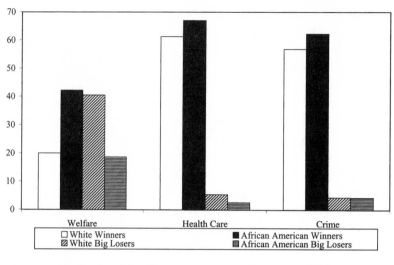

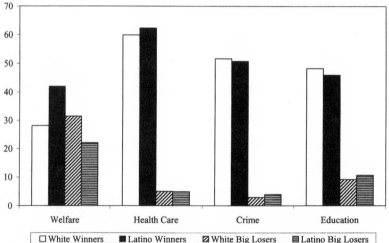

FIGURE 6.1. Percentage of policy winners in salient domains for minority groups (Office of Management and Budget 2004; General Social Survey [6.1a: 1972–94, 1996, 1998, 2000, 2002]; Roper poll [6.1a: 1979, 1981, 1992; 6.1b: 1979–94]).

"big losers" compared to African American "big losers." Indeed, nearly the same proportion of whites were big losers as African Americans were winners in this domain. The story is much the same for Latinos. In chapter 4 we saw that white winners outnumbered Latino winners by 4–7 percentage points in domains not distinctively salient to Latinos. However, for

welfare, 42% of Latinos were winners, compared to 28% of whites.[2] This 14-point difference doubles the largest gap we saw in chapter 4 (7 points on defense spending). In addition, about 30% of whites were big losers, compared to 21% of Latinos.

We also note that African Americans' and Latinos' advantage on welfare extends even into the 1990s, during which major welfare reform was enacted (in 1996), significantly scaling back welfare spending. For example, the increase in welfare outlays from fiscal year 1996 to 1997 was a mere 1%, which pales in comparison to many of the earlier years, which averaged a 10.4 % increase in outlays between fiscal years 1972 and 2003. Many will certainly wonder how African Americans could be winners on welfare when this major reform was opposed by many African American leaders. Since this was a major policy change, it would be harmful to our expectations if African Americans won most of the time, but lost with regard to big decisions. However, Katherine Tate (2007) has noted that African Americans' preferences for welfare policies shifted so that by the mid-1990s a sizeable number of African Americans favored welfare reform. In fact, she notes that in the 1996 NES, more African Americans favored a decrease in welfare spending than favored an increase in spending. We found similar patterns in our data.

To explore whether minorities continued to be equally or more likely to win than whites in the 1990s, we generated year-by year comparisons of policy winners for racial and ethnic groups (see fig. 6.2). Breaking down the results over time provides a more interesting and nuanced story, but does not alter our conclusions. We do see a steady erosion in the percentage of African American (and, to a lesser degree, Latino) winners on welfare spending from 1973 to 2002. By the late 1990s (after the 1996 welfare reform) African Americans and whites were about equally likely to be policy winners. Although the percentage of African American and Latino winners generally declined over time, even after welfare reform *African Americans and Latinos remained as likely as whites to be winners, or more so.*

Our finding that African Americans' policy representation may be greatest in the area of welfare policy is particularly interesting in light of the racialized nature of welfare in the United States (e.g., Gilens 1999 and 2003). According to Gilens (1999), white Americans are generally supportive of many social programs, but hold a certain animus toward welfare. This animus is rooted in whites' overestimation of the proportion of welfare re-

---

2. The percentages of white winners differ in figure 6.1a and 6.1b because the analyses are based on different years.

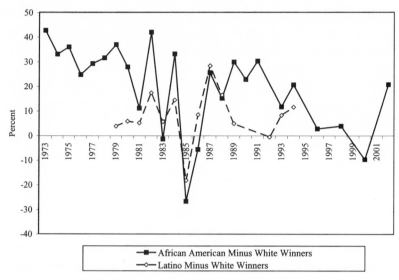

FIGURE 6.2. Year-by-year analyses of African American and Latino policy winners on welfare spending (Office of Management and Budget 2004; General Social Survey 1972–94, 1996, 1998, 2000, 2002; Roper poll 1979–94).

cipients who are African American, and in a consequent attitude that welfare recipients are undeserving. He argues that the impression that welfare programs primarily serve African Americans is rooted in "racialized" media portrayals of welfare. We provide an additional basis for whites' negative assessments of welfare spending that does not require that whites be hostile toward African Americans or that media sources appeal to whites' biases (though both may be true)—welfare is one national policy area where whites are much more likely than African Americans or Latinos to "lose."

Moving on from welfare, the results in other domains continue to support the finding that minority citizens win as often or even slightly more often than whites on issues distinctively salient to their groups (see fig. 6.1). On spending for health care, which also is particularly salient for African Americans and Latinos, both groups are more likely to be winners than whites—African Americans by about 6 percentage points and Latinos by about 3 percentage points. On spending to fight crime, 6 percentage points more African Americans than whites were policy winners, and Latinos' rate of winning rivals that of whites.[3] Finally, whites are more likely than

3. Our finding that Latinos are equally represented in the area of spending to fight crime might be disputed on the grounds that while Latinos want government to fight

Latinos to be winners on education spending, but only by a little more than 2 percentage points. In sum, the proportion of African American and Latino winners on federal outlays rivals and often exceeds that of whites in policy domains that these groups care more about than do whites. These results offer the first wave of evidence that the American political system satisfies a pluralist standard of political equality with respect to racial and ethnic groups.

ISSUE SALIENCE AND SENATOR RESPONSIVENESS

As we noted in chapter 4, examining collective representation through the lens of our policy analyses can only provide a partial view of relative representation. Significantly, since the extent of collective representation tends to be greater than dyadic representation (Weissberg 1978), evidence that minority groups are politically equal in these domains in the sense of collective representation may not mean they are politically equal in the sense of dyadic representation. Therefore, to test the pluralist standard even further, we turn to our other approaches. For the next two waves of evidence, we examine the two chambers of Congress to see whether members are more responsive and proximate to their minority constituents on distinctively salient issues.[4]

We begin in the Senate. To examine whether senators are more responsive to minorities' salient concerns, we extend our prior analysis of senators' responsiveness to specific issues that are more salient for minorities. This

---

crime by attacking the roots of criminality, including poverty and unequal educational opportunity, government efforts to fight crime primarily involve putting more police on the streets, building prisons, and otherwise enhancing the criminal justice system. For instance, a 2004 poll commissioned by the National Council of La Raza found that nearly three-quarters of Hispanics prefer dealing with the "causes of crime, with an emphasis on job training, counseling, and neighborhood activity centers for young people" (74%) rather than "a tougher approach to crime with an emphasis on stricter sentencing, capital punishment for more crimes, and fewer paroles for convicted felons" (22%). However, this evidence does not show that if Latinos had to choose between spending additional money to fight crime through a tougher approach to crime or redirecting those funds to another policy domain, they would choose the latter.

4. This is not to say only Congress protects minority interests. Others have observed that the federal courts (Barnum 1985; Frymer 2003; but see Dahl 1956) and the president, independently and through executive appointments to the courts (Gates and Cohen 1988; Cohen 1997; Riley 1999; Mayer 2001; Conley 2005), have intervened in the policy process to protect the interests of racial minorities.

analysis requires measures of senators' roll-call behavior on issues salient to minorities as well as measures of minorities' corresponding opinions on these issues.

We follow others in relying on the Leadership Council on Civil Rights' (LCCR) identification of key votes (Lublin 1997; Whitby 1998; Canon 1999) to locate roll calls on issues particularly salient for African Americans in the 107th Senate. Some have argued that LCCR votes are not in every case of greater interest to African Americans, and that in some instances the LCCR's position has diverged from the mean attitudes of African Americans (e.g., Canon 1999). Therefore, we examine only LCCR votes that relate to explicitly racial issues or to implicitly racial issues that are also more salient for African Americans, such as income security. Seven of the fourteen LCCR votes in the 107th Senate met these criteria (see table 6.1).[5] Using these votes, we calculated the proportion of votes on which each senator opposed the LCCR among votes in which that senator participated.

To locate roll calls in the 107th Senate that were more salient for Latinos, we rely on key votes identified by the National Hispanic Leadership Agenda (NHLA), a nonpartisan coalition of major Latino organizations whose mission is to "provide the Hispanic community with a clearer, stronger voice" in the country's affairs.[6] Fortunately, the NHLA groups the key congressional votes it identifies into subcategories, including votes related to two of the issue domains we have identified as distinctively salient for Latinos—economic security and education. Unfortunately, the NHLA does not identify key votes related to crime control or health care. Using the NHLA votes enumerated in table 6.1, we calculated the proportion of votes in each policy area in which senators took part and opposed the position of the NHLA to measure senators' positions on economic security and education policy.

For measures of citizens' preferences in these domains, we again rely on the NAES. First, we combined two NAES items related to "LCCR-like" issues to measure citizens' general attitudes on issues are salient for African Americans: whether the federal government should do more to end

5. Omitted from the creation of the index are votes concerning bilingual education, the prohibition of groups that deny membership on the basis of sexual orientation from meeting in public schools, and education funding, among others.
6. For additional information about the NHLA, and the NHLA congressional scorecards, see the Web site of the League of United Latin American Citizens: http://www .lulac.org/.

TABLE 6.1. VOTES USED TO CREATE ROLL-CALL SCORES ON SALIENT
ISSUES, 107TH SENATE

Votes used to create LCCR scores

Date	Roll-call #		Brief description
	Senate	*LCCR*	
2.1.01	—	1	Ashcroft Confirmation as Attorney General
3.8.01	18	2	Hatch motion to table Durbin amendment to predatory lending bill that would invalidate claims against borrowers if the lender had violated the Truth in Lending Act
5.10.01	98	5	Tax cuts limiting spending increases in various domestic programs
5.26.01	107	9	Conference bill to cut taxes, limiting increases in domestic programs
2.14.02	31	11	Vote on amendment that would restore right to vote in federal elections to felons who have fully served their prison sentences
2.27.02	38	12	Motion to amend the Election Bill so other means of identification could substitute for photo identification for first-time voters registering by mail
6.11.02	147	13	Motion to invoke cloture on bill to extend federal hate-crime status to all crimes committed on the basis of race, color, religion, or national origin

Votes used to create NHLA scores

Date	Roll-call #		Brief description
	Senate	*NHLA*	
			Economic Security
5.10.01	98	1	Tax cuts limiting spending increases in various domestic programs
5.26.01	107	2	Vote on conference bill to cut taxes, limiting increases in various domestic programs; $1.35 trillion in tax relief
5.23.01	159	3	Amendment 741 to H.R. 1836; refundable children's tax credit
1.29.02	6	6	Amendment 2714 to H.R. 622; to enhance unemployment benefits
			Education
6.14.01	192	1	S. 1; ESEA reauthorization
5.15.01	103	2	Amendment 378 to S. 1; class-size reduction amendment
5.10.01	100	3	Amendment 451 to S. 1; increase authorization levels for Bilingual Education Act to $1.2 billion in 2002

(continued)

TABLE 6.1. (*continued*)

	Votes used to create NHLA scores		
Date	Roll-call #		Brief description
	Senate	NHLA	
5.16.01	108	4	Amendment 525 to S. 1; $1.6 billion authorization for public school infrastructure
5.10.01	99	5	Amendment 403 to S. 1; ensure Title I assessments are fair
6.5.02	132	6	Amendment 3608 to H.R. 4775; $150 million for summer school programs in high-poverty communities

job discrimination against African Americans, and whether poverty is a serious national problem.[7] We used these questions to generate individual states' "white LCCR ideology" and "African American LCCR ideology" for each of the twenty-six states we analyzed in chapter 4.[8]

To measure citizens' attitudes in the two issue areas more salient for Latinos, we use a single NAES item for each domain. The first item asked whether the federal government should work to reduce income differences among Americans (yes or no), and the second asked how much money the

7. We did this using principal-components factor analysis. The first principal factor of this analysis had an eigenvalue of 1.23, with factor loadings of 0.71 for the two items. The question wording of these items was as follows: "Trying to stop job discrimination against blacks—should the federal government do more about this, the same as now, less, or nothing at all?" "The amount of poverty in the United States—is this an extremely serious problem, serious, not too serious, or not serious at all?" To assess whether this measure is equally reliable for whites and African Americans, we created separate factor scores for each group. The items load on a single factor for both African Americans and Latinos (eigenvalue is 1.53 for whites and 1.24 for African Americans). Furthermore, factor loadings for whites are somewhat larger than those for African Americans, so African Americans' better representation in this domain cannot be attributed to racial differences in measurement error. After extracting these factors, we generated a factor score for each respondent answering both items, and use the state white and African American means of these scores in the twenty-six states we analyzed in chapter 4 to measure each state's white LCCR ideology and African American LCCR ideology.

8. Under standard definitions of reliability (see Jones and Norrander 1996), state-level mean white attitudes for LCCR ideology were highly reliable (.94). In contrast, African Americans' state-level means for LCCR ideology were moderately reliable (.57). To compensate for the lower reliability of the measures for African Americans, we use an errors-in-variables estimator in some of the estimations we report.

federal government should invest in the educational system (more, the same, less, or none). Focusing on the twenty-one states we analyzed in chapter 4, we use state-level mean white and Latino opinion on the income differences item to model senators' NHLA economic security scores, and state mean white and Latino opinion on the education item to model senators' NHLA education scores.[9]

Our modeling approach to assess the representation of minority groups on distinctively salient issues in most respects mirrors our approach in chapter 5 to examine the responsiveness of senators to groups on issues equally salient or more salient to whites. The principal departure is that we are less eager to use the errors-in-variables estimator in these models in order to "stack the deck" against the hypothesis that minority preferences are equally represented by using less reliable measures for the minority groups. This is simply because we want to provide a more conservative test of pluralist claims.

As table 6.2 shows, the pattern of senators' responsiveness to group attitudes is unique on the LCCR and NHLA votes. First, on LCCR roll calls, senators' votes responded *more to African Americans' preferences* than to whites' preferences. In the bivariate models, the responsiveness coefficient is 1.65 for whites (column 1) and 1.95 for African Americans (column 2). When we include both preference measures in the same model (column 3), we find that senators' estimated responsiveness to African American opinion is 75% greater than their responsiveness to white opinion. In fact, senators appear not to be responsive at all to white opinion once we control for African American opinion. After we control for measurement error, responsiveness to African Americans' preferences grows sharply relative to that of whites, whose preferences are estimated to have a negative effect on roll-call voting. Given the quite dramatic change in estimates when using the errors-in-variables estimator, we are inclined to downplay these results and focus on the more conservative OLS results in the rest of the table. However, since controlling for measurement error further supports our findings, rather

9. The reliability of state-level opinion on the income differences item was .86 and .39 for whites and Latinos, respectively, and on the education item was .75 and .29 for whites and Latinos, respectively. Given the unreliable nature of these measures of Latino opinion, we must interpret the results with considerable caution. However, unreliable measures of Latino opinion work against finding significant Latino representation. Thus, to the extent we find any positive Latino representation, we can fairly confidently infer that Latinos really are represented in these domains. Still, we account for these differences in measurement error in some of the models we report below.

TABLE 6.2. MODELS OF LCCR VOTES, 107TH SENATE

Estimator	OLS	OLS	OLS	Errors in Variables
White LCCR ideology	1.65** [.52]	—	.83 [.60]	-.70 [1.09]
African American LCCR ideology	—	1.95** [.50]	1.45* [.61]	4.12* [1.62]
Constant	.35** [.08]	1.81** [.33]	1.40** [.44]	3.31** [1.17]
p-value	—	—	.55	.07
N	52	52	52	52
R^2	.17	.23	.26	.41

Sources: 2000 National Annenberg Election Survey; LCCR.
Notes: Dependent variable: Senators' revised LCCR scores. Reported p-value is from two-tailed hypothesis test that the white and African American LCCR ideology estimates are equal.
*$p < .05$; **$p < .01$; standard errors in brackets.

than raising a red flag by generating different results, we are a bit more confident about our conclusions. On issues distinctively important to African Americans, senators are more responsive to African Americans' preferences than to whites' preferences.

The substantive impact of these differences is substantial. To gauge this, we predict senators' probability of opposition to the LCCR using the parameter estimates reported in the third column of table 6.2. As African Americans' LCCR ideologies changed from the 25th to the 75th percentile in the distribution, becoming more opposed to the LCCR, senators opposed the LCCR's position about 20 percentage points more often, from 48% to 68% (see fig. 6.3). In contrast, a similar, conservative change in white LCCR ideology produces a 12 percentage-point loss in LCCR support.[10]

When we model NHLA economic security scores as a function of white or Latino opinion separately (see table 6.3, columns 1 and 2), we see senators are somewhat more responsive to white opinion (compare the 2.38 coefficient for white opinion to the 1.48 coefficient for Latino opinion). However, once we control for the relationship between whites' and Latinos' opinions on welfare policy (column 3), only the Latino opinion estimate approaches statistical significance ($p = .08$). In the multivariate errors-in-variables model presented in column 4, senators are only responsive to Latinos; only

10. The ranges of white (0.64) and African American (0.50) opinion are similar.

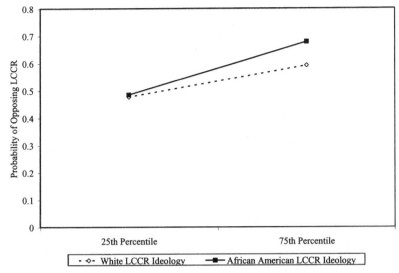

FIGURE 6.3. Responsiveness of senators on issues distinctively salient for African Americans, 107th Congress (2000 National Annenberg Election Survey; Leadership Conference on Civil Rights, online at http://www.civilrights.org/research_center/voting_scorecards/voting_scorecards.html [all links relating to 107th Congress]).

TABLE 6.3. MODELS OF NHLA VOTES, 107TH SENATE

	Economic security				Education			
Estimator	OLS	OLS	OLS	Errors in variables	OLS	OLS	OLS	Errors in variables
White opinion	2.38** [1.12]	—	1.28 [1.25]	−5.28 [4.16]	.86 [.90]	—	.56 [.95]	−.97 [2.68]
Latino opinion	—	1.48* [.56]	1.15 [.64]	7.23* [3.55]	—	.62 [.49]	.52 [.53]	2.74 [2.97]
Constant	−3.34 [1.72]	−1.62* [.74]	−3.16 [1.68]	−1.07 [2.16]	−.95 [1.34]	−.41 [.60]	−1.13 [1.36]	−1.53 [1.69]
p-value	—	—	.94	.11	—	—	.98	.50
N	42	42	42	42	42	42	42	42
R^2	.10	.15	.17	.50	.02	.03	.05	.14

Sources: 2000 National Annenberg Election Survey; NHLA.
Note: Dependent variable: Revised NHLA economic security or education scores. Reported p-value is from two-tailed hypothesis test that the white and Latino opinion estimates are equal.
*$p < .05$; **$p < .01$; standard errors in brackets.

the estimate for Latinos is positive and statistically significant. We interpret these results as evidence that senators are at least equally responsive to and perhaps somewhat more responsive to Latinos than to whites on economic security policies.

When we examine the NHLA education votes, we first see that when we model these votes as a function of white opinion and Latino opinion separately (columns 5 and 6), senators once again appear to be more responsive to whites than Latinos, although the standard errors for both models are too large to conclude much with certainty. However, when both Latinos' and whites' preferences are included (column 7), senators appear equally responsive to whites and Latinos. Finally, the results of the errors-in-variables model (column 8) suggest that senators are more responsive to Latinos than whites, although the standard errors are once again too large to draw conclusions confidently. We draw the conservative conclusion that there is no evidence to suggest that senators respond more to whites on education policy. In general, senators' votes on economic security and education policies, which are more important to Latinos than whites, appear to be at least as responsive to this group's preferences as to the preferences of whites.

Putting more precise figures on these conclusions, using the results from columns 3 and 7 in table 6.3, where Latinos' economic security opinions are more opposed to the NHLA's positions, we see that senators opposed the NHLA's position about 15 percentage points more often (see fig. 6.4). Where whites' opinions are more opposed to the NHLA's position, senators' opposition to NHLA economic security positions increased about 9 percentage points (reflecting a smaller difference between the 25th and 75th percentile). As Latinos' education funding opinion changed from the 25th to the 75th percentile, becoming more opposed to NHLA positions, senators opposed the NHLA's position about 5 percentage points more often. In contrast, a similar change in white education funding opinion is anticipated to reduce support 4 percentage points. The main point is that Latinos are roughly equally represented (or may be slightly better represented) compared to whites in these domains.

ISSUE SALIENCE AND PROXIMITY

So far we have seen that both in terms of dyadic and collective representation, minorities are represented as well as whites are in domains of distinctive salience. However, as we saw in chapter 5, such evidence may mask important

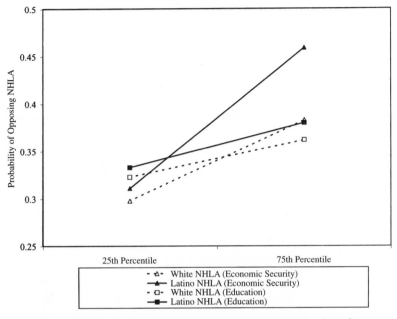

FIGURE 6.4. Responsiveness of senators on issues distinctively salient for Latinos, 107th Congress (2000 National Annenberg Election Survey; National Hispanic Leadership Agenda, online at http://www.lulac.org/publications/107thcongress-1-2.pdf.).

aspects of representation. In particular, evidence that senators are more responsive to African Americans on LCCR votes may not prove to be terribly important in a normative sense. As we noted in chapter 5, it may be that senators are more *responsive* to African American opinion on these issues, but are actually acting in ways that are *closer* to the preferences of whites.

To complete our picture of relative representation on these issues and to be sure minority groups really are meaningfully gaining relative representation, we turn to the third wave of evidence, looking at constituents' proximity to members of the House of Representatives. Are minority constituents also "closer" to their elected representatives on issues that minorities care more about? This will tell us more definitively that when minorities care about an issue, legislators pay greater heed to them in that domain. We compared groups' overall ideological proximity in chapter 5; now we measure the proximity of citizens to their House representatives on specific issues that are more salient for these groups. We limit our analysis to representatives who are not the same race or ethnicity as the racial

or ethnic minority group.[11] We do so because descriptive representation is an alternative factor potentially affecting the political equality of minority groups (we explore this factor in the next chapter).

Here again, we rely on representatives' voting behavior on selected LCCR and NHLA House votes, listed in table 6.4. Many of these votes parallel the votes we analyzed in the Senate, but some are unique. As above, these scores indicate the proportion of votes on which the representative participated and opposed the LCCR or NHLA. We use the same measures of citizen preferences described above. Based on these preferences and MC votes, we generate proximity measures on these scales using three of the techniques described in chapter 5.[12]

To see which group is closer to its representatives, we calculate the proximity gap on LCCR votes, with higher gaps indicating that whites are closer than African Americans to their MCs. We follow an equivalent strategy for whites and Latinos on NHLA votes. Figure 6.5 shows these proximity gaps, along with the proximity gap for all issues, which we presented in chapter 5. If minorities are equally represented on issues that are distinctively salient for them, we expect that the proximity gaps on LCCR and NHLA votes and citizens' related opinions will be near to zero, indicating equal distance across groups.

As we saw in the previous chapter, on all issues, African Americans are between 0.07 and 0.09 points farther than whites from their MCs, depending on the specific proximity measure (see solid black columns). By all three measures available for the present analysis, the proximity gap decreases substantially when we shift to LCCR votes (see columns with horizontal lines). The proximity gap shrinks to about 0.05 by the Powell measure and about 0.01 by the other two. The gap is statistically indistinguishable from zero according to these two measures.

We find similar results for Latinos. On all issues, whites are 0.09 or 0.10 points closer to their MCs than are Latinos (see columns with lines slanting up to the right). However, the proximity gap shrinks dramatically when we examine only NHLA votes (see columns with diagonals slanting down to the right). There is even some evidence that Latinos are better represented

11. As in chapter 5, this means we include all non–African American MCs in our comparison of white and African American constituents' proximity and non-Latino MCs in our comparisons of white and Latino constituents' proximity.
12. We do not report analyses using the binned measure because citizens' placements of their MCs on LCCR and NHLA issues are not available.

TABLE 6.4. VOTES USED TO CREATE ROLL-CALL SCORES ON SALIENT
ISSUES, 107TH HOUSE

Votes used to create LCCR scores

Date	Roll-call #		Brief description
	House	*LCCR*	
3.1.01	23	1	Democratic substitute amendment to Bankruptcy Abuse Prevention and Consumer Protection Act (H.R. 333)
5.9.01	104	2	Tax cuts limiting spending increases in various domestic programs
10.24.01	404	6	Vote on Economic Security and Recovery Act of 2001 (H.R. 3090), which includes a $1.3 trillion tax cut
12.6.01	478	7	Racial profiling at the border by customs officials
12.12.01	488	8	Election reform, including protection of laws intended to make voter registration easier (e.g., motor voter)
5.16.02	170	11	Welfare reauthorization, including increased work requirements for welfare recipients and a freeze of TANF funding for five years

Votes used to create NHLA scores

Date	Roll-call #		Brief description
	House	*NHLA*	
			Economic security
5.09.01	104	1	H. Con. Res. 83; tax cuts
5.26.01	149	2	Conference Report on H.R. 136; $1.35 trillion in tax relief
10.24.01	404	3	Economic Security and Recovery Act of 2001, H.R. 3090
5.16.02	170	5	Reauthorization of Temporary Assistance to Needy Families Block Grant
4.23.02	106	6	Farm Security Act, including food stamps for immigrants
			Education
5.23.01	145	1	ESEA reauthorization
5.22.01	132	2	Amendment 51 to H.R. 1; Title I consolidation
5.22.01	138	3	Amendment 55 to H.R. 1; allowing schools to expel students with disabilities
5.23.01	143	4	Amendment 69 to H.R. 1; limitation on aggregate increase in authorizations for fiscal year 2002 to 11.5 percent
3.20.02	79	5	Budget Resolution, including level funding of many educational programs

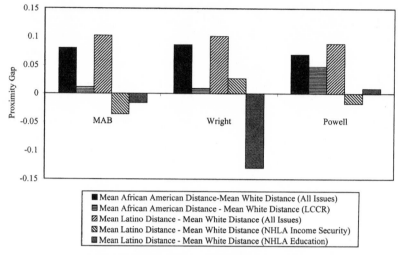

FIGURE 6.5. The proximity gap on issues uniquely salient for minorities, 107th Congress (2000 National Annenberg Election Survey; Leadership Conference on Civil Rights; National Hispanic Leadership Agenda).

than whites, but this evidence is uneven across the particular measures. The Wright measure suggests that Latinos are better represented than whites on education issues, while the MAB and Powell measures suggest that Latinos are better represented on economic security issues. The main point for our purposes is that in these domains the proximity gap that exists across all issues is negated. In short, we find that, on these issues, *minority constituents are represented as well as, if not better than, white constituents.* This is the third wave of evidence to support the conclusion that minorities are politically equal to whites when judged by a pluralist standard of equality.

THE RELEVANCE OF PARTY AFFILIATION

Before concluding this chapter, we pause to make a few observations relating to MC party affiliation and the size of racial and ethnic minority populations in congressional districts. We saw in the last chapter that when minorities are represented by Democrats in Congress, the gap between minority and white political representation is smaller than when minorities are represented by Republicans. Interestingly, this does not always hold when looking at issues of distinctive salience to minority

TABLE 6.5. PARTY DIFFERENCES IN RESPONSIVENESS, SALIENT ISSUES

(a) Whites and African Americans

MC party	Dem	GOP	Dem	GOP
White LCCR ideology	—	—	.825* [.327]	.307* [.140]
African American LCCR ideology	.447 [.313]	.416** [.128]	−.229 [.391]	.361** [.121]
N	28	24	28	24
R²	.07	.32	.26	.45

(b) Whites and Latinos

	Economic security				Education			
MC party	Dem	GOP	Dem	GOP	Dem	GOP	Dem	GOP
White economic security opinion	—	—	2.254* [1.032]	.796 [.991]	—	—	—	—
Latino economic security opinion	.748 [.399]	−.323 [.629]	.029 [.494]	−.435 [.691]	—	—	—	—
White education opinion	—	—	—	—	—	—	.528 [.417]	−1.05 [1.07]
Latino education opinion	—	—	—	—	.228 [.291]	−.124 [.335]	.092 [.307]	−.025 [.351]
N	24	18	24	18	24	18	24	18
R²	.14	.01	.30	.06	.03	.01	.10	.07

Sources: 2000 National Annenberg Election Survey; LCCR; NHLA.
Note: Dependent variable: Senators' revised LCCR, NHLA economic security, and NHLA education scores.
*$p < .05$; **$p < .01$; standard errors in brackets.

groups. If we estimate the bivariate OLS models in table 6.2 separately for Democratic and Republican senators, we see that the relationship between African Americans' preferences and senators' roll-call voting is of about the same size for Democrats and Republicans, but the relationship is only statistically significant for Republicans (see table 6.5a, columns 1 and 2). When we include African Americans' preferences and whites' preferences in the model, *only Republican senators respond to African Americans' preferences* (table 6.5a, columns 3 and 4). In fact, the Republican responsiveness coefficients are about the same for whites and African Americans. Thus, Republican senators' roll-call votes respond to state-level variation in

minority sentiment on these issues to a degree that Democratic senators' votes do not.

Before we make too much of this counterintuitive finding, we first note that these results are based on relatively few observations. We also note that responsiveness to state-level variation in preferences can arise even when senators are not particularly "close" to their constituents' preferences (recall fig. 5.3). Finally, and most importantly, Figure 6.6 presents proximity to House members on LCCR issues. Comparing the proximity of whites to their Democratic MCs (first white column) to the proximity of African Americans to their Democratic MCs (second white column) reveals that Democratic members are in fact closer to their African American constituents' preferences than they are to their white constituents' preferences. In contrast, Republican members are far closer to their white constituents' preferences (first black column) than they are to their African American constituents' preferences (second black column). In fact, Republican MCs are between two and three times as far from their African American constituents as Democratic MCs are. These proximity results suggest that although Republican senators may be sensitive to geographic variation in African Americans' preferences such that Republicans representing liberal

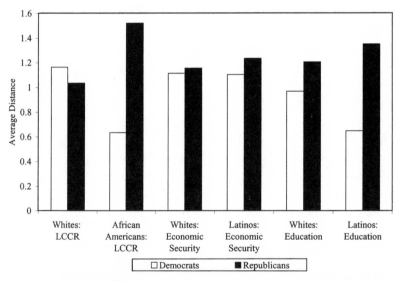

FIGURE 6.6. Party differences in groups' mean distance from MCs on salient issues (2000 National Annenberg Election Survey; Leadership Conference on Civil Rights; National Hispanic Leadership Agenda).

African American constituencies tend to be more liberal than other Republican senators, overall, Democrats' roll-call votes are much more in line with their African American constituents' preferences.[13]

The results for Latinos hold few surprises. The bivariate responsiveness models show that only Democratic senators respond to changes in Latino opinion on economic security, and neither party responds to Latinos' opinions on education (see table 6.5b). The latter finding may be driven by the small number of observations and relatively unreliable measures of preferences. The proximity results are more revealing. Figure 6.6 shows that Democratic MCs were about as close to Latinos as they were to whites on roll calls relating to economic security (compare the third and fourth white columns), while Republicans were farther from Latinos than whites (compare the third and fourth black columns). Similarly, Democrats were significantly closer to Latinos than whites on education votes (compare the fifth and sixth white columns), while Republicans were significantly farther from their Latino constituents compared to their white constituents on these votes (compare the fifth and sixth black columns).

IMPLICATIONS

The previous two chapters presented evidence that whites are better represented under the race-conscious egalitarian standard and to some degree under the proportional standard of political equality. This chapter shows that Latinos and African Americans are not completely locked out of the system. Despite historic and ongoing discrimination against these groups, often explicitly aimed at political marginalization, the American political system appears to fulfill, at least in some minimal way, the pluralist model of democracy. Despite their numerical minority status in a system in which the majority rules much of the time, African Americans and Latinos maintain significant representation in issue domains that are distinctively salient for these groups. The three waves of complementary evidence presented here add to the findings of other studies that even relatively small minority groups can achieve more than proportional representation on

13. Parallel analyses for the Senate find that African Americans are only closer than whites to their senators on LCCR votes when African Americans are represented by Democrats. Similarly, Latinos are only closer than whites to their senators on NHLA votes when Latinos are represented by Democrats.

issues that are particularly salient to them (e.g., Hutchings 1998), a key element of pluralist models of democracy.[14]

Theoretically, these results demonstrate the connections among issue salience, reelection concerns, and minority group representation. They show that the reelection incentive helps to protect minority rights. Although Dahl (1956) concluded that it is impossible to forge constitutional guarantees that intense minorities will influence policy, we show that the electoral incentives outlined by Downs and Fiorina, which compel elected officials to consider the salience of issues for various groups of voters, largely solve "the intensity problem." The groups that care most about an issue appear to have disproportionately positive outcomes on government actions in that domain, even when they are in the minority. Finding that responsiveness to groups' preferences varies by salience of the issue domain reinforces earlier findings that the connection between constituency preferences and representatives' votes is stronger for salient issues (Hutchings 1998 and 2003). More importantly, it shows a further implication of the importance of salience—different groups are represented in different issue domains, just as pluralistic models of democracy suggest should happen.

14. This chapter has shown that minority preferences are equally reflected in their representatives' voting behavior on issues of distinctive importance to the minority group. This is especially true in districts with significant minority populations. We saw in the previous chapter that African Americans are generally not much better off when they make up a large portion of an electoral district (at least when they are not represented by members of the same race). This is not true for the distinctively salient issues we examine in this chapter. In districts where African Americans make up less than 12% of constituents, MCs are closer to whites than African Americans on LCCR votes. However, in districts with more than 12% African Americans, House members are equally far from African Americans and whites. In districts with at least 40% African Americans, House members are much closer to African Americans than they are to whites on these issues. We take this as at least suggestive evidence that not only does issue salience matter for equality in and of itself, it may improve proportional equality as well. Whereas we saw that African Americans did not make relative representation gains *on most issues* across districts where their numbers increased, here we see that on distinctively salient issues, districts with more African Americans enjoy relative representation gains. Recall from chapter 5 that where the size of Latino populations in electoral districts is large, Latinos tend to gain ground on their white counterparts when we look at all issues across the board. This is also true when looking at the NHLA issues. Latinos are closer than whites to their House members on both the NHLA's education and economic security votes in districts with large Latino populations.

More practically, these results suggest important ways that leaders of minorities groups can improve their groups' political equality. First, they can go to greater lengths to identify emerging concerns important to these communities, to assess attitudes on these issues, and to convey to office-holders that these preferences are salient. Second, these leaders may be able to garner greater representation by working to get salient issues on the legislative agenda (Kingdon 1984; Baumgartner and Jones 1993). Minorities appear to hold an advantage when distinctively salient issues are under consideration, so if these issues are considered more frequently, minorities will be better off. We discuss these strategies in greater detail in our concluding chapter.

In short, we have seen that adopting a pluralist standard of equality reveals far more frequent political equality among African Americans, Latinos, and whites. Whether this pattern of findings is satisfying depends on one's preferred standard of equality. Some will be content to know that minority groups are more than proportionally represented in issue domains that are distinctively salient. Others, however, will demand that minority groups be better represented not only on a small set of "African American issues" or "Latino issues," but in political decisions more broadly. Some may also argue that the extent to which minority groups "win" on these salient issues is limited. After all, if a citizen prefers a very large increase in welfare spending and outlays rise by 6%, we consider this citizen a winner even though this is clearly not the citizen's most preferred outcome. In addition, the policies that some minority citizens may prefer, like slavery reparations or mandating equal per-pupil educational expenditures, may never come to a roll-call vote in Congress.

Because the issues that minorities care about more than whites are few, does this mean that minorities must be resigned to unequal representation most of the time? One additional avenue for reducing political inequality more broadly is to promote descriptive representation. In the next chapter, we explore the implications of descriptive representation for political equality.

Descriptive Representation and Political Equality

One prominent potential hurdle to minorities' political equality is the present racial and ethnic composition of Congress. In the current (110th) House of Representatives, 40 of 435 members are African American (9% of all members) and 26 are Latino (6% of members). There is one African American senator and there are three Latino senators.[1] According to 2005 census estimates, African Americans make up 13.4% of the nation's population, and Latinos comprise 14.4% of the population, so a Congress that matched the nation's racial and ethnic composition would include 18 more African American members of the House, 37 more Latino House members, 12 more African American senators, and 11 more Latino senators.

Many argue that the unrepresentative face of government necessarily biases against the interests of minorities, among other groups (e.g., Canon 1999; Mansbridge 1999; Haynie 2001; Dovi 2002; Tate 2003a; but see Swain 1993).[2] Thus, another way to produce political equality among racial and ethnic groups may be to elect more African Americans and Latinos, increasing the "descriptive representation" of minority constituents. This possibility relates to a more general theoretical question that dates at least as far back as Hannah Pitkin's (1967) foundational book *The Concept of Representation*: does descriptive representation (the election of representatives who share a trait with a group of citizens) enhance a group's substantive

---

1. Data from the Congressional Research Service Web site: http://opencrs.cdt.org/document/RS22555.
2. The literature on descriptive and substantive representation also includes many studies that ask whether women are better represented by women (e.g., Swers 2002). The political equality of women and men is an important question that we explore elsewhere (Griffin, Newman, and Wolbrecht 2006).

representation (the extent to which the group's political preferences are reflected in the representative's official activities)?

We devote this chapter to exploring how descriptive representation matters. First we ask whether descriptive representation improves minorities' relative proximity to their members of Congress (MCs) on all issues. Then, we see if descriptive representation improves the relative representation of minorities over and above electing a Democratic MC. We make these comparisons "dyadically" by comparing citizens' preferences to the behavior of their MCs by race/ethnicity, and collectively by seeing if a larger African American or Latino congressional delegation correlates with more preferred outcomes for minorities nationally. Third, we study whether descriptive representation leads to equality under the proportionality standard. Fourth, we examine the effects of descriptive representation on issues that are uniquely salient for minorities, asking whether descriptive representation yields equality by the standards of pluralism. Finally, we explore one way that more African Americans and Latinos might become descriptively represented by examining the relationship between political knowledge and interest on the one hand and descriptive representation on the other.

In short, we find that African Americans represented by African American MCs and Latinos represented by Latino MCs enjoy substantive representation equal (or nearly equal) to that of whites. In some cases this is largely or entirely related to the fact that African American and (somewhat less so) Latino MCs are usually Democrats. However, there are some conditions under which descriptive representation brings gains in relative representation beyond those associated with electing a Democrat. There is also evidence that descriptive representation improves collective outcomes for minority groups. In addition, descriptive MCs exhibit more attentiveness to the racial/ethnic composition of their districts than do white MCs. Moreover, on issues uniquely salient for minorities, descriptive representation brings representation benefits beyond electing a Democrat. Finally, we present evidence suggesting that levels of descriptive representation among African Americans and Latinos might increase if levels of political knowledge and interest were to rise.

DESCRIPTIVE REPRESENTATION AND POLITICAL EQUALITY

There is some disagreement about whether we can expect minority representatives to better serve minority citizens' interests. Some argue that white

elected officials can represent minority constituents just as well as African American and Latino officials can (Swain 1993). In this view, the electoral incentive for MCs to be accountable to their constituents obtains regardless of whether the officials share their constituents' race or ethnicity. However, others claim that descriptive representation enhances substantive representation by changing the nature of deliberation (Mansbridge 1999), altering the legislative agenda (Canon 1999), engaging minorities in the political process (Gay 2002; Barreto, Segura, and Woods 2004; Banducci, Donovan, and Karp 2004), improving individuals' assessments of their MCs' performance in office (Tate 2003a), decreasing political alienation (Pantoja and Segura 2003), and placing in office representatives who may be more likely to share the preferences of these groups (Tate 2003a).

Currently, the balance of empirical evidence generally indicates that descriptive representation promotes minorities' interests. For instance, Latino and especially African American MCs tend to vote fairly liberally, both in general and in policy areas that these groups care more about than do whites (Cameron, Epstein, and O'Halloran 1996; Whitby 1998; Canon 1999; Tate 2003a; but see Swain 1993). Since Latino and African American constituents tend to be more liberal than whites, this would appear to be evidence of greater responsiveness. Moreover, African American MCs' votes on Leadership Council on Civil Rights (LCCR) issues appear to be more responsive than white MCs' votes to alterations in the racial composition of their districts over time (Whitby 1998, 130). Again, it appears that descriptive representation yields gains in African Americans' absolute levels of substantive representation.

However, despite great attention to descriptive representation, we know relatively little about its impact on political equality. Advances in absolute representation do not guarantee improvements in relative representation, much less equal representation compared to whites. Although African American MCs tend to vote more liberally than any other group of MCs (e.g., Lublin 1997; Canon 1999), this does not definitively tell us whether African American MCs tend to represent their African American constituents *better than* their white constituents for two reasons. First, African Americans are not a monolithic political community; there is significant variation in African Americans' political opinions (e.g., Dawson 1994; Gilliam 1996; Tate 2003a; Gay 2004), so more liberal MCs may not be more representative of their African American constituents.

Second, whites in districts represented by an African American MC tend to be more liberal than whites in other districts, perhaps because African

American MCs tend to hail from more urban districts. In the National Annenberg Election Survey (NAES), the proportion of whites represented by African American MCs who identified themselves as very or somewhat liberal (28%) was substantially more than that of whites represented by white MCs (21%). Additionally, the proportion of African Americans who identify themselves as very or somewhat liberal is only a little greater among African Americans who are descriptively represented than among those who are not (30% versus 28%). Thus, African American MCs may still be responding to their white constituents more than their African American constituents.

Similarly, more whites represented by Latino MCs identified themselves as very or somewhat liberal in the NAES compared to whites not represented by Latinos (by about 3.5 percentage points). Meanwhile Latinos represented by Latino MCs are actually more *conservative* on average than other Latinos: 39% of Latinos represented by Latinos identify themselves as very or somewhat conservative, compared to 35% of those who are not so represented. Taken together, whites are somewhat more liberal than Latinos when both groups are represented by Latinos. Again, Latino MCs' tendency to vote more liberally may reflect the attitudes of whites in these districts as much as the attitudes of Latinos. Thus, while we have learned from previous research that minorities who are descriptively represented are *better* represented compared to those who are not, we do not know if they are *equally* represented compared to white constituents, or whether considerable political inequalities remain.

DESCRIPTIVE REPRESENTATION AND RACE-CONSCIOUS EGALITARIANISM

Our analyses focus on the House of Representatives, for this is where descriptive representation of minorities primarily takes place in the federal policy process. During the 107th Congress, the focus of our empirical analyses, there were no African American or Latino senators. Our focus on the House brings us back to the measures of proximity. We first compare MCs' voting behavior, as measured by their W-NOMINATE roll-call coordinates for the 107th Congress to their constituents' preferences, as expressed in the 2000 NAES ideological orientation self-placement item (see chapter 3 for details on the opinion items). We again use the proximity measures we introduced in chapter 5: those by Miller (1964), Achen (1978), and Burden (2004), hereafter cited as MAB; Powell (1982); and Wright (1978); and our binned measure using NES data.

Our first task is to ask whether descriptively represented minorities are politically equal under the demands of race-conscious egalitarianism. We begin by comparing the relative ideological distance of groups represented by African Americans and Latinos. To do so, we measure the distance between each respondent and his or her MC. We then compare the average distance between whites and their MCs with the average distance between African Americans and their MCs and Latinos and their MCs, as we did in chapter 5 (see fig. 5.4). We once again refer to these differences as the "proximity gap." If descriptive representation yields political equality under a race-conscious egalitarian standard, these differences in means will decline to approximately zero, indicating equality of distance.

We report the proximity gap for districts in which African Americans and Latinos are descriptively represented in figure 7.1, using three distance measures.[3] For comparative purposes, we also include the gaps in districts where these groups are not descriptively represented (these are the same as in fig. 5.4). When African Americans are not descriptively represented, they are between 0.07 and 0.09 points farther than whites from their MCs (see fig. 7.1, white columns). However, this proximity gap declines substantially where African Americans are descriptively represented (see solid black columns). In fact, these gaps are so small (less than 0.02 points) that the measures reveal no systematic difference in the distance of African Americans and whites from their MCs. Thus, African American MCs are just as close to their African American constituents as they are to their white constituents.

Latinos also make relative representation gains in districts represented by Latino MCs. When Latinos are not descriptively represented, they are roughly 0.10 points farther than whites from their MCs (see columns with horizontal lines). In contrast, in districts represented by Latino MCs, the proximity gap decreases by more than half, to a size that only approaches statistical significance for two of the three measures and is clearly insignificant for the third ($p = .11$ for the MAB and Wright measures; $p = .20$ for the Powell measure).[4] Thus, descriptive representation is associated with relative representation

3. The binned measure, which is excluded from the figure, actually finds that descriptively represented African Americans are *much closer* on average to their representatives. In fact, we do not include this measure in the figure because it finds that African Americans are so much closer (0.30 points) that including it alters the scale such that the other differences are hard to see.
4. Again, the binned measure reports that Latinos are significantly closer to Latino MCs than are white constituents.

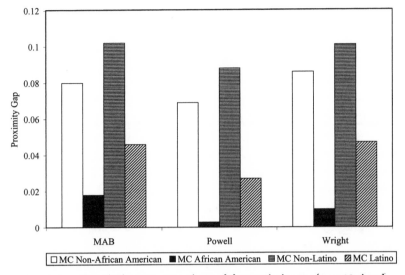

FIGURE 7.1. Descriptive representation and the proximity gap (2000 National Annenberg Election Survey; Lewis and Poole 2004; for MC race and ethnicity, see Amer 2004; Library of Congress Web site: http://www.loc.gov/rr/hispanic/congress/).

gains for Latinos, but Latinos remain somewhat more distant than whites even from these MCs. In every case, however, these results demonstrate a substantial improvement over African Americans' or Latinos' relative representation when they are not descriptively represented.

Descriptive Representation and Party Affiliation | Before we conclude that electing more African Americans and Latinos would make representation more equal, we must examine whether it is the MCs' race or ethnicity that brings equal representation across these groups or if other factors are inducing these MCs to represent the groups equally. For example, certain kinds of districts that are currently represented by an African American or Latino MC might induce greater political equality regardless of the MC's race or ethnicity. That is, the factors leading to the election of a minority MC may independently lead to greater political equality. Therefore, we control for some of these factors.

We do this by estimating an OLS model of ideological distance from one's MC. Since the dependent variable is each respondent's distance from his or her MC, negative coefficients indicate greater proximity to MCs. For instance, we include an indicator for African American constituents, whether

the constituent is represented by an African American MC (0 no, 1 yes), and an interaction between constituent race and MC race equal to 1 if both are African American. If descriptive representation is associated with gains in representation relative to whites, the interaction term will be negative. The models only include African Americans and whites (or Latinos and whites), so the indicators for African Americans or Latinos signify the additional distance of African Americans or Latinos relative to their white counterparts. In terms of controls, we saw in chapter 5 that high-income earners tend to be closer to their MCs, so we control for respondents' income. We also know that voters tend to be better represented than nonvoters (Griffin and Newman 2005), so we include reported turnout in the 1996 election. We also saw in chapter 5 that the proximity gap in so-called threat districts, where minority groups make up a significant minority of the constituency, tends to be especially pronounced. Consequently, we control for these threat districts (25–40% African American or 40–50% Latino).

In addition, it is especially important to explore the connections between descriptive representation and MCs' party affiliation. Some have claimed that since virtually all African American MCs are Democrats, electing a descriptive representative may do little more to advance this minority group's interests than simply electing a Democrat (e.g., Swain 1993). After all, we saw in chapter 5 that Democrats represent minority group preferences to a much greater extent than do Republicans. In fact, Carol Swain (1993, 215) showed that after controlling for MCs' party affiliations, the effect of MCs' race on their general pattern of roll-call voting was negligible.[5] Others have subsequently challenged this position, sometimes by showing that on issues more salient for African Americans, descriptive Democratic MCs represent this group better than nondescriptive Democrats (e.g., Lublin 1997; Canon 1999).

We enter this debate by asking whether descriptive representation boosts African Americans' *relative* proximity to their MCs compared to representation by a nondescriptive Democrat. We do so by analyzing only those districts represented by a Democrat. This is a tougher hurdle for descriptive representation than simply testing, as Swain did, whether descriptive representation improves substantive representation, controlling for MC party.[6] As the first column in table 7.1 demonstrates, the African American * African American

5. Swain (1993) examined voting behavior on Americans for Democratic Action (ADA) scores, which include voting on a wide range of issues.
6. We estimated a model parallel to that reported in table 7.1, column 1 for all MCs, controlling for MC party affiliation, and appeared to find that descriptively represented

TABLE 7.1. EFFECT OF DESCRIPTIVE REPRESENTATION, BY PARTY

MC party	Whites and African Americans		Whites and Latinos		
	Democrat		Democrat		GOP
Districts	All	Threat	All	Threat	All
African American*	0.038	0.227			
African American MC	[0.042]	[0.148]			
African American	−0.061*	−0.160			
	[0.024]	[0.125]			
African American MC	0.123**	−0.048			
	[0.027]	[0.079]			
Latino*			−0.014	−0.733**	−0.166
Latino MC			[0.059]	[0.235]	[0.133]
Latino			0.048*	0.385*	0.080**
			[0.023]	[0.161]	[0.025]
Latino MC			0.014	0.101	−0.065
			[0.042]	[0.160]	[0.095]
Household income	−0.001	0.009	−0.000	−0.057	−0.013**
	[0.003]	[0.017]	[0.003]	[0.033]	[0.003]
Turnout	0.056**	−0.088	0.067**	0.069	−0.162**
	[0.015]	[0.074]	[0.015]	[0.125]	[0.014]
Threat district	−0.087*		0.362**		−0.223*
	[0.034]		[0.051]		[0.098]
Constant	1.009**	1.079**	1.003**	1.537**	1.265**
	[0.020]	[0.113]	[0.019]	[0.205]	[0.019]
N	13,057	542	13,305	226	17,024

Sources: 2000 National Annenberg Election Survey; Lewis and Poole 2004; for MC race and ethnicity, see Amer 2004; http://www.loc.gov/rr/hispanic/congress/.
Note: Dependent variable: Distance from MC (Wright measure of distance).
*p < .05; **p < .01; standard errors in brackets.

African Americans were better represented relative to whites. However, this model is not well specified to test the effect of descriptive representation over and above MC party.

MC interaction is positive and statistically insignificant. Thus, in the context of all issues, descriptive representation appears to add little to African Americans' representation relative to that of whites beyond representation by a Democrat. This is true across all districts represented by Democrats as well as in threat districts represented by Democrats (see column 2).

The story is a bit different for Latinos. Across all districts represented by Democrats, descriptive representation provides no extra boost in Latinos' relative representation, as demonstrated by the statistically insignificant Latino * Latino MC coefficient (see column 3). However, in threat districts represented by Democrats, descriptive representation is associated with significant gains in relative representation (see column 4). In these districts, Latinos represented by non-Latino Democrats are 0.39 points farther than whites from those MCs. In contrast, Latinos represented by Latino Democrats in threat districts are 0.35 points closer than whites to those MCs (0.733 – 0.385). Finally, column 5 indicates that among districts represented by Republicans, descriptive representation provides no gain in relative representation for Latinos. After controlling for turnout, income, and threat districts, the proximity gap is about the same for Latino Republican MCs and non-Latino Republican MCs.[7]

An important reason that Latinos are so much farther than whites from their MCs in threat districts is that when Latinos are not represented by other Latinos in these districts, they are often represented by African American MCs. African American MCs tend to be quite liberal as a group and especially liberal in these particular districts. As a result, they tend to be quite distant from many Latinos. Earlier in this chapter, we saw that whites represented by African Americans tend to be significantly more liberal than whites in other districts. In contrast, Latinos in districts represented by African American MCs tend to be a bit more conservative than Latinos elsewhere (the mean ideology of Latinos in districts represented by African American MCs is 3.13, compared to 3.10 everywhere else). Moreover, for reasons that are not immediately obvious to us, African American MCs representing these specific districts tend to be significantly more liberal than other African American MCs (compare the average w-NOMINATE score of –0.61 for those in Latino

---

7. We did not estimate these models for African Americans represented by Republican MCs because there were no African American Republicans in the 107th Congress. Similarly, we did not estimate a model for Republican MCs in Latino threat districts because there are so few of them.

threat districts to –0.44 for all other African American MCs).[8] Consequently, Latinos are 0.17 points further than whites from their MCs when they are represented by African American MCs. In threat districts, this proximity gap jumps to 0.50. However, we are hesitant to draw firm conclusions on these matters because there are relatively few Latino respondents who are represented by African American MCs (around 450).

These findings, tentative as they are, raise two important points. First, in general, Latinos may not be much closer to African American MCs than they are to white MCs.[9] Thus, for Latinos, descriptive representation's benefits may require a specific match—a Latino MC, not just any minority MC.[10] Second, these findings may shed some light on why Latinos and African Americans sometimes view each other with animosity (Kaufmann 2003). One potential reason for this may be that political figures from these groups may not represent constituents from the other group nearly as well as they represent constituents from their own group. This may lead to competition rather than cooperation among minority groups.

To summarize this section, we note that when we look at all issues, descriptively represented African Americans and Latinos are just as close as whites to their MCs. These gains are mostly due to party effects for African Americans, but extend beyond party for Latinos in threat districts.

Descriptive Representation and Collective Representation | Before we proceed to discuss how descriptive representation relates to the other two standards of political equality, we shift briefly to discuss descriptive representation in the context of collective representation. Although descriptive representation does not appear to bring African American constituents relative representation gains beyond those associated with electing a Democrat in terms of the ways a specific MC represents his or her specific constituents, it may be that African Americans nationally benefit from the presence of more African American MCs in Congress. At least some African American

8. One likely reason that African American MCs who represent many Latino constituents are more liberal is that these MCs may be representing predominantly African Americans and Latinos rather than African Americans and whites. If Latinos are more liberal than whites, these MCs will be more liberal if they are attentive to constituent opinion.

9. In contrast, both Latinos and African Americans make relative representation gains in districts represented by Latino MCs.

10. Suzanne Dovi (2002, 729) explores similar issues, asking, "Will just any woman, black, or Latino do" as a representative of these groups?

MCs see themselves as representatives of the African American community nationally, representing African Americans whether or not they reside in the MC's district (recall, for example, Tate's [2003a] comments about Adam Clayton Powell quoted in chapter 4). Moreover, if more African Americans serve in the House, there is a greater African American presence on committees and the size of the African American voting bloc on the House floor obviously increases, potentially yielding policies more aligned with the preferences of the national African American community.

To determine whether a larger African American delegation in the House of Representatives boosts African Americans' policy representation, we return to our analyses of winners and losers on spending, using GSS and Roper opinion data on whether respondents preferred federal spending in various domains to increase, stay the same, or decrease (see chapter 4). Simply put, we assessed whether the number of African American MCs in the House is related to the probability of African Americans' "winning" in terms of government spending. To do this, we summed the nine binary indicators of policy winning that we analyzed in chapter 4. Thus, a respondent who "won" on three issues, but "lost" on six would have a score of three. We modeled this dependent variable using OLS and robust standard errors (clustering by year) as a function of the size of the African American delegation in the House. If descriptive representation boosts African Americans' collective representation, then African Americans should be more likely to win as the size of the African American delegation increases. If so, the African American delegation coefficient will be positive. Since we have seen that Democrats tend to represent African Americans better than do Republicans, we also controlled for the size of the Democratic delegation in the House. Finally, we included controls for the average level of winning for whites to account for the general level of winning by year, as well as a year time trend to account for changes in the level of winning for groups that are not attributable to the size of their congressional delegations.

Table 7.2 presents the results, which indicate that African Americans' collective representation benefits from greater presence of African Americans in the House. As the positive and statistically significant African American delegation coefficient in column 1 indicates, when the size of the African American delegation increased, African Americans nationally were more likely to win. Over the period of study, the African American delegation rose from a low of 13 members to 41, an increase of 28 members. Multiplying the African American delegation coefficient of .045 by 28 estimates that this increase led to African Americans "winning" on about 1.25 more issues (out

TABLE 7.2. DESCRIPTIVE REPRESENTATION AND COLLECTIVE
REPRESENTATION

	African Americans	Latinos
Size of African American congressional delegation	0.045** [0.015]	
Size of Latino congressional delegation		−0.022 [0.066]
Size of Democratic congressional delegation	0.009* [0.004]	0.006 [0.012]
Average level of policy winning among whites	1.214** [0.101]	1.170** [0.165]
Year	−0.055* [0.020]	0.012 [0.058]
Constant	105.743* [40.372]	−25.681 [115.262]
N	2,956	764
R^2	0.28	0.24

Sources: Office of Management and Budget 2004; General Social Survey; Roper Poll; for MC race and ethnicity, see Amer 2004; http://www.loc.gov/rr/hispanic/congress/.
Note: Dependent variable: Policy winning (comparison of spending preferences and federal allocations in subsequent fiscal year).
* $p < .05$; ** $p < .01$; standard errors in brackets.

of 9). We note that this is above and beyond the effect of electing Democrats. African Americans are more likely to win when there are more Democrats in the House as well, although the size of the African American delegation has a larger impact. For African Americans to win on one more issue would require increasing the Democratic delegation by more than 100 members (over this period the size of the Democratic delegation varied by 88 members).[11] Thus, African Americans are more likely to win when there are more Democrats in the House, but they also win more often as the size of the African American delegation increases. Thus, descriptive representation appears to bring some collective gains to African Americans, benefiting some African American constituents who are not represented by an African American MC in a dyadic sense. We consider a different issue relating to dyadic and collective representation in the chapter's final section.

11. Adding an indicator for years in which Democrats were in the majority did not significantly alter the results just described.

In contrast, we did not find evidence that Latinos have benefited collectively from the growing Latino congressional delegation (see column 2).[12] There are several possible reasons for this. First, our data for Latinos end in 1994, just as the Republicans gained a majority. Second, we cannot observe the effects of the large increase in Latino MCs that took place after the 1992 congressional redistricting. Third, we have four times more data on the collective representation of African Americans than we have on the collective representation of Latinos. Finally, as we noted at the beginning of this chapter, the ratio of Latino MCs to the size of the Latino population is much smaller than the same ratio for African Americans. So, Latinos may not benefit collectively from descriptive representation as much as African Americans do, or our data may be too limited to illuminate this.

DESCRIPTIVE REPRESENTATION AND PROPORTIONALITY

Thus far we have seen that descriptive representation leads to gains in relative representation independent of MC party affiliation, but only in some contexts. We shift now to exploring descriptive representation's impact on equality under the proportionality standard. We begin by assessing whether African American and Latino representatives are more sensitive than nondescriptive MCs to the racial/ethnic composition of their districts. Recall from chapter 5 that nondescriptive MCs were not especially responsive to the percentage of African Americans among their constituents (see fig. 5.6). Even in majority African American districts, African Americans remained farther than whites from non–African American MCs. MCs were more attentive to the concentration of Latinos in their districts, at least if we control for threat districts. Here we ask whether these patterns also hold for districts with Latino or African American representatives.

First, we examine districts that are at least 40% African American or Latino and simply compare the ideological proximity gaps in these districts. When minorities are not descriptively represented, as we saw in chapter 5, even when they make up a large proportion of a district they tend to be further from their MCs than whites (see fig. 7.2, white columns). This is especially true for Latinos. However, in districts with significant minority populations, descriptive representation substantially improves the relative representation of minorities (see black columns). Under these

12. The data for Latinos ends in 1994, so the Democrats were in the majority for the entire period.

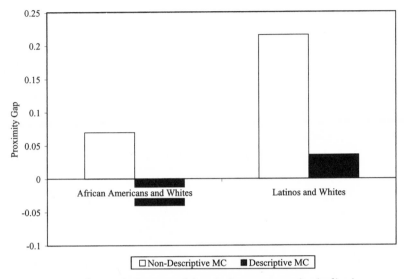

FIGURE 7.2. The proximity gap and descriptive representation in districts at least 40% African American or Latino (2000 National Annenberg Election Survey; Lewis and Poole 2004; for MC race and ethnicity, see Amer 2004; Library of Congress Web site: http://www.loc.gov/rr/hispanic/congress/).

circumstances, African Americans are actually somewhat closer than whites to their MCs ($p = .10$). For Latinos, descriptive representation shrinks the proximity gap from more than 0.20 points to less than 0.05 points, a clear movement toward equality, although still falling a bit shy of the proportionality standard in its purest form.

Next, we examine this in a multivariate setting by modeling ideological proximity as a function of a familiar set of variables, including indicators for African American and Latino respondents, the percentage of the district population made up of African Americans or Latinos, and an interaction term between "African American/Latino respondent" and "percentage of the district African American/Latino." We limit the sample to those respondents who are represented by African Americans and Latinos. The results of these estimations, presented in table 7.3, show that descriptive representation also advances the proportional standard of political equality across groups. African American MCs' votes are attuned to the composition of their districts (see column 1). As the "African American * district percentage African American" interaction indicates, in districts where African Americans make up a larger portion of the constituency, the proximity gap decreases. Latino representatives are also sensitive to district ethnic composition, as indicated

TABLE 7.3. DESCRIPTIVE REPRESENTATION AND PROPORTIONALITY

MC race/ethnicity	African American	Latino
African American	0.352**	—
	[0.128]	
African American*	−0.701**	—
district percentage African American	[0.228]	
District percentage African American	0.633**	
	[0.162]	
Latino	—	0.373
		[0.221]
Latino*	—	−0.574
district percentage Latino		[0.356]
District percentage Latino	—	0.284
		[0.263]
Household income	−0.015*	−0.002
	[0.007]	[0.010]
MC Republican	0.057	−0.136**
	[0.098]	[0.050]
Constant	0.908**	0.925**
	[0.095]	[0.165]
N	3,071	1,550

Sources: 2000 National Annenberg Election Survey; Lewis and Poole 2004; for MC race and ethnicity, see Amer 2004; http://www.loc.gov/rr/hispanic/congress/.
Note: Dependent variable: Distance from MC (Wright measure of distance).
* $p < .05$; ** $p < .01$; standard errors in brackets.

by the large magnitude of the estimate on the interaction term in table 7.3, column 2, an estimate that approaches statistical significance ($p = .11$).[13]

We conclude from these two analyses that in districts where the African American or Latino proportion of constituents is large, having an African American or Latino MC improves African American or Latino constituents' relative proximity. In short, descriptive representation is associated with political equality by the proportionality standard.

13. An alternative interpretation of these results is that most African American and Latino MCs are Democrats, and Democrats are sensitive to the African American or Latino proportion of their district. To explore this interpretation, we reestimated the models in table 7.3 for white, Democratic MCs. We found that in neither case were white Democrats attentive to the racial or ethnic composition of the district.

DESCRIPTIVE REPRESENTATION AND PLURALISM

Thus far we have examined the broad range of issues captured by constituents' ideology and MCs' W-NOMINATE scores, measures that showed significant inequality among groups in earlier chapters. Recall, though, that in chapter 6 we also showed that minorities are roughly equally proximate to their MCs on the issues they care more about than whites. Thus, if descriptive representation brings additional relative representation gains, these minority groups will actually be better represented than whites on these issues when they are descriptively represented. To test whether this occurs, we analyzed MCs' roll-call behavior on votes of particular concern to African Americans. As in chapter 6, for our analyses of African Americans and whites, we rely on LCCR key votes from the 107th Congress and constituents' LCCR ideology (see chapter 6 for details). We measure MCs' tendency to oppose the LCCR's position on these votes using the proportion of MCs' voting decisions opposed to the LCCR's position on the votes listed in table 6.4.

Figure 7.3a shows the proximity gap for the issues of distinctive concern to African Americans. We do not report analyses using the binned measure because we do not possess citizen placements of their MCs on LCCR issues. As we saw in the previous chapter, even nondescriptively represented MCs were about the same distance from whites and African Americans on these issues (see the white columns), where the proximity gap is between 0.02 and 0.05 points. When they are represented by African American MCs, however, African Americans' opinions are much closer to the votes of their MC than are whites' for all three measures (see the black columns). In fact, the proximity gap is 0.10 points in favor of African Americans by one estimate and 0.65 points in African Americans' favor by another. By all three measures, this gap is at least as great as the ideological proximity gap working against African Americans overall (see fig. 5.4). The average distance of African Americans is only about two-fifths that of whites when both groups are represented by African Americans. That is, African Americans are *twice as close as whites* to their African American representatives on these issues.

The results are less dramatic for Latinos (see fig. 7.3b), but they suggest that Latinos may make some gains relative to whites on issues of distinctive salience when descriptively represented. The MAB and Powell measures reveal tiny changes in the proximity gap related to descriptive representation. For example, Latinos were about 0.04 points closer than whites to their non-Latino MCs on economic security issues (see white columns), and

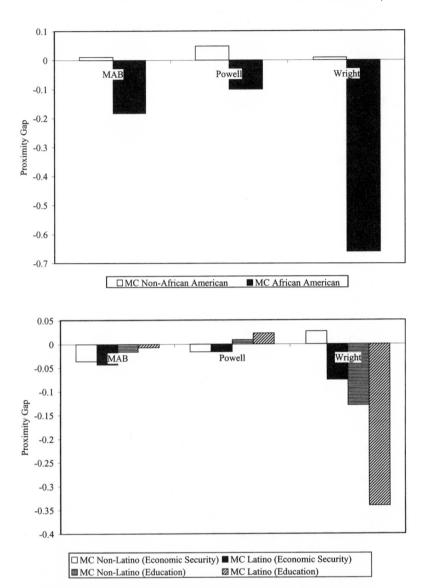

FIGURE 7.3. Descriptive representation and the proximity gap, salient issues (2000 National Annenberg Election Survey; Leadership Conference on Civil Rights, online at http://www.civilrights.org/research_center/voting_scorecards/voting_scorecards.html [all links relating to 107th Congress]; National Hispanic Leadership Agenda, online at http://www.lulac.org/publications/107thcongress -1-2.pdf.; for MC race and ethnicity, see Amer 2004; http://www.loc.gov/rr/hispanic/congress/).

about 0.045 points closer than whites when their MC was Latino (see black columns). For education issues, Latinos were about 0.02 point closer than whites to non-Latino MCs, but only 0.01 points closer than whites to Latino MCs. The Powell measures reveal similarly minute changes. However, the Wright measures indicate that descriptively represented Latinos were significantly closer to their MCs on these issues. Where Latinos were not descriptively represented, they were about 0.03 points *farther* than whites from their MCs on economic security issues. In contrast, descriptively represented Latinos were about .07 points *closer* than whites to their MCs. For education issues, nondescriptively represented Latinos were 0.13 points closer than whites, a gap that increased to 0.34 points for descriptively represented Latinos.

These results hold when we control for the effects of income, turnout, threat districts, and even representation by Democrats. To assess descriptive representation's impact in this multivariate setting, we model the distance of each respondent from his or her MC using the Wright measure of distance.[14] Table 7.4 presents the results. If we focus on the coefficients for African American MCs in column 1, we see that whites represented by African American MCs are 0.21 points farther from their MCs than other whites. Compare this to the combined effect of the African American indicator (–0.01), representation by an African American MC (0.21), and the African American * African American MC interaction (–0.69). All else equal, African Americans represented by African Americans are about 0.70 points closer than whites to these MCs (compare 0.21 to the combined effects just described, –0.49).

Perhaps more importantly, when we look only at districts represented by Democrats, we see that African Americans represented by African American Democrats are also almost 0.70 points closer than whites to these MCs. In large part this is because all Democratic MCs are 0.50 points closer to African American constituents than white constituents on these issues (see the African American indicator in column 2). In addition though, African Americans represented by African American Democrats are estimated to be 0.19 points closer than whites represented by African American Democrats (see the coefficient for the interaction term). Thus, on these salient issues African American MCs represent African Americans' preferences better than

14. We repeated these analyses using the MAB and Powell measures, and in each case descriptive representation improved the relative representation of minorities and was statistically significant at $p < .01$.

whites' preferences to a degree that exceeds that of non–African American Democrats. This extends prior work showing that African Americans are better represented on salient issues when they are descriptively represented (Lublin 1997; Canon 1999). We go farther to show that, on these issues, descriptive representation improves the representation of African Americans compared to whites such that African Americans are significantly better represented than whites in these districts.

The results in table 7.4 suggest, however, that African Americans' gains in relative representation associated with descriptive representation do not accrue as much from African American MCs being closer to African American constituents than other Democratic MCs. Rather, African American MCs tend to be farther from white constituents than are other Democratic MCs. This is seen more clearly in figure 7.4, which simply presents the proximity of African Americans and whites to their Democratic MCs. Notice that the distance from whites to non–African American MCs is 1.18 points, much smaller than the distance between whites and their African American MCs (1.32). African Americans represented by Democrats, on the other hand, are about equally distant from their MCs whether they are African American or not.[15] Therefore, most of African Americans' relative gains are a consequence of African American MCs being more distant from whites than are other Democrats.

This highlights two differences between our relative representation approach and extant studies of descriptive representation, which tend to focus on African Americans in isolation. First, by looking at the representation of both African Americans and whites, we note the impact of MCs' race on whites' representation. Second, our analyses do not find that African American MCs represent African American constituents appreciably better in an absolute sense than do other Democrats, which is contrary to some studies (e.g., Canon 1999; Lublin 1997). This may simply be due to our use of opinion data to estimate African American constituents' preferences, while other studies tend to assume that African Americans' opinions are uniformly liberal. Earlier studies tend to show that African American MCs vote more in line with LCCR positions than other Democrats. Our use of opinion

15. This holds in the multivariate setting of table 7.3 as well. Holding constant turnout and income, whites represented by African American Democrats are an estimated 0.19 points farther from those MCs than whites represented by other Democrats. In contrast, the distance between African Americans and African American Democratic MCs (0.187–0.193) is only slightly smaller than the distance between African Americans and other Democratic MCs.

TABLE 7.4. EFFECT OF DESCRIPTIVE REPRESENTATION, SALIENT ISSUES

MCs	LCCR All	LCCR Democrats	NHLA: Education All	NHLA: Education Democrats	NHLA: Economic security All	NHLA: Economic security Democrats
African American	-0.013 [0.017]	-0.505** [0.028]				
African American MC	0.211** [0.026]	0.187** [0.032]				
African American* African American MC	-0.690** [0.039]	-0.193** [0.049]				
Latino			-0.088** [0.030]	-0.240** [0.047]	0.039* [0.018]	0.066* [0.029]
Latino MC			0.059 [0.068]	0.061 [0.089]	0.083 [0.044]	0.120* [0.056]
Latino* Latino MC			-0.134 [0.093]	-0.004 [0.122]	-0.145* [0.059]	-0.140 [0.075]
MC Republican	-0.039** [0.009]		0.292** [0.017]		0.074** [0.011]	
Household income	-0.003 [0.002]	0.037** [0.004]	0.014** [0.004]	0.026** [0.007]	-0.004 [0.003]	0.037** [0.004]

Turnout	−0.031** [0.010]	0.033 [0.018]	0.042* [0.020]	0.185** [0.033]	−0.034** [0.012]	−0.001 [0.020]
Threat district	0.021 [0.021]	0.006 [0.039]	0.018 [0.074]	0.024* [0.100]	−0.113* [0.047]	−0.100 [0.061]
Constant	1.148** [0.015]	0.946** [0.023]	0.833** [0.028]	0.682** [0.044]	1.137** [0.017]	0.901** [0.027]
N	29,055	12,784	8,297	3,787	21,062	9,473

Sources: 2000 National Annenberg Election Survey; LCCR; NHLA; for MC race and ethnicity, see Amer 2004; http://www.loc.gov/rr/hispanic/congress/.

Note: Dependent variable: Distance from MC (LCCR and NHLA Wright measures).

* $p < .05$; ** $p < .01$; standard errors in brackets.

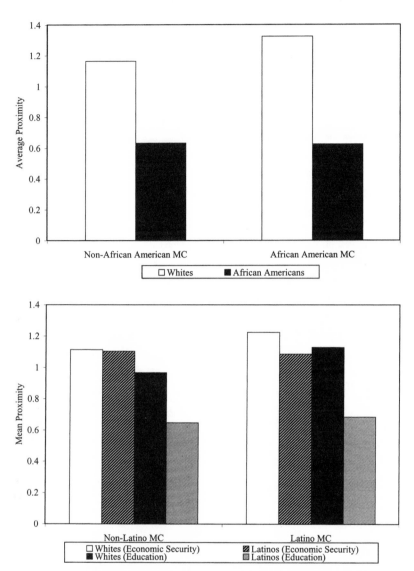

FIGURE 7.4. Proximity to Democratic MCs on salient votes (2000 National Annenberg Election Survey; Leadership Conference on Civil Rights; National Hispanic Leadership Agenda; for MC race and ethnicity, see Amer 2004; Library of Congress Web site: http://www.loc.gov/rr/hispanic/congress/).

data, which suggests that at least some African Americans are moderate or even conservative on such issues, suggests that the almost universally liberal group of African American MCs may not be particularly close to some of their African American constituents.

This resonates with Tate's (2003a) work that finds African American MCs are generally quite liberal, more liberal than some of their African American constituents. As she put it, "First and most importantly, Blacks are very divided in opinion on most social and economic policy matters, more so than Black legislators. Secondly, Black opinion has become somewhat more conservative over time. This makes the distinctively liberal policy representation of Blacks less representative of their real policy interests" (93). Tate's observation that preferences among the African American community have become somewhat more conservative over time (see also Tate 2007) points to a second potential explanation for the difference between our results and those of earlier studies. If African American MCs have remained relatively liberal, but their African American constituents have become more conservative, the distance between the two will have increased over time. Thus, the benefits of policy representation associated with descriptive representation noted in earlier studies may have diminished.

Returning to table 7.4, the results are somewhat mixed for Latinos, but they point to similar conclusions. On education votes, Latinos were generally about 0.09 points closer to their MCs than whites (see table 7.4, column 3), and the Latino * Latino MC interaction indicates additional gains, but the estimate is imprecise ($p = .15$, two-tailed). However, descriptive representation registered no gain compared to other Democratic MCs (see the near-zero coefficient for the interaction term in column 4). For economic security issues, Latinos were about 0.10 points closer than whites to their Latino MCs (see column 5, where the coefficient for the Latino indicator is 0.039 and the interaction term is –0.134). In this case, descriptive representation's effect appears to be over and above that of MC party, as Latinos represented by Latino Democrats were 0.07 points closer to those MCs than whites were (see column 6, where the Latino indicator is 0.066, and the interaction term is –0.140; for the interaction term, $p = .06$, two-tailed). Thus, in the context of all issues and no descriptive representation, the proximity gap between whites and Latinos is about 0.10 points in whites' favor (see fig. 5.4), but on issues of distinctive salience, Latino MCs are 0.07 points *closer* than whites to their MCs. Again, descriptive representation turns the tables, making Latinos better represented than whites in these districts.

Once again, most of these gains relative to whites came at the expense of white constituents. Figure 7.4b illustrates this, showing that whites represented by Latino MCs are farther from those MCs on economic security and education issues than whites who are not represented by Latinos (compare the white columns for economic security and the black columns for education). Meanwhile, there is little difference between the distance of Latinos from their Democratic MCs on these issues, regardless of the MC's ethnicity (compare the heavy diagonal columns for economic security and the light diagonal columns for education).[16] In general, then, descriptive representation appears to bring with it additional relative representation gains for African Americans and (to a lesser extent) for Latinos. In these issue domains, descriptive representation appears to turn the tables on whites so that minorities are actually better represented than whites.

SUMMING UP AND LOOKING FORWARD

The host of analyses and findings we present in this chapter lead to three main points. First, in some contexts, African Americans and Latinos are represented just as well as whites or even better than whites. The overall patterns of African American MCs' roll-call votes equally reflect their African American and white constituents' preferences. The same is true of Latino MCs and their Latino and white constituents. Moreover, these African American and Latino MCs' roll-call votes on issues of distinctive salience to their groups are actually *more reflective* of their African American or Latino constituents' preferences than their white constituents' preferences. Even though this equality may not always be the direct result of descriptive representation, it is still significant that African Americans and Latinos enjoy

16. This conclusion holds in the multivariate setting of table 7.4 as well. For example, on economic security, whites represented by Latino Democrats are an estimated 0.12 points farther from those MCs than whites represented by other Democrats (see the Latino MC indicator in column 6). In contrast, Latinos represented by Latino Democrats are only 0.02 points closer to those MCs than are Latinos to other Democratic MCs (this is the estimate from combining the coefficient of the Latino MC indicator, 0.12, with the descriptive representation interaction term, –0.14). Although there is relatively little upon which to form conclusions, it is notable that in education votes, Latinos gain in absolute terms when they are represented by a Latino Republican MC as compared to a non-Latino Republican MC.

political equality in some contexts. The story of political inequality is not simply a story of white dominance in American politics.

Second, under some conditions descriptive representation appears to have a direct impact on African Americans' and Latinos' relative representation over and above district racial/ethnic composition, income, turnout, and even MCs' party affiliations. Like others who have shown that minority group MCs tend to represent members of their group more closely than whites do (e.g., Lublin 1997; Whitby 1998; Canon 1999; Tate 2003a), we find that descriptively represented African Americans or Latinos sometimes see their policy preferences reflected in government action more than their fellow African Americans or Latinos who are not descriptively represented. Our greatest contribution, however, is to show that African Americans' and Latinos' gains in absolute representation often translate into equality with whites in terms of substantive representation.

To summarize, descriptive representation independently improves the relative representation of minorities, often leading to equality under each of the three standards of political equality. Specifically, descriptive representation leads to relative representation gains over and above the effects of MCs' party under the following conditions:

RACE-CONSCIOUS EGALITARIANISM (ALL ISSUES)
- Descriptively represented Latinos in threat districts are significantly closer than whites to their MCs.

PROPORTIONALITY (ALL ISSUES)
- African American MCs are more sensitive to district racial and ethnic composition than are non-African American MCs at all levels of district percentage African American.
- Descriptively represented African Americans in districts with at least 40% African American populations are just as close as whites to their MCs.
- For Latinos in districts that are at least 40% Latino, the proximity gap shrinks considerably when Latinos are descriptively represented, although a relatively small gap remains.

PLURALISM
- On LCCR votes, descriptively represented African Americans are significantly closer than whites to their MCs.
- On NHLA economic security votes, descriptively represented Latinos are significantly closer than whites to their MCs.

This list of conditions highlights not only that descriptive representation can improve the relative representation of minority constituents, but also that descriptive representation on its own is not a panacea for political inequality. Under many conditions, descriptive representation appears to offer gains in policy representation beyond electing Democrats to office, but under others it does not. In some contexts, it appears that electing a Democrat is an equally useful tool for making relative representation gains. This points to the importance of the tension between electing minority MCs and electing Democrats of any racial or ethnic background. One of the main ways to increase the number of minority MCs is by racial redistricting, drawing congressional districts to increase the number of minority constituents. Racial redistricting has increased the number of minority MCs (Canon 1999). However it also tends to dilute the Democratic voting bloc in nearby districts, at least in the South. Therefore, racial redistricting can lead to more Latino and African American members, but fewer Democrats in Congress overall (Cameron, Epstein, and O'Halloran 1996; Lublin 1997). Thus, while minority citizens benefit from racial redistricting by the election of Latinos and African Americans, those benefits are potentially undercut in a more conservative House. The question, then, is whether the benefits of racial redistricting and descriptive representation outweigh any costs in substantive representation stemming from electing more conservative Republicans.

Our finding that African Americans win more often when there are more African Americans in office (see table 7.2) suggests that this trade-off works to the benefit of minority representation, but our results echo Lublin's (1997) conclusion that descriptive representation helps minority representation most if it does not come at the cost of electoral losses for Democrats. When thinking about the potential trade-off between more minority House members and more Democratic House members, it is important to remember that we are focusing only on policy representation. Some argue that descriptive representation brings other types of representation benefits. For instance, descriptive representation may enhance the representation of minority interests in MCs' committee work or the way they frame debates (Whitby 1998; Canon 1999; Tate 2003a). In addition, simply including more minority voices in the deliberation that occurs within committee rooms and on the House floor increases the number of viewpoints presented to the benefit of minorities (Bessette 1994; Gutmann and Thompson 1996). However, in terms of policy responsiveness, those who prefer to boost minorities' relative representation should consider ways of increas-

ing descriptive representation of minorities without altering district lines in ways that hurt Democrats' electoral prospects.

Our third and concluding point, then, is to offer some suggestive evidence for one potential route of doing just this: increasing political knowledge and interest among minority constituents, which may increase the incidence of descriptive representation. Doing so would not require a trade-off between electing minority MCs and Democrats, nor would it require facing the legal challenges that racial redistricting encounters. Political knowledge and interest levels are closely related to whether or not a district elects a minority member. Certainly some of this association occurs because minority MCs will enhance their descriptively represented constituents' interest in and knowledge about politics (Bobo and Gilliam 1990; Burns, Schlozman, and Verba 2001; Banducci, Donovan, and Karp 2004). However, some of this relationship may arise because politically knowledgeable and interested minority constituents are more able or likely to elect minority MCs than similarly situated minority constituents with lower levels of knowledge and interest. These more interested and knowledgeable constituents are more likely to vote and participate in politics in other ways (Verba, Schlozman, and Brady 1995), they tend to prefer descriptive representation (Tate 2003b), and tend to have more political resources like education and income at their disposal (Verba, Schlozman, and Brady 1995).

To demonstrate the connection between political knowledge and interest on the one hand and descriptive representation on the other, we estimated a probit model of the probability of being represented by an African American MC (for African American respondents) or a Latino MC (for Latino respondents) as a function of knowledge or interest.[17] According to Lublin (1997), district racial composition has a profound effect on whether the district elects a minority MC, while other district level factors have only marginal or no impact on the election of minority MCs. Following Lublin, we control for the percentage of a district's population composed of African Americans or Latinos. We also expect that more politically conservative

17. Political interest was measured using the following item: "Some people seem to follow what is going on in government and public affairs most of the time, whether there is an election or not. Others are not that interested. Would you say you follow what is going on in government and public affairs most of the time, some of the time, only now and then, or hardly at all?" Political knowledge was measured by an interviewer assessment at the completion of the interview. "What grade would you give for how knowledgeable the respondent is about politics? A, Excellent; B, Good; C, Average; D, Poor; F, Very Poor."

TABLE 7.5. KNOWLEDGE, INTEREST, AND DESCRIPTIVE
REPRESENTATION

	African Americans		Latinos	
Political knowledge	0.086*		0.078	
	[0.042]		[0.048]	
Political interest		0.045		0.098
		[0.047]		[0.056]
Turnout	−0.041	−0.027	−0.114	−0.141
	[0.102]	[0.104]	[0.116]	[0.116]
District percentage	9.065**	8.948**	−4.048**	−4.062**
African American	[0.467]	[0.459]	[0.737]	[0.745]
District percentage Latino	−1.837**	−1.835**	9.124**	9.077**
	[0.473]	[0.473]	[0.426]	[0.427]
District partisanship	2.985**	3.091**	2.770**	2.749**
	[0.512]	[0.506]	[0.692]	[0.699]
Constant	−5.669**	−5.560**	−6.027**	−5.990**
	[0.287]	[0.291]	[0.448]	[0.442]
N	3,413	3,396	3,250	3,199

Sources: 2000 National Annenberg Election Survey; for MC race and ethnicity, see Amer 2004;
http://www.loc.gov/rr/hispanic/congress/.
Note: Dependent variable: Whether respondent is descriptively represented (0 no, 1 yes).
*$p < .05$; **$p < .01$; standard errors in brackets.

districts will be less likely to elect minority MCs. As a measure of district political predispositions, we included the percentage of the district that voted for Bill Clinton in the 1996 presidential election. We also included turnout as a control.

Table 7.5 suggests that politically knowledgeable and interested minority constituents are more likely to secure descriptive representation. Political knowledge was clearly related to descriptive representation for African Americans (see column 1), though interest was not (see column 2). For Latinos, political knowledge and interest were related to descriptive representation, though the estimates are a bit more imprecise ($p = .10$ for knowledge; $p = .08$ for interest). Substantively, these effects can be important. For example, where African Americans make up 40% of a district, an African American with the lowest knowledge score had a 40% chance of being represented by an African American MC. In contrast, an African American with the highest knowledge rating had a 56% chance of being descriptively

represented.[18] Thus, in districts that could conceivably be descriptively represented, political knowledge can tip the scales from a greater probability of not electing an African American MC to a greater probability of descriptive representation. In fact, knowledge and interest levels among African Americans and Latinos were higher in descriptively represented districts than those not descriptively represented. This was true across various district racial compositions.[19]

This suggests that one way to increase the number of minority office holders—potentially garnering for minority constituents the benefits of greater relative representation outlined in this chapter without decreasing the number of Democrats—is to boost interest and knowledge among minority citizens. We hasten to note that these results remain somewhat suggestive at this point because it is impossible to tell how much of the observed relationships arise because descriptive representation inspires greater interest and knowledge among constituents (e.g., Burns, Schlozman, and Verba 2001; Banducci, Donovan, and Karp 2004), and how much derives from greater interest and knowledge leading to the election of minority MCs. However, the possibility that boosting knowledge and interest can increase the incidence of descriptive representation, presumably because they boost minority turnout turns our attention to the importance of political action, especially electoral participation. The next chapter examines how turnout shapes relative representation.

18. In a district that is 40% Latino, a Latino with the lowest knowledge score had a 12% chance of being descriptively represented, compared to a 20% chance for a Latino who had the highest knowledge score.
19. The only exception to this is that in districts that are more than 40% African American, political interest among African Americans was significantly lower in districts represented by African Americans.

EIGHT

The Rewards of Voting

Our nettlesome task is to discover how to organize our strength into compelling power.

DR. MARTIN LUTHER KING JR.,
"Where Do We Go From Here? Chaos or Community?" 1967

Does the Democrat [*sic*] Party take African American voters for granted? It's a fair question. I know plenty of politicians assume they have your vote. But do they earn it and do they deserve it? Is it a good thing for the African American community to be represented mainly by one political party? That's a legitimate question. How is it possible to gain political leverage if the party is never forced to compete? Have the traditional solutions of the Democrat [*sic*] party truly served the African American community?

GEORGE W. BUSH,
in a July 23, 2004, address to Urban League

The previous two chapters point to two conditions under which minority representation is closer to that of whites. We saw that minority groups' representation is often on par with whites' representation on issues of distinctive salience to the groups. We also saw that descriptive representation sometimes improves minorities' relative proximity to members of Congress (MCs). A third way minorities may be able to improve their representation compared to that of whites is by participating in elections. Indeed, one of the principal aims of the civil rights movement was to encourage racial minorities to vote in order to overcome centuries of political, economic, and social inequality. It is well known that African Americans and especially

Latinos have historically been less likely than whites to participate in elections (e.g., Verba and Nie 1972; Wolfinger and Rosenstone 1980; Rosenstone and Hansen 1993; Verba, Schlozman, and Brady 1995). At least for African Americans, this gap has long been attributed to group disparities in education and income (e.g., Verba and Nie 1972) and to the infrequency of attempts to mobilize African American voters (e.g., Rosenstone and Hansen 1993). Therefore, improvement in these groups' relative socioeconomic status along with major mobilization efforts by interest organizations such as the National Association for the Advancement of Colored People (NAACP), the Urban League, the National Association of Latino Elected Officials (NALEO) and the National Council of La Raza (NCLR) have been associated with a recent rise in African American and Latino turnout. For instance, according to the NAACP National Voter Fund, the organization registered one hundred sixty thousand African Americans to vote in 2000 and mobilized two million voters.[1] According to census data, in the 2004 election African American and Latino reported voter turnout was the highest ever, at 60.0% of eligible citizens for African Americans and 47.2% for Latinos (compared to 65.4% for whites). For some perspective, consider that as recently as 1988, African American turnout was 51.5%, while Latino turnout was 28.8%.

These efforts to get African Americans and Latinos to the polls on election day are driven by the hope that boosting political participation among these groups will lead to improved representation. As V. O. Key (1949, 527) once asserted, "[T]he blunt truth is that politicians and officials are under no compulsion to pay much heed to classes and groups of citizens that do not vote." Walter Dean Burnham (1987, 99) stated that truth even more bluntly: "[I]f you don't vote, you don't count."[2] Normatively, some argue that voting should not be a prerequisite for representation. Verba and Orren (1985, 8) argue that "no preferences ought to be totally ignored in the political system." Whether or not voters should be better represented than nonvoters, few political scientists have tested Key's claim that they are better represented (for exceptions, see Campbell 2003; Martin 2003; Griffin and Newman 2005). As Larry Bartels (1998, 45) has pointed out, differences in turnout among

---

1. See the NAACP Web site: http://naacpnvf.org/c_history.php.
2. This assumption extends beyond academic circles. For example, columnist Bob Herbert laments that "[t]he inclination of many politicians to give short shrift to the interests of the young, the poor, the working classes, the black and the brown, has been encouraged by the consistently poor voting records of those groups" (quoted in Highton and Wolfinger 2001, 189).

various groups "are seldom explicitly related to any observed or potential impact they may have upon the strategic decisions of candidates or the policy outcomes produced by the electoral process." Simply put, we are still learning about turnout's political impacts.

One point upon which Key and many after him were silent was the equality of voting's rewards. Those who don't vote may not count, but *do those who vote count equally?* Equal rewards for voting (coupled with targeted turnout efforts) are important if boosting turnout across all groups is to promote their political equality. Otherwise, if whites gain more from voting, then the relative representation gains made by mobilizing minorities will be offset by greater gains among whites. Certainly, as a result of court decisions establishing the legal principle of "one person, one vote," votes have a roughly equal influence on electoral outcomes in a legal sense. However, Bartels (1998) argues that political conditions may render votes politically unequal, meaning that different groups among the public have different "voting power." If so, voting's rewards may not be distributed evenly. More specifically, Bartels argues that current political conditions theoretically work to the disadvantage of African Americans compared to whites, so that African Americans have less voting power in elections. Thus African Americans' votes may yield fewer political gains than whites' votes do. President Bush argued as much in his 2004 speech to the Urban League, asserting that African Americans lack "political leverage" due to their affinity for Democratic candidates. Some of the reasons that African Americans have less voting power may extend to Latinos, and this group may also face unique circumstances that affect its voting power. We develop these expectations below.

In this chapter, we examine whether and how much political participation promotes the political equality of African Americans and Latinos. We ask four principal questions. First, are minorities who vote better represented than those who do not? The answer to this question will tell us whether, if minorities were to vote at higher rates, while whites continued to vote at the same rate, minority representation would improve relative to whites. Second, are the representational rewards for voting equal across groups? If whites gain more from voting, then boosting turnout equally across all groups would not improve minorities' relative representation. Third, in electoral districts with larger minority populations, are the rewards for voting greater for minorities than in other districts? Knowing this will tell us whether voting advances equality in a proportional sense. Finally, are minorities' rewards for voting greater with regard to issues that

they care more about than whites do? Knowing this will tell us whether voting advances equality in a pluralist sense.

THE REWARDS OF VOTING

Studies of political participation often argue that political activity is crucial to political representation because it is the chief means by which citizens make their preferences known to elected officials. Verba (1996, 1) summarized this position well, explaining that "participation is a mechanism for representation, a means by which governing officials are informed of the preferences and needs of the public and are induced to respond to those preferences and needs." If citizens do not communicate their preferences, they make the task of responding to their preferences much more difficult for representatives. Of course, of the many ways to participate in American politics, voting is among the least communicative (e.g., Verba, Schlozman, and Brady 1995). However, those who vote communicate more than those who do not simply by virtue of "saying" something about their preferences regarding the candidates presented to them and their reaction to the state of the country and the state of their electoral district. Moreover, voters tend to participate in politics in other ways that communicate more specific information about their preferences (Verba and Nie 1972).

A second, important way for citizens' views to be represented is through the election of relatively like-minded officials (e.g., Miller and Stokes 1963). Presumably, voters support candidates who most closely match their preferences, so the candidate who is elected typically shares preferences with many in the electorate, a link that may not extend to nonvoters. Many studies have analyzed part of this claim, testing whether turnout patterns advantage the Republican Party (e.g., DeNardo 1980; Tucker, Vedlitz, and DeNardo 1986; Nagel and McNulty 1996; Highton and Wolfinger 2001; Citrin, Schickler, and Sides 2003) or racial majorities (Hajnal and Trounstine 2005), but these studies typically stop at election outcomes, leaving unexplored the representational consequences of turnout.

Both of these mechanisms for voter representation require relatively little of elected officials. That is, these mechanisms do not require that officials know who voters are or what their preferences are in order to represent them better than nonvoters. If officials respond to their perceptions of their constituents' preferences on the basis of messages directly communicated to them, then voters' preferences will be disproportionately represented. Further, if voters select like-minded representatives who simply vote according

to their own preferences, these votes will reflect voters' preferences to some degree, but that may not be true for nonvoters.

Of course, the more obvious reason that voters are better represented than nonvoters is simply because voters, not nonvoters, give elected officials their jobs and decide whether they will be retained. Consequently, officials seeking reelection will pay special attention to the preferences of likely voters (e.g., Key 1949; Arnold 1990; Bartels 1998). Rosenstone and Hansen (1993, 11) argue that in this way participation "is a source of policy benefits for citizens" because politicians have every incentive to keep politically active citizens relatively satisfied. As they put it, "[T]he active contribute directly to [politicians'] goals: they pressure, they contribute, they vote. The inactive offer only potential, the *possibility* that they might someday rise up against rulers who neglect them. Only the rare politician would pass up the blandishments of the active to champion the cause of those who never take part" (247; emphasis in original). Thus, reelection-oriented politicians have far greater incentives to represent voters than nonvoters when the two disagree.

We are still learning exactly how voter preferences are translated into voter-friendly policies. Two early studies took a step in that direction, showing that enfranchisement of southern African Americans pushed southern legislators in a liberal direction (Bullock 1981; see also Keech 1968). More recent studies show that patterns of participation affect various public policies from Social Security (Campbell 2003) to redistributive policies (Hill and Leighley 1992) and the distribution of federal discretionary funds (Martin 2003). In some of our earlier work (Griffin and Newman 2005), we continued down this path, showing that senators' roll-call behavior responded more to the preferences of voters than nonvoters in the 101st to 107th Congresses (1989–2002). We also showed that among the reasons voters are rewarded with greater representation is that voters are more likely to communicate their preferences to public officials, voters select like-minded representatives, and only voters can decide whether their representatives will remain in office. In this chapter, we take a natural next step in this analysis, asking whether voting's rewards are equal across groups.

THE EQUALITY OF VOTING'S REWARDS

Although prior investigations suggest several reasons why voters might be better represented than nonvoters, not all voters may be rewarded equally. In particular, the factors that bring voters representation gains may play out in ways that make the benefits of voting greater for white voters than

for African American or Latino voters. First, if white voters are more active in other participatory domains such as contacting public officials, working on political campaigns, and contributing to candidates, their rewards for voting will be greater. According to Verba, Schlozman, and Brady's comprehensive study of political participation, African Americans are quite a bit less likely than whites to report contacting public officials, which is one of the most clear and effective ways of communicating one's preferences. Only 24% of African Americans reported contacting officials, compared to 37% of whites. Latino citizens, meanwhile, report contacting officials at *much* lower rates than whites, with just 17% reporting such interaction (Verba, Schlozman, and Brady 1995, 233). Since this disparity between whites and minorities in "contacting" in general also extends to white and minority voters,[3] whites should be rewarded more for voting than minorities, and Latinos should be especially disadvantaged.

Second, because African Americans and Latinos are numerical minorities in most electoral districts, they have less control over who gets elected and consequently less ability to select like-minded officials. Simply by virtue of numbers, whites may tip the electoral scales so that African Americans and Latinos are often represented by officials who do not share their preferences. This is especially true for large electoral districts, like states and congressional districts, where African Americans and Latinos are more likely to be numerical minorities.

Third, reelection-seeking officials have greater incentive to appeal to some potential voters in their constituencies than others. In defining the concept of "voting power," Bartels (1998, 43) argued that strategic, election-oriented politicians will "[tailor] their appeals to those prospective voters who are both likely to turn out and susceptible to conversion." Officials have little incentive to spend scarce resources like time, money, or even roll-call votes in trying to win the approval of those who are unlikely to vote. Similarly, all else equal, politicians have more incentive to appeal to those whose minds are not yet made up than to those whose votes are

---

3. In pooled data from the National Election Studies (1978–1994), 18% of white voters indicated that they had contacted their incumbent MCs, compared to just 10% of African American voters. More recently, the question has been altered to refer to contacting a "government official" to express views on a public issue. Pooling across the three most recent National Election Studies (2000–2004), which are closest to the time period we analyze here, shows that 29% of white voters, 14% of African American voters, and 23% of Latino voters claimed that they contacted an official (we pooled to increase the small size of the Latino sample).

already virtually cast no matter what the candidates do. Of course, officials must tend to their "base," keeping core supporters satisfied and mobilized, but it is the "swing voters" or "marginal voters" (Kelley 1983) who receive disproportionate attention. If their votes are lost, the opponent likely gains them, while disaffected loyalists will more likely just stay home. This being the case, some citizens' votes are more highly sought after than others and "disparities in the force of [candidates' strategic imperative to compete for individuals' votes] can produce disparities in electoral influence" (Bartels 1998, 48). We contend that a natural consequence of unequal electoral influence will be unequal rewards for voting. That is, since some voters are especially important, officeholders seeking reelection will disproportionately represent their preferences.

The notion of voting power is important for our purposes because, as Bartels shows, African Americans have significantly less voting power than the population at large. Part of this stems from African Americans' numerical minority status and somewhat lower turnout rates. As we have noted, African Americans vote at only slightly lower levels than whites—60% compared to 65% in the 2004 presidential election (see also Verba, Schlozman, and Brady 1995, 233 and Bartels 1998). More significantly, African Americans overwhelmingly and consistently support the Democratic Party and its candidates. Over the past three decades of National Election Studies (NES), typically more than 80% of African Americans identified themselves with the Democratic Party, and around 90% of those claiming to have voted for one of the two major party presidential candidates said they voted for the Democrat. According to Bartels, this makes African Americans "by far the least pivotal group in the American electorate" (Bartels 1998, 65; Burkett 2002–2003). Given that, as Republican Jack Kemp recently declared, "one party [takes] minorities for granted and our party blows them off,"[4] the party system has pushed African Americans to the margins of party competition, decreasing their voting power (see also Frymer 1999). In fact, Bartels calculates that African Americans' *per capita* voting power in presidential elections is only two-thirds that of whites. As a result, many officeholders have less incentive to reward African American voters by casting roll-call votes consistent with their preferences. If this notion of voting power is correct, one of its politically significant implications is that African American voters will reap fewer representational benefits than will white voters.

4. *New York Times*, July 22, 2004.

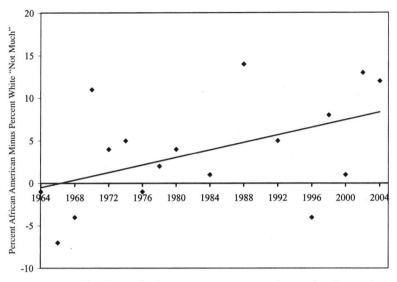

FIGURE 8.1. "Elections make the government pay attention to what the people think": Difference in African Americans and whites responding "not much" (National Election Studies, 1964–2004).

According to data from the NES, African Americans appear to perceive such a difference, more often claiming that their votes are ineffectual. As figure 8.1 shows, when asked how much elections make the government pay attention to what the people think, more often than not more African Americans than whites have answered "not much" over the past forty years (there is too little data for Latinos, typically fewer than one hundred observations in a year, to make meaningful parallel comparisons). The figure plots the difference between the percentage of African Americans who answered "not much" and the percentage of whites offering the same answer. As the plot shows, whites outnumbered African Americans in thinking that elections make little difference only five times over the last forty years (just three times to a significant degree). In fact, as the regression line shows, the racial disparity in perceived effectiveness has increased quite a bit over time. Below, we evaluate whether this perception has any bearing in reality.

The expectation that African Americans' votes are less consequential than those of whites also extends to Latinos. Latino citizens are much less likely than whites to report voting. In addition, because only citizens can vote, and more Latinos than whites and African Americans are noncitizens, the actual Latino turnout rate among all persons of voting age is even lower.

For instance, data from the Census Current Population Survey indicate that turnout among the full Latino population (citizen and noncitizen) in the 2004 election was much lower (28%).[5]

In addition, Latinos tend to support Democrats, though less uniformly than do African Americans. Perhaps with the exception of Cuban Americans, who overwhelmingly support the Republican Party (Brischetto 1987), within Latino groups of different national origins, commitment to either the Democratic or Republican Party is weaker than among African Americans. Still, since 1972, between 60% and 70% of Latinos identified themselves as Democrats, while typically between 55% and 65% of Latinos voted for Democratic presidential candidates. In short, African Americans and Latinos may gain fewer representational rewards from voting than do whites.

PUBLIC POLICY REWARDS FOR VOTING

Having laid out some theoretical expectations, we now turn to the evidence. In this section, we ask whether the policy rewards of voting are equal across groups. Are white, African American, and Latino voters more likely to be policy winners, compared to white, African American, and Latino nonvoters, respectively? Are the rewards of voting equal across groups? Finally, are minority voters and whites who do not vote equally represented?

To assess the consequences of voting on citizens' policy representation, we turn to the 2000 National Annenberg Election Survey (NAES). The NAES queried respondents about their desired level of federal spending or effort in three issue domains: education, defense, and the environment. Consistent with our method in chapter 4, we code respondents as policy winners in these three areas if they desired no change in spending or effort, since spending increases were relatively minor in these three domains.[6] All remaining respondents—those who expressed a preference for increased or decreased spending—were coded policy losers.[7] We code respondents as voters if they

5. Data obtained from http://www.census.gov/prod/2006pubs/p20-556.pdf.
6. Spending on education, defense, and the environment increased 5.9%, 3.7%, and 2.4%, respectively, from fiscal 2000 to 2001. Education is a domain in which spending has regularly increased much more than 5% (8.5% on average), and so we judged a 5.9% increase the same as we judged a 0–5% increase in chapter 4 as "no increase."
7. Recall that our comparisons of policy winning in chapter 4 also relied on GSS data. The advantage of this data is that it compares citizens' attitudes and government outlays in multiple years, so a racial group that is a policy winner in one year but generally a loser will be identified as such. The disadvantage of this data for our present analysis

reported voting in the 1996 presidential election in order to retain in our analyses the many respondents who were interviewed prior to the 2000 election.[8]

Figure 8.2 presents the percentage of voters and nonvoters who were policy winners in 2000 for each group.[9] As the figure shows, white voters were significantly more likely to be winners than nonvoters for spending on education and the environment. In the domain of education spending, 23% of nonvoting whites were winners, compared to 28% of voting whites. The difference was slightly larger for environmental spending, where voting winners (28%) outnumbered nonvoting winners (21%). The reverse was true for defense spending, probably because fiscal year 2000 was a relatively peaceful one which did not produce spending changes to reward whites' generally greater support for more defense spending.

When white voters received a boost, did African American and Latino voters receive a comparable boost? In two of the three domains, African Americans clearly did not. In education spending, where we have seen that African Americans' relative representation is somewhat greater, 8% of nonvoting African Americans were winners and 11% of African American voters were winners. Even that modest improvement exceeds the changes in the other domains, where there is virtually no difference between African American voters and nonvoters. On defense spending, 40.8% of African

---

is that there are relatively few respondents in each year, and this problem is exacerbated when the sample is divided into voters and nonvoters. An additional disadvantage of the GSS is that it does not consistently identify Latinos.

8. In doing so, we are assuming that voting is "habitual," as others have shown (e.g., Gerber, Green, and Shachar 2003). Relying on respondents' self-reported turnout raises a potentially confounding factor in our analysis—the tendency of survey respondents to overreport voting (i.e. "false voters"). This may not affect our results much because the error in independent variables induced by overreporting typically only leads to minor biases in models of turnout and candidate choice (e.g., Sigelman 1982). However, if false voters had preferences similar to those of actual voters, evidence that voters are better represented would be misleading—the estimated relationship between being a nonvoter and the likelihood of being a policy winner would be attenuated, with the actual relationship more like that between being a voter and the probability of being a policy winner. Evidence that false voters tend to be highly educated and generally most likely to vote suggests that false voters may indeed be similar to voters in many respects (Silver, Anderson, and Abramson 1986). However, in previous analyses of NES-validated voter data, we found no systematic evidence that voters' attitudes are carbon copies of false voters' attitudes (Griffin and Newman 2005).

9. Note that these data parallel those presented in chapter 4, but the opinion data are drawn from a different source (the NAES) and only span a single year (2000).

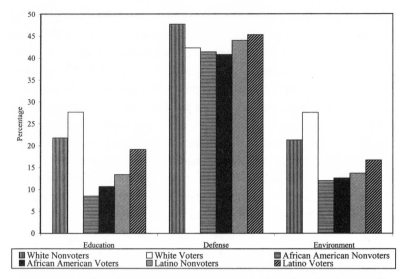

FIGURE 8.2. Policy winners by group and turnout in three domains, 2000 (Office of Management and Budget 2004; 2000 National Annenberg Election Survey).

American voters were winners, compared to 41.4% of African American nonvoters. On environmental spending, 12.6% of African American voters were winners compared to 12.0% of African American nonvoters. Neither difference is statistically significant.

In contrast, Latino voters do enjoy higher rates of winning. In fact, the gains from voting are even slightly greater than those for whites in education spending, where 19% of Latino voters were winners compared to just 13% of nonvoters, a 6-point turnout boost compared to the 5-point boost for whites. More Latino voters were winners in environmental spending (17%) compared to nonvoters (14%). Latinos were the only group for which voters were more likely to win (albeit modestly) on defense spending. In short, to answer our first question, African Americans gain little from voting, but Latinos tend to gain more consistently from turning out.

Figure 8.2 also allows us to assess how voting affects Latinos' representation relative to that of whites, which addresses our second question of whether the rewards of voting are equal across groups. When we compare white and Latino nonvoters in the area of education spending, whites are about 8 percentage points more likely to be policy winners.[10] When we

10. At first glance, this appears to contrast with our earlier finding in chapter 3 that Latinos are more influential in this domain, but this is just one year of data, and in this

compare Latino voters to white *nonvoters* in this domain, this gap narrows to about 3 percentage points. So, stimulating turnout *only* among Latinos would greatly improve the equality of representation among these groups. Note, however, that the percentage of winners among Latino voters remains significantly smaller than the percentage of winners among white nonvoters. Turnout offers Latinos some relative representation gains, but those gains do not yield equal rates of winning. In the area of environmental protection, Latino voters also are less likely than white nonvoters to be policy winners, and turnout again helps to diminish but not eliminate the representation gap. In contrast, even mobilization efforts that increase turnout only among African Americans may yield only nominal representation gains for African Americans. More broad-based turnout campaigns designed to mobilize all voters would appear to yield little relative gains for Latinos, and would actually set back African Americans' efforts for greater equality.

In sum, to this point we have shown that white and Latino voters are more likely than the nonvoting members of these groups to be policy winners. In contrast, African American voters only rarely win more often than African American nonvoters. For further evidence on this point, we turn to the House of Representatives and our measures of ideological proximity.

PROXIMITY REWARDS FOR VOTING

Are MCs more proximate to their voting constituents than their nonvoting constituents? To examine this question, we model the Wright (1978) ideological proximity measure we used in chapters 5 and 6. This approach enables us to investigate the factors that amplify or dampen the effect of voting on greater political proximity. First, for each group, we model the ideological proximity of citizens from their representatives as a function of reported turnout and household income using OLS regression (see table 8.1). Recall that greater distance means less representation, so factors that decrease distance (which means their coefficients have a negative sign) indicate greater proximity. As table 8.1 shows, whites who vote are about 0.07 points closer ideologically to their representatives than whites who do not vote (column 1).

The effect of voting on proximity for African Americans and Latinos is much weaker, both substantively, as reflected by the smaller magnitude of

---

year Latinos might have been more likely to be policy losers even if over the course of many years they are generally more likely to be policy winners.

TABLE 8.1. VOTING AND IDEOLOGICAL PROXIMITY, 107TH CONGRESS

	Whites	African Americans		Latinos	
	(1)	(2)	(3)	(4)	(5)
Turnout	−0.070**	−0.021	0.058	−0.007	−0.017
	[0.011]	[0.031]	[.051]	[.033]	
Turnout * district percentage African American			−0.286 [0.147]		
District percentage African American			−0.071 [0.163]		
African American MC			0.113 [0.061]		
Turnout * district percentage Latino					0.048 [0.139]
District percentage Latino					0.194 [0.133]
Latino MC					−0.180* [0.071]
Household income	−0.006* [.002]	−0.028** [.008]	−0.029** [0.008]	−0.018* [.008]	−0.018* [0.008]
Constant	1.148** [0.015]	1.266** [0.039]	1.259** [0.053]	1.219** [0.036]	1.203** [0.044]
N	26,349	3,019	3,019	2,761	2,761

Sources: 2000 National Annenberg Election Survey; Lewis and Poole 2004.
Note: Dependent variable: Distance from MC (Wright measure of distance).
$*p < .05; **p < .01$; standard errors in brackets.

the estimates in columns 2 and 4, and statistically. The estimated effect of voting is no more than one-third the size of the estimated effect for whites. Moreover, statistically speaking, we cannot even be sure minority voters make representation gains. For these groups, the rewards of voting, if any, pale compared to the rewards whites receive, contrary to the standards of race-conscious egalitarianism and proportionality, which require that individual citizens be equally represented.[11] Here we again have evidence

11. Some further probing found slightly more certain results—nondescriptively represented Latinos who voted were estimated to be 0.05 points closer to their MCs than nondescriptively represented Latinos who did not vote ($p = .10$). Once again, these rewards for voting are still short of those whites enjoy.

that the average African American or Latino citizen does not gain as much policy representation as the average white citizen from voting.[12]

Next, we evaluate whether the racial or ethnic composition of districts conditions the effect of voting. Are minorities more likely to be rewarded for voting when they reside in a district with a larger proportion of their group? This seems likely, given that voting power depends not only on the proportion of the group that is politically active and the distribution of party support, but also on the size of the group (Fiorina 1974; Bartels 1998). Individuals who belong to large groups have more voting power. To test this, we determined whether the percentage of a congressional district that is African American or Latino magnifies the effect of turnout for minorities by interacting reported turnout with the percentage of a district that is Latino or African American. If the effect of turnout is greater in districts with larger minority populations, the interaction term will be negative and statistically significant. We also control for MCs' race or ethnicity since virtually every congressional district that is at least 40% African American is represented by an African American MC. The results, reported in columns 3 and 5 of table 8.1, indicate that district racial and ethnic composition matters only for African Americans. The statistically significant and negative Turnout * Percentage African American coefficient demonstrates that when African Americans reside in districts with higher concentrations of African Americans, voting yields them greater proximity (p = .052). In contrast, the statistically insignificant interaction for Latinos (see column 5) indicates that turnout offers Latinos no relative representation gains across districts as the size of the Latino population rises linearly.[13]

To interpret the effect of district racial composition on African American voters' proximity more generally, we simulated the predicted distance

12. For comparative purposes, we also tested whether African American and Latino voters are closer than nonvoters to their senators. We found that they are not. However, white voters are closer than white nonvoters to their senators.

13. We can only speculate about why Latinos are not similarly benefited when they vote and live in districts with many other Latinos. One possibility is that districts that contain many Latinos may have higher rates of Latino noncitizenship or non-English speaking populations; thus, larger Latino populations may not necessarily mean larger concentrations of potential Latino voters. In addition, if Latino citizens are less likely to vote when they reside in districts with large concentrations of Latinos (but see Barreto, Segura, and Woods 2004), this will work to offset the greater voting power we would expect Latinos to enjoy in these districts.

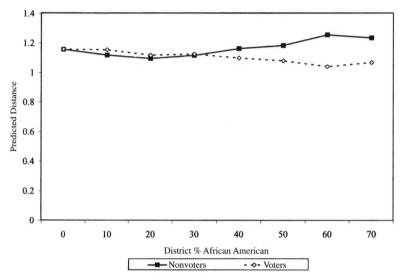

FIGURE 8.3. Predicted ideological proximity of African American nonvoters and voters to MCs, by district percentage African American (2000 National Annenberg Election Survey; Lewis and Poole 2004).

of African American nonvoters and voters from their MCs when they reside in differently constituted districts (see fig. 8.3). In districts with relatively few African Americans, African American voters are no better off than African American nonvoters. This changes once African Americans make up at least 40% of the district's population. When African Americans make up 50% of a district, the model estimates that African American voters will be about 0.09 points closer to their MCs than African American nonvoters. This gap roughly doubles in districts that are 60% African American.

To further illustrate the representation gains associated with voting in districts with significant African American populations, we turn to figure 8.4(a), which presents the mean distance of African American and white voters and nonvoters from MCs in districts where African Americans comprise at least 40% of the population. If we look first at nonvoters in these districts, we see that African Americans are a bit farther than whites from their MCs (see the first set of columns). However, in these districts, voting clearly brings rewards for African Americans. African American voters were about 0.07 points closer to their MCs than were African American nonvoters (compare the black columns). Note that this gain is about the

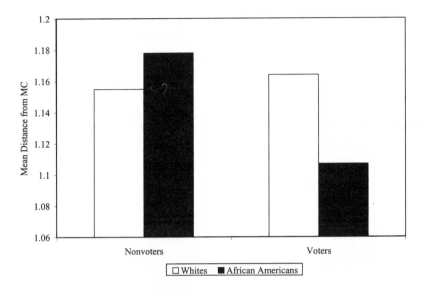

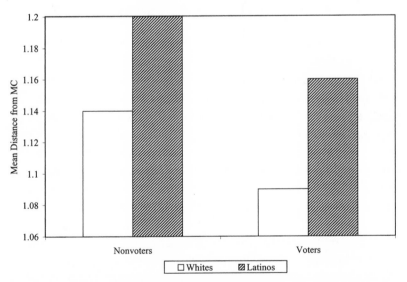

FIGURE 8.4. Rewards for voting in districts that are more than 40% African American or Latino (2000 National Annenberg Election Survey; Lewis and Poole 2004).

same size as the gain white voters generally enjoy (see table 8.1, column 1). In these specific districts, whites actually do not gain from voting (compare the white columns). In fact, in these districts, African American voters are about 0.05 points closer to their MCs than are white voters. Thus, in these districts, voting appears to turn the tables, leading to better representation for African Americans compared to whites.

In some contrast, in districts that are at least 40% Latino, both Latinos and whites appear to benefit from voting (see fig. 8.4b). That is, when Latinos approach or exceed a majority of an electoral district, they appear to realize absolute gains from voting as the average distance between Latinos and their MCs is 1.20 points for nonvoters, but 1.16 points for voters, a 0.04-point gain. However, whites also make absolute gains from voting, as the average white nonvoter in these districts was about 1.14 points away from his or her MC, but a voter was 1.09 points away, a 0.05-point gain. Thus, Latinos' gains in absolute representation do not translate into equal representation with whites.

To summarize, the gains African Americans and Latinos earn from voting are focused in districts where there are more African Americans and Latinos, where their voting power is greater. Where African Americans comprise at least 40% of the district, they gain more from voting than do whites. In these districts, African American voters are closer to their MCs than both African American nonvoters and white voters. In 40% Latino districts, however, Latino voters make absolute, but not relative representation gains. They are closer to their MCs than are Latino nonvoters, but since whites gain about as much from voting, Latino voters remain farther than white voters from their MCs.

REWARDS FOR VOTING BY PARTY

Do the representatives affiliated with each political party reward minority voting similarly? As discussed above, Democrats and Republicans have strategic reasons to respond (or not respond) to voting by African Americans and Latinos. Our finding that African Americans and Latinos typically receive only small proximity rewards for voting may indicate that neither political party rewards minorities for voting, or that the rewards bestowed by one party are attenuated by the other party's failure to reward.

We compared the ideological proximity of African American and Latino voters and nonvoters represented by Democrats to their nondescriptive MCs. Then we did the same for those represented by Republican MCs. As

figure 8.5 shows, Republicans reward African Americans for voting slightly less than Democrats do. Democrats were about 0.02 points closer to African American voters compared to African American nonvoters. Republicans were only about 0.01 points closer. The most important point is that both parties rewarded African Americans weakly for voting, leading to the insignificant estimate in table 8.1.

The story is different for Latinos. If we look only at Republican MCs, we would conclude that Latinos are rewarded with greater proximity for voting.[14] Republican MCs were about 0.05 points closer to Latino voters than Latino nonvoters. However, because Democrats do not reward Latinos at all, when we combine both parties we obtain the insignificant result in table 8.1. This result speaks to one of this chapter's puzzles, namely, why Latinos appear in figure 8.1 to enjoy policy rewards for voting but in table 8.1 not to enjoy proximity rewards. The answer appears to be that only Republicans reward Latinos for voting with greater proximity, and that Republicans' greater influence on policy outcomes in fiscal 2001, when they controlled both the legislative and executive branches, allowed them to reward Latino voters with more favorable policy outcomes as well. These results are also important because they may document in a systematic way recent GOP efforts to court Latino voters.

REWARDS FOR VOTING IN SALIENT DOMAINS

Thus far, we have seen that voting is associated with a greater likelihood of Latinos being policy winners, but it brings Latinos and African Americans small and inconsistent relative proximity gains. This may not mean that minorities never make substantial gains from voting irrespective of district racial or ethnic composition. Even if African Americans generally do not improve their outcomes when they vote, voting may improve African Americans' representation in issue areas that this group cares about more than whites. For instance, we have seen that African Americans do realize small rewards for voting on education spending (fig. 8.1), a domain where African Americans are generally more likely to be policy winners (see chapter 4). More generally, this seems likely because citizens tend to pay greater attention to roll-call votes their legislators cast that are salient to them. Their voting decisions in subsequent elections are then weighted heavily by their

14. This is not driven by Cuban Americans. If they are excluded, the decline in mean distance is about the same as reported in figure 8.6 (0.08), from 1.22 to 1.14.

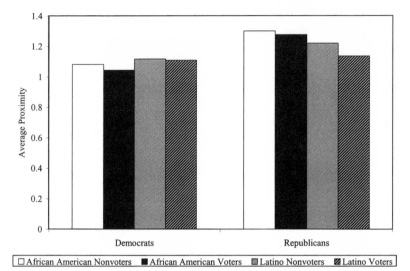

FIGURE 8.5. Party differences in voting's rewards (2000 National Annenberg Election Survey; Lewis and Poole 2004).

legislators' perceived performance on these important issues (Hutchings 1998, 2003). Furthermore, we observed in unreported analyses that African American voters, while generally not better represented than nonvoters, are somewhat better represented in domains that are salient for this group, such as welfare spending and health care spending.[15]

To test this notion, we modeled African Americans' proximity to their representatives' standardized LCCR votes, first as a function of reported turnout (see table 8.2, column 1). As the significant and negative turnout coefficient shows, voting African Americans are better represented than nonvoting African Americans in their MCs' LCCR votes. Furthermore, on these issues, African Americans' rewards for voting far exceed those of whites.[16] Thus, on these issues, turnout can enable African Americans to make significant representational gains relative to whites. As we found with respect to representatives' voting patterns in general, on these salient

15. Among African Americans, voters are more likely to be policy winners on health care and welfare spending after controlling for income, educational attainment, age, gender, and ideology.
16. Estimating a parallel model for whites showed that whites' rewards for voting on these issues (−0.021) are less than one-third the rewards that African Americans receive.

TABLE 8.2. AFRICAN AMERICANS' REWARDS FOR VOTING ON SALIENT
ISSUES, 107TH CONGRESS

Turnout	−0.075**	0.026
	[0.028]	[0.045]
Turnout* district		−0.287*
percentage African American		[0.130]
District percentage		−0.276
African American		[0.145]
African American		−0.261**
MC		[0.055]
Household		−0.003
income		[0.007]
Constant	1.005**	1.154**
	[0.023]	[0.047]
N	3,326	3,018

Sources: 2000 National Annenberg Election Survey; LCCR.
Note: Dependent variable: Distance from MC (Wright measure of distance).
* $p < .05$; ** $p < .01$; standard errors in brackets.

issues African American voters are better represented when they reside in districts with larger proportions of African Americans. The negative and statistically significant Turnout * Percentage African American interaction in column 2 indicates that voting in districts with a large African American population brings additional representation benefits on these salient issues, even when controlling for MCs' race.

To determine the magnitude of this effect, we once again simulated nonvoting and voting African Americans' predicted distance from their representatives (this time on LCCR votes), conditioned by the size of the African American population in their congressional districts. As shown in figure 8.6, both nonvoting and voting African Americans are better represented on salient issues when they reside in districts with a larger percentage of African Americans, but the effect of district racial composition on proximity is greater for African American voters. In districts where African Americans make up at least 30% of the population, African Americans gain from voting on these issues. In a district that is 50% African American, the predicted distance of 0.81 points for an African American nonvoter is 0.09 points farther than that predicted for an African American voter (0.72). This 0.09-point gain from voting again rivals whites' 0.07-point gain (table 8.1).

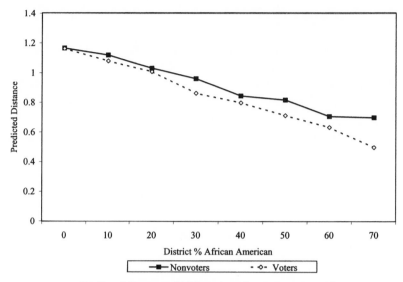

FIGURE 8.6. Predicted distance of African American nonvoters and voters on LCCR votes, by district percentage African American (2000 National Annenberg Election Survey; Leadership Conference on Civil Rights, online at http://www .civilrights.org/research_center/voting_scorecards/voting_scorecards.html [all links relating to 107th Congress]).

These results indicate that the proportional standard of political equality is satisfied with respect to voting's rewards on uniquely salient issues for African Americans. Where African Americans comprise about half of an electoral district's population, African American voters make gains similar to those white voters enjoy.

In contrast to the additional gains on salient issues that African Americans earn from voting, Latinos appear to benefit little from voting in these domains (data not shown). In a bivariate context, Latino voters are closer to their MCs than nonvoters on economic security votes, but actually worse off than nonvoters on education votes. We pay relatively little attention to these findings because, once we control for the other factors, voting appears to have no impact on Latinos proximity to their MCs. Further probing did reveal one condition under which voting brings significant rewards to Latinos beyond the other controls: on economic security issues, Latino voters represented by non-Latino MCs were 0.07 points closer to their MCs than similarly situated Latino nonvoters ($p < .05$). Thus, Latinos may enjoy some rewards for voting in these distinctively salient domains, but those gains are focused on only some of the Latino community.

IMPLICATIONS

In this chapter we have seen that voters are better represented than non-voters, but that this mainly applies to whites. African American voters are not similarly advantaged, except in special issue domains or districts with large African American populations. Latinos make some gains from voting, but they are not as consistent as those whites enjoy. Stated another way, we reveal a political consequence of minorities' lower rates of voting and contacting public officials, of their minority status, and of their lesser voting power: asymmetric rewards for voting. These results suggest that although the "one person, one vote" principle may be met in the sense that each voter has about the same influence on the election's outcome, the representational benefits of these votes may not be equal.

All of this suggests that stimulating minority turnout, taken alone, may be a limited strategy for improving the relative representation of minorities' preferences in many policy areas. However, we would not go so far as to say that turnout is irrelevant to minority representation. As we have seen, the asymmetric rewards of turnout appear to depend on the size of an electoral district's African American population. This suggests that African Americans have greater incentives to vote for offices representing smaller geographical units where African Americans have a better chance of constituting a substantial portion of the population. Moreover, even in electoral districts with small African American populations, African Americans' voting power would be even less if they turned out at lower rates. If African Americans dropped out of the political arena altogether, representatives would presumably pay them even less attention. Finally, on issues they care about more than whites, voting by African Americans yields greater representation gains for this group. A drop in African American turnout may significantly depress African Americans' representation on these issues.

In many ways similar to African Americans, Latinos are only sometimes rewarded for voting with greater proximity and a higher frequency of being policy winners on a wider range of policies. The many ongoing efforts to naturalize, register, and mobilize Latinos appear to contribute to advancing this group's effectiveness in Washington. However, those advances have their limits. In the end, boosting minority turnout offers minorities the possibility of some gains in relative representation, but does not appear to be a sure-fire strategy for overcoming existing inequalities of representation.

NINE

Conclusion:
The Future of Political (In)Equality

We set out to assess the equality of political representation in the racially and ethnically diverse context of the United States in the late twentieth and early twenty-first centuries. In short, we found that whites are often better represented than African Americans and Latinos. This is true even beyond the effects of income differences between the groups and even when minorities make up a substantial proportion of a constituency. However, we showed that Democrats tend to represent minorities and whites more equally than do Republicans, although even Democrats sometimes advantage their white constituents. In addition, we found that three factors, aside from being represented by a Democrat, can even the extent of white and minority representation, at least under some conditions: distinctive issue salience, descriptive representation, and mobilizing minority turnout. Our aim for this last chapter is to take stock of what we have learned and to speculate about what this might mean for the decades to come. In doing so, we touch on important normative questions, public policy debates, and the state of research on political inequality in the United States.

Two of the most unique elements of our analysis—its explicit focus on the relative representation of different groups, and its inclusion of three racial/ethnic groups—bring to light several important features of the current political landscape. In describing the extent to which African Americans, Latinos, and whites are politically equal, we told a complex story. At one level, the story is much as many have come to expect: the system advantages whites. When whites want government spending to increase or decrease in a variety of areas, they are more likely to get their way than are African Americans and Latinos. This holds for issues ranging from defense spending to the environment and space exploration. Furthermore, in general, senators as a group are more responsive to whites' general ideological

perspectives within the states they represent than they are to their Latino or African American constituents, and senators' and House representatives' roll-call votes are generally ideologically "closer" to their white constituents' preferences than they are to their Latino or African American constituents' preferences. In fact, even where minority groups make up 25% or even 40% of electoral districts, they remain significantly "farther away" from the roll-call votes of their members of Congress (MCs) than are whites. In short, to the extent that any citizens get what they want, whites get what they want more often than do Latinos or African Americans. In this broad sense, whites are more often winners in public decision making than are the minority groups.

This in itself may not be news to anyone. Race continues to divide American society and politics (e.g., Kinder and Sanders 1996; Sniderman and Carmines 1997), and whites constitute a majority of the population in the vast majority of electoral districts operating under plurality rule. Had we found that African Americans or Latinos have just as much political clout as whites, this would have been either startling news or a sign that we had made a wrong turn somewhere. However, beyond rigorously confirming what we already believed, showing just how large racial and ethnic gaps in representation are, and establishing a baseline of inequality against which we can compare relative representation under various conditions, our analyses reveal an important and novel point. The political inequality of these groups is related to, but not completely explained by, income inequality. Recent studies have demonstrated that high-income earners tend to get what they want from government more than low-income earners do (e.g., Bartels 2008; Gilens 2005; Jacobs and Skocpol 2005). We find further evidence that this is true. However, income is not the only source of political inequality in American politics. African Americans and Latinos are less likely than whites to get what they want from government—over and above their disadvantage stemming from earning lower incomes. Thus, in understanding the sources of inequality in American politics, we must consider both race/ethnicity *and* class.

This initial finding that whites more often get what they want, even after we account for whites' larger incomes, although significant, is not the whole story. The first complication is the standard by which we judge equality. If instead of comparing groups' representation regardless of size, we look at groups' clout relative to their size, viewing political equality through a proportional lens, the story is more mixed. At least when represented by white MCs, African Americans remain somewhat disadvantaged compared to

whites, even when African Americans comprise a sizeable portion or even a majority of their electoral district's population. Latinos fare somewhat better on this score, but still are significantly less well represented compared to whites, even when this group comprises between 40% and 50% of a constituency. These findings, perhaps at first glance surprising, comport with earlier studies showing that, where the African American population in districts is somewhat larger, MCs are more conservative (Key 1949; Giles and Buckner 1993).

Our finding does more than just confirm the conclusions of earlier studies. Recall that even if MCs tend to vote more liberally when representing districts with significant African American populations, this may not mean that African Americans are making relative representation gains since (1) African Americans who reside in districts with large African American populations are not clearly more liberal, and (2) whites in these districts tend to be much more liberal. Our evidence suggests that African Americans are more likely to get what they want in districts where this group constitutes a rather large share of the population, but even in majority African American districts, whites are still closer than African Americans to their MCs, so long as these MCs are not African American. It is true that in districts that are 40% African American, descriptively represented African Americans are closer than whites to their MCs. However, short of achieving descriptive representation (and even then in limited issue domains), whites hold a slight representation advantage over African Americans in districts where African Americans make up a significant but nonmajority portion of the constituency. The story is different for Latinos. Although they are particularly poorly represented compared to whites in districts comprised of 40–50% Latinos, in majority Latino districts, Latinos are represented in a fashion equal to whites, even when represented by white MCs.

Further complicating the story, three other factors can shrink the gap between minority group representation and white representation. First, the balance of representation among groups changes over issue domains. In general, reelection-minded representatives support the majority in their district, but when the minority cares more about an issue than does the majority, these representatives often side with the minority on that issue. It appears that this version of pluralism is alive and well in American politics. African Americans, even by the strict standard of race-conscious egalitarianism, are more than proportionally represented when it comes to spending decisions on welfare, health care, and crime, along with many of the issue domains closely watched by the Leadership Conference on Civil

Rights (LCCR). The same holds for Latinos, whose lesser representation overall is minimized and even reversed in domains like welfare and education, where specific votes are monitored by the National Hispanic Leadership Agenda (NHLA).

Second, descriptive representation provides African Americans and Latinos some gains in relative representation, though descriptive representation appears not to bring political equality automatically wherever it occurs. Descriptive representation is certainly associated with equal representation among groups. African Americans' and Latinos' greater distance from their white MCs largely disappears when they are represented by members of their own group. However, much of this is due to MCs' party affiliations rather than to their race or ethnicity. Descriptive representation on its own offers some gains in relative representation over and above electing Democratic MCs, but those gains are limited to certain types of districts and specific issues. Descriptive representation can also improve the representation of all African Americans, even those who do not live in a district represented by an African American MC. When there are more African Americans in the House of Representatives, more African Americans see their views reflected in national policies.

A third factor, voter turnout, also provides mixed results. Perhaps one of the most disheartening findings for those who seek greater equality of representation between minorities and whites relates to the limited effects of turnout for African Americans and Latinos. Certainly the franchise has dramatically improved the political standing of African Americans over the second half of the twentieth century (e.g., Thernstrom 1987). However, at present, African Americans who vote are sometimes no more likely to get what they want from government than African Americans who do not vote. In general, when whites and African Americans turn out at similar rates, whites' advantage does not shrink. This renders the vote, often an effective political tool, a relatively weak instrument for equalizing the representation of whites and African Americans. Of course, this does not mean voting does no good for African Americans. In districts where African Americans comprise 40% or more of the district population, voting brings rewards for African Americans that exceed those whites enjoy. The threshold for representation gains is even lower for issues of distinctive salience. African American voters are closer to their MCs on LCCR votes than are nonvoting African Americans once districts reach the 30% African American mark. Moreover, African Americans gain as much as whites do from voting when it comes to representation on issues distinctively salient to African Americans

in districts where African Americans make up a majority of the population. Note, however, that this means African Americans enjoy rewards of voting that equal whites' rewards in rather narrow circumstances. Around 40% of the African American population lives in majority African American districts (Lublin 1997, 35). Even there, African American voters benefit as much as white voters do only on specific issues.

Latinos also reap some representational rewards from voting, but again only in some contexts. Under some conditions, these rewards rival those that whites receive. Latino voters are more likely to be policy winners and in some instances may be a bit closer to their MCs than nonvoters. However, these gains are typically not as large as those enjoyed by white voters. So, boosting turnout across the board may not benefit Latinos' representation relative to that of whites. Increasing turnout only among Latinos would help to increase this group's equality of representation. However, voting Latinos are still less likely than *nonvoting* whites to be on the winning side of government's decisions.

Thus, looking at the relative representation of these three groups and judging against three standards of equality yields a more nuanced story of racial/ethnic politics in the United States than we might have guessed. The answer to the "who governs?" question changes depending on what one means by equality, the issue at hand, whether descriptive representation is part of the picture, and who votes.

NORMATIVE IMPLICATIONS

What one makes of these findings depends largely on the standard of equality one prefers. Although the normative import of these findings depends on readers' perspectives on equality, the empirical results inform the three normative positions we staked out, giving advocates of each standard of equality reason to celebrate and take pause. To put the most positive face on our results, some readers may argue that although whites are clearly advantaged, the system is still providing for the representation of African Americans and Latinos to some degree. Although whites are policy winners more often than Latinos and African Americans, the disparity is seldom greater than 10 percentage points across a host of issues. In addition, Democratic MCs tend to represent African Americans and Latinos better than Republican MCs, and a majority of African Americans (63%) and Latinos (57%) in our data were represented by Democrats. Moreover, we have seen many contexts in which minority groups are represented just as well as or even better than whites.

Race-conscious egalitarians, however, will not view our results nearly as favorably. From this perspective, most of our findings are disappointing. In general, on most issues, most of the time, whites are better represented than African Americans and Latinos. Furthermore, Latinos and African Americans as groups are not more than proportionally represented. In fact, our results may even mute the degree to which the system disadvantages African Americans and Latinos. Our measure of spending preferences, for example, only asks if respondents want more, less, or the same amount of spending. If African Americans or Latinos want spending on welfare to increase by 25%, labeling respondents as "policy winners" in years when welfare spending increases more than 5% may be overly optimistic.[1] Race-conscious egalitarians may think that this pattern of results indicates a failure to live up to the goals of strict equality among racial and ethnic groups. However, even the race-conscious egalitarian has something to celebrate, as minority groups are more than proportionally represented in issue domains that these groups care more about than the does the majority, especially when they are descriptively represented. However, these conditions are exceptions rather than the rule. Of the 996 votes in the House of Representatives during the 107th Congress, the LCCR only selected a dozen as "key votes."[2] Similarly, in our data only about 30% of African Americans and 18% of Latinos were descriptively represented in the 107th Congress. Therefore, on balance, race-conscious egalitarians will find much more to be concerned about than to celebrate here.

The advocate of proportionality also finds reason for both celebration and concern. One major point of concern is MCs' limited sensitivity to the percentage of African Americans in electoral districts. This finding applies only to nondescriptive MCs and only when we look across the broad spectrum of issues, but again, this is the normal state of things. In addition, MCs respond to whites' preferences more than to African Americans' preferences at both the group level and the individual level (recall table 5.5). Finally, even though African Americans are better represented in an absolute sense in districts that are 40% or 50% African American, whites remain somewhat better represented than African Americans even in these districts. Thus, on

1. We have no evidence that a significant portion of African American or Latino communities prefer these kinds of increases, but note the possibility that our results are understating the extent of underrepresentation of minority interests.
2. Of these, we only used seven because the NAES did not include questions related to the subject of the other votes.

most issues most of the time, the proportionalist must conclude that the system is not upholding the notion of representation according to group size for African Americans.

The principle of proportionality is somewhat more fulfilled for Latinos, giving the proportionalist something to cheer. White MCs are sensitive to the size of their Latino constituencies and are just as close to Latino constituents as they are to white constituents in majority Latino districts. However, Latinos fare worst compared to whites in districts that are just shy of a Latino majority (40–50% Latino).

Of the three standards, the pluralist standard is most often satisfied with respect to minority representation. However, even here the evidence is mixed. The general pattern of our results—that whites are better represented on most issues, but Latinos and African Americans are more than proportionally represented on issues of distinctive salience for these groups—is precisely what pluralism demands. Even though Robert Dahl (1956), a leading light among pluralists, worried over the lack of institutional means to guarantee greater minority representation on salient issues, the system largely produces this result nonetheless.

However, we may have underappreciated the extent to which some of the most important issues for minorities in absolute terms—including, most prominently, redistributive programs—are also very important to the white majority. Under a pluralist standard of equality as we define it, minorities should be more than proportionally represented on issues that they care about *more than whites*. When minority groups and whites both care deeply about an issue, the theoretical logic we spell out suggests that MCs will generally support the larger group. Only when the minority is more concerned with an issue than is the majority does the MC have an electoral incentive to support the minority position. We identify several issues that meet this criterion, test the relative representation of groups, and conclude that on these issues the pluralist standard of equality is largely satisfied. We are mindful, though, that some of the most important issues for minorities in absolute terms, like issues dealing with economic and social inequalities manifested in the quality of schools, health care, job training and opportunity, and the accumulation of wealth and capital, are *also* deeply important to whites. Certainly, policies designed to alter these conditions, like affirmative action, are hotly contested and highly salient to both minority groups and whites. As a result, according to the electoral logic we spell out, minorities will not be represented more than proportionally on these issues. This is somewhat invisible in a study like ours that focuses on proposals that reach a roll-call

vote. Many important issues for minorities, such as slavery reparations or mandating equal per-pupil educational expenditures, will never reach a roll-call vote, and if they do, the salience of these issues for whites means that whites will probably carry the day. While this may not violate our conception of pluralism, it will limit the extent of minority representation.

Pluralists may also be troubled by the impact of descriptive representation. In districts represented by African Americans, whites and African Americans are equally represented across the broad spectrum of issues, and whites are represented worse than African Americans on issues distinctively salient to African Americans. The problem for pluralists is that whites may never be better represented in these districts. Indeed, in analyses that we did not include in chapter 7 for brevity's sake, we examined key roll-call votes on the environment, as identified by the League of Conservation Voters. Since whites tend to care much more about the environment than African Americans do (see fig. 3.6), the pluralist would expect whites to be better represented. However, we found that when African Americans are descriptively represented, they are at least as close as whites to their MCs and maybe even closer on these environmental votes. We can press this concern only so far, though. Descriptive representation may limit whites' clout in districts with minority members, denying pluralism in those specific districts, but many of these whites still may find themselves "winners" when it comes to national policy. In the language of representation studies, pluralism may not hold for these whites in the dyadic sense, but it does in terms of collective representation (Weisberg 1978).

In the end, our empirical findings hold a complex set of normative implications. The question of whether any of these groups is represented "too much" is a multifaceted and nuanced one. Those proposing answers to that question must grapple with the complicated reality that these groups are more and less equal under a variety of conditions. No simple answer is likely to do justice to this complex reality. There are ways in which the American political system clearly advantages whites, but there are ways in which it promotes the preferences of Latinos and African Americans as well.

THE FUTURE OF POLITICAL (IN)EQUALITY

Given what we have learned, what can we expect in the future? How might the story of (in)equality change over the next few decades? Our analyses point to institutional and political factors that may alter the balance of representation among the groups.

In general, we might expect that Latinos may gain ground on whites over the next several decades, probably to a greater degree than African Americans will. Some Latino leaders have noted the political gains this group has enjoyed and anticipate more gains in the future. For example, César Chávez noted that one "trend that gives us hope is the monumental growth of Hispanic influence in this country . . . [including] increased population, increased social and economic clout, and increased political influence."[3] Several factors point toward potential gains for Latinos, primarily Latinos' population growth. Latinos as a group constitute an increasing share of the U.S. population, recently becoming the nation's largest minority group. In contrast, the African American share of the population is relatively stable. Furthermore, the rise in the Latino population is not limited to the American southwest. The Latino population in the southern United States grew from 7.9% to 11.6% of the population between 1990 and 2000, and from 7.4% to 9.8% of the population in the Northeast. Moreover, there are large Latino populations in states that are potentially key "swing" states in presidential elections, like Florida, North Carolina, New Mexico, and Colorado. It may be that forward-looking politicians in various states not only see the current political benefits of appealing to Latinos, but may view current appeals as investments that will pay increasingly rich dividends as the Latino population continues to grow and disperse.[4] For example, in commenting on major 2006 protests by Latinos and other immigrants on immigration reform, Senator Lindsey Graham (R-SC) noted, "I understand clearly that the demographic changes are real in America and how we handle this issue in terms of fairness will be very important for the future of both parties. . . . Those who believe that they have no political vulnerability for the moment don't understand the future" (Swarns 2006).

In addition to population growth, Latinos' political preferences may lead to future gains. As a group, Latinos are more similar to whites in their political preferences than are African Americans. This will limit the extent to which government can respond to whites more than Latinos. When these groups agree, government cannot grant one group its wishes and not the

3. Commonwealth club address delivered November 8, 1984. See the American Rhetoric Web site: http://www.americanrhetoric.com/speeches/cesarchavezcommonwealth clubaddress.htm.
4. Along these lines, Espino (2004) found that MCs representing districts that border districts with significant Latino populations tended to be responsive to Latino opinion, presumably in anticipation of a growing Latino population in their own districts, whether by population movement or by redistricting.

other. In addition, although Latinos as a group tend to identify with and support Democratic candidates, Latino party identification and the Latino vote are more heterogeneous and fluid than is true for African Americans. Over the last three decades, typically more than 80% of African Americans identified themselves as Democrats and more than 90% have voted for Democratic presidential candidates. In contrast, 60–70% of Latinos identified as Democrats over the same period. In fact, in the 2000 and 2004 National Election Studies (NES) not many more than half of all Latinos identified themselves as Democrats. Latino support for Democratic presidential candidates is also less stable than that of African Americans. Typically between 55% and 65% of Latinos voted for Democratic candidates. In the 2004 NES, 60% of Latinos reported voting for John Kerry, compared to 88% of African Americans. In short, more Latino votes are up for grabs, so elected officials have more incentive to appeal to Latinos. Thus, we might expect Latinos' representation to improve relative to that of whites, but the same factors that suggest gains in Latinos' future suggest minimal changes for African Americans.

Our findings point to three potential tools that may lead to greater political equality more generally. First, descriptive representation appears to hold some promise as a tool for equalizing African American, Latino, and white representation. Although descriptive representation does not guarantee political equality and under some conditions provides few relative representation gains beyond electing Democrats, descriptive representation does appear to boost minority representation relative to that of whites under some conditions. Therefore, increasing the extent of descriptive representation by electing more African American and Latino MCs would presumably lead to at least some gains in political equality. However, these gains may be undercut if electing minority MCs requires drawing congressional districts in ways that ultimately dilute the strength of Democratic voting blocs (e.g., Lublin 1997).

Given this potential trade-off, it is vital to consider strategies for electing more minority members that do not alter district lines in favor of Republican candidates. Our results in chapter 7 point to one such potential strategy: increasing the extent of political knowledge and interest among African Americans and Latinos. Doing so may lead to more widespread descriptive representation. Thus, interest groups and other minority group leaders may do well to consider the benefits of trying to increase interest and knowledge. Particularly where they can take advantage of "niche" media outlets that target minority groups, it may be possible for interest groups, grassroots movements, and minority group leaders to stir up

greater political interest and knowledge among Latinos and African Americans. We do not mean to suggest that this will be easy. Boosting political interest and knowledge among any group of Americans poses challenges.[5] Despite the challenges, this avenue holds some promise for those looking to make relative representation gains among minority groups.

In addition to boosting political interest and knowledge, a second way minority groups could increase their representation relative to whites is to exploit the benefits of distinctive issue salience. Minority group leaders and interest groups may be able to boost minority groups' relative representation by identifying concerns important to these communities, assessing group members' attitudes on these issues, and conveying to office holders that these preferences are salient. To date, such efforts by group leaders to learn more about the communities they serve have been limited, primarily due to the enormous cost of polling. On the one hand, the National Association for the Advancement of Colored People (NAACP) regularly commissions polls. On the other hand, the National Council of La Raza (NCLR), the "largest national Latino civil rights and advocacy organization in the United States,"[6] has commissioned just one poll of the Latino community, according to our discussions with them. The poll assessed the issues of greatest importance to the Latino community and Latinos' attitudes on issues such as education, immigration, and health care. The League of United Latino American Citizens (LULAC), a key member of the NHLA, conducted its first poll as an organization in February 2005, to determine Latinos' attitudes on President Bush's proposed privatization of Social Security. The National Association of Latino Elected and Appointed Officials (NALEO), "the leading organization that empowers Latinos to participate fully in the American political process," has yet to commission a poll of Latinos. To be sure, these organizations rely on polling by policy institutes and academics, but there is little question that more frequent, in-depth polling of African Americans and Latinos would provide information that politicians and interest organizations could use to help minorities be more influential in the policy process.

Beyond understanding what issues are salient, another strategy for improving minorities' representation is to increase publicity for minorities'

5. Niche media open new possibilities for stimulating the electorate, but the proliferation of news outlets also opens possibilities for avoiding political information altogether (Prior 2005). When politically disinterested people are watching one television channel and political information is thrust at them, they can simply switch to something nonpolitical.

6. See the Web site of the National Council of La Raza: http://www.nclr.org/.

issue concerns—to convey to officeholders and the media the issues that are salient for these groups. The first step in doing this is for interest organizations to gain credibility as representatives of the group (Wilson 1981). As Wilson puts it, it is important to determine "what success interest groups have had in establishing a sense that they are the legitimate spokesmen for the interests they claim to represent" (15). This is the goal for organizations such as the NAACP, the National Urban League, the National Council of La Raza, and LULAC—to be trusted by elected officials as the accurate representatives of African Americans' and Latinos' interests. The next step is to communicate minorities' concerns. For example, after LULAC completed its Social Security reform poll, it pursued an advertising campaign aimed at the constituents of House member Heather Wilson (R-NM) and then Ways and Means Committee Chairman Bill Thomas (R-CA) in an effort to reverse their support for reform.

Finally, minority group leaders can advance minorities' interests a great deal just by getting salient issues placed on the policy and legislative agenda (Kingdon 1984; Baumgartner and Jones 1993). Minorities appear to have a built-in advantage when issues they deem salient are under consideration, so the more often that salient issues are considered, the better off minorities will be. This again is not easy because it is much easier for minorities to block new policies than to implement them (Bachrach and Baratz 1962; Kingdon 1984). If the status quo tends not to favor minorities, then efforts to improve minorities' representation via agenda-setting are limited. Moreover, many of the concerns of minorities are not new—discrimination, economic assistance, education, health care—and we know that policy change is more likely to be incremental than radical when this is the case (Baumgartner and Jones 1993, 5). Finally, minorities' efforts to affect the agenda will be less successful if a minority group is not cohesive (Kingdon 1984, 55). This is more likely to be a concern for Latino leaders, due to the relative diversity of opinions among this population.

Electoral mobilization is a third strategy for changing the balance of representation in the future. Latino voters tend to be policy winners more often than nonvoters, and African American voters tend to be closer than nonvoters to their MCs' votes on distinctively salient issues and in districts with significant African American populations. However, since Latinos' and African Americans' rewards for voting are typically smaller than those of whites, if nothing else changes and if turnout is to provide relative gains compared to whites, turnout will have to rise more for the minority groups than it does for whites.

What can we expect from mobilization as a lever for altering the future balance of representation? Recall that voting power is a function of group size and the likelihood that the group's votes could be won by either candidate. In terms of group size, the African American population appears to be relatively stable. Therefore, the only way for African Americans to increase voting power is to selectively boost turnout or to loosen their affiliation with the Democratic Party. Regarding the former, it may be difficult to increase African Americans' voting rate when the factors that affect turnout (e.g., income and education) change slowly and when African Americans already vote at a higher rate than we would expect on the basis of socioeconomic factors. Moreover, African Americans' preferences are not equally represented, which makes turnout gains unlikely due to the effect of representation on efficacy and, in turn, the effect of efficacy on participation (Abramson and Aldrich 1982). In terms of the latter possibility, there are some early signs that African Americans' strong support for Democratic candidates may be cracking. In 2002, the Joint Center for Political and Economic Studies, a liberal think tank, asked African American respondents in a national survey to identify themselves as either Democrats, Independents, or Republicans. Although 63% claimed to be Democrats, the number was down from 74% in 2000. The decrease occurred in nearly every age group. There was a significant increase in those calling themselves Independents, especially between the ages of 26 and 35. Respondents identifying themselves as Republicans also increased: between ages 26 and 35, the number tripled, going from 5% in 2000 to 15% in 2002. Finally, among African American Protestants, 3.5% reported voting for George Bush in 2000, while 17.2% voted for Bush in 2004. If these trends continue, African Americans' voting power may look very different in coming elections. In the end, since Democratic MCs tend to be closer to African Americans than are Republican MCs, gaining voting power by voting more frequently for Republicans may not be an appealing trade-off for African Americans.

Latinos' voting power, on the other hand, looks much more likely to rise. The Latino population is growing rapidly, but much will depend on whether they are captured by one party or the other. Recent signs suggest that Latinos as a group are actually becoming more split among the two major parties. The percentage of Latinos identifying with the Democratic Party has declined since the late 1990s, as have the percentages of Latinos voting for Democratic presidential and House candidates. Clearly Republican leaders believe the GOP can successfully court Latino voters. In 2004 the GOP created a Spanish-language Web site and posted an initiative called "Abriendo Cami-

nos" (Forging New Paths), which serves as the party's platform for extolling what it identifies as President Bush's efforts to aid Latinos. In 2000, the Republicans employed a Team Leader Project, in which speakers from the Bush administration informed local communities about Republican legislative proposals to assist Latinos. Whether the Republican Party can successfully court Latino support while at least some Republicans are pushing for immigration reform, including harsh penalties for assisting undocumented immigrants and the construction of a wall on the border remains to be seen. Republicans' success in appealing to Latinos will shape the political opportunities open to this group.

Any prognosticating about the future is dangerous in the social sciences. As political conditions change, the nature of minority representation will respond. Two recent phenomena remind us that the state of minority representation could change quickly. First, the Democrats regained majorities in both the House of Representatives and the Senate in the dramatic 2006 midterm elections. African Americans hold forty-two seats in the 110th House elected in 2006 (including two nonvoting members), while Latinos hold twenty-six seats. Many minority MCs now hold more powerful committee positions as a result of being in the Democratic majority. According to David Bositis of the Joint Center for Economic Studies, "this is by far the peak—ever—for the Congressional Black Caucus" (cited in Terhune 2006). Second, as of this writing there appears to be a real possibility that Senator Barack Obama (D-IL) could be elected as the nation's first minority president in 2008. Thus, we recognize that the nature of minority representation will continue to shift in both predictable and unpredictable ways.

As we close, we note that although we have taken a significant step toward recognizing the diverse racial and ethnic makeup of American society by examining African Americans, Latinos, and whites together, there is much more to be done. We have neglected other important and growing ethnic and racial minority groups. For example, the Asian American population is growing and may play an increasingly important role in American politics. At this point, though, Asian Americans' attitudes are much more similar to those of whites, minimizing the possibility of disparities in representation. In any case, future efforts to comprehend who governs American politics have to reckon with an increasingly diverse electorate. As we have seen, examining the relative representation of three different groups reveals new insights into the complex phenomena of representation and political equality in democratic politics.

References

Abramson, Paul R., and John H. Aldrich. 1982. "The Decline of Electoral Participation in America." *American Political Science Review* 76:502–21.

Achen, Christopher. 1978. "Measuring Representation." *American Journal of Political Science* 22:475–510.

Adamson, Joni, Mei Mei Evans, and Rachel Stein. 2001. *The Environmental Justice Reader: Politics, Poetics, and Pedagogy.* Tucson: University of Arizona Press.

Amer, Mildred L. 2004. "Black Members of the United States Congress: 1870–2004." Library of Congress, Congressional Research Service. Online at http://www.senate.gov/reference/resources/pdf/RL30378.pdf.

Anaya, S. James. 2000. "On Justifying Special Ethnic Group Rights: Comments on Pogge." In *Ethnicity and Group Rights*, ed. Ian Shapiro and Will Kymlicka, 222–31. New York: New York University Press..

Ansolabehere, Stephen, James M. Snyder, and Charles Stewart III. 2001. "The Effects of Party and Preferences on Congressional Roll Call Voting." *Legislative Studies Quarterly* 26:533–72.

Arnold, R. Douglas. 1990. *The Logic of Congressional Action.* New Haven, CT: Yale University Press.

Bachrach, Peter, and Morton S. Baratz. 1962. "Two Faces of Power." *American Political Science Review* 56:947–52.

Bafumi, Joseph, and Michael Herron. 2007. "Representation and American Political Institutions." Paper presented at the annual meeting of the Midwest Political Science Association, Chicago, IL.

Banducci, Susan A., Todd Donovan, and Jeffrey A. Karp. 2004. "Minority Representation, Empowerment, and Participation." *Journal of Politics* 66:534–56.

Barnum, David G. 1985. "The Supreme Court and Public Opinion: Judicial Decision Making in the Post–New Deal Period." *Journal of Politics* 47:652–66.

Barreto, Matt, Gary M. Segura, and Nathan D. Woods. 2004. "The Mobilizing Effect of Majority-Minority Districts on Latino Turnout." *American Political Science Review* 98:65–75.

Bartels, Larry M. 1991. "Constituency Opinion and Congressional Policy Making: The Reagan Defense Build Up." *American Political Science Review* 85:457–74.

————. 1998. "Where the Ducks Are: Voting Power in a Party System." In *Politicians and Party Politics*, ed. John Geer, 43–79. Baltimore, MD: Johns Hopkins University Press.

————. 2002. "Economic Inequality and Political Representation." Paper presented at the 2002 meeting of the American Political Science Association, Boston, MA.

————. 2008. *Unequal Democracy: The Political Economy of the New Gilded Age*. New York: Russell Sage.

Baumgartner, Frank R., and Bryan D. Jones. 1993. *Agendas and Instability in American Politics*. Chicago: University of Chicago Press.

Bennett, Stephen Earl and David Resnick. 1990. "The Implications of Nonvoting for Democracy in the United States." *American Journal of Political Science* 34:771–802.

Bessette, Joseph. M. 1994. *The Mild Voice of Reason*. Chicago: University of Chicago Press.

Binder, Sarah, Forrest Maltzman, and Lee Sigelman. 1998. "Senators' Home-State Reputations: Why Do Constituents Love a Bill Cohen So Much More Than an Al D'Amato?" *Legislative Studies Quarterly* 23:545–60.

Blalock, Hubert M., Jr. 1967. *Toward a Theory of Minority-Group Relations*. New York: John Wiley.

Bobo, Lawrence, and Frank D. Gilliam. 1990. "Race, Sociopolitical Participation, and Black Empowerment." *American Political Science Review* 84:377–93.

Boninger, D. S., J. A. Krosnick, and M. K. Berent. 1995. "The Origins of Attitude Importance: Self-Interest, Social Identification, and Value Relevance." *Journal of Personality and Social Psychology* 68:61–80.

Brace, Paul, Kellie Sims-Butler, Kevin Arceneaux, and Martin Johnson. 2002. "Public Opinion in the American States: New Perspectives on Using National Survey Data." *American Journal of Political Science* 46:173–89.

Brischetto, Robert. 1987. "Latinos and the 1984 Election Exit Polls: Some Findings and Some Methodological Lessons." In *Ignored Voices: Public Opinion Polls and the Latino Community*, ed. Rodolfo O. de la Garza, 76–94. CMAS Publications. Austin: University of Texas.

Bullock, Charles S., III. 1981. "Congressional Voting and the Mobilization of a Black Electorate in the South." *Journal of Politics* 43:662–82.

Bullock, Charles S., III, and David W. Brady. 1983. "Party, Constituency, and Roll-Call Voting in the U. S. Senate." *Legislative Studies Quarterly* 8:29–43.

Bullock, Charles S., and Harrell R. Rodgers Jr. 1976. "Coercion to Compliance: Southern School Districts and School Desegregation Guidelines." *Journal of Politics* 38:987–1011.

Burden, Barry C. 2004. "A Technique for Estimating Candidate and Voter Locations." *Electoral Studies* 23:623–39.

Burden, Barry C., Gregory A. Caldeira, and Tim Groseclose. 2000. "Measuring the Ideologies of U.S. Senators: The Song Remains the Same." *Legislative Studies Quarterly* 25:237–58.

Burkett, Maxine. 2002–3. "Strategic Voting and African-Americans: True Vote, True Representation, True Power for the Black Community." *Michigan Journal of Race and Law* 8:425–69.

Burnham, Walter Dean. 1987. "The Turnout Problem." In *Elections American Style*, ed. A. James Reichley, 97–133. Washington, DC: Brookings Institution.

Burns, Peter F. 2006. *Electoral Politics Is Not Enough: Racial and Ethnic Minorities and Urban Politics*. Albany, NY: SUNY Press.

Burns, Nancy, Kay Schlozman, and Sidney Verba. 2001. *The Private Roots of Public Action: Gender, Equality, and Political Participation*. Cambridge, MA: Harvard University Press.

Calhoun, John C. 1953. *A Disquisition on Government and Selections from the Discourse*. Ed. C. Gordon Post. Indianapolis, IN: Bobbs Merrill.

Camacho, David E. 1998. *Environmental Injustices, Political Struggles: Race, Class and the Environment*. Durham, NC: Duke University Press.

Cameron, Charles, David Epstein, and Sharyn O'Halloran. 1996. "Do Majority-Minority Districts Maximize Substantive Black Representation in Congress?" *American Political Science Review* 90:794–812.

Campbell, Andrea L. 2003. *How Policies Make Citizens: Senior Political Activism and the American Welfare State*. Princeton, NJ: Princeton University Press.

Canon, David T. 1999. *Race, Redistricting, and Representation: The Unintended Consequences of Black Majority Districts*. Chicago: University of Chicago Press.

Carmines, Edward G., and James A. Stimson. 1989. *Issue Evolution: Race and the Transformation of American Politics*. Princeton, NJ: Princeton University Press.

Carter, Stephen H. 1994. "Foreword." In *The Tyranny of the Majority: Fundamental Fairness in Representative Democracy*, vii–xx. New York: Free Press.

Citrin, Jack, Eric Schickler, and John Sides. 2003. "What If Everyone Voted? Simulating the Impact of Increased Turnout in Senate Elections." *American Journal of Political Science* 47:75–90.

Cohen, Jeffrey E. 1997. *Presidential Responsiveness and Public Policy-Making: The Public and the Policies that Presidents Choose*. Ann Arbor: University of Michigan Press.

Colker, Ruth. 1986. "Anti-Subordination Above All: Sex, Race, and Equal protection." *New York University Law Review* 61:1003–66.

Combs, Michael W., John R. Hibbing, and Susan Welch. 1984. "Black Constituents and Congressional Roll Call Votes." *Western Political Quarterly* 37:424–34.

Conley, Patricia. 2005. "The American Presidency and the Politics of Democratic Inclusion." In *The Politics of Democratic Inclusion*, ed. Christina Wolbrecht and Rodney E. Hero, 314–34. Philadelphia, PA: Temple University Press.

Converse, Philip E. 1964. "The Nature of Belief Systems in Mass Publics." In *Ideology and Discontent*, ed. David Apter, 206–61. New York: Free Press.

Dahl, Robert A. 1956. *A Preface to Democratic Theory*. Chicago: University of Chicago Press.

———. 1961. *Who Governs? Democracy and Power in an American City*. New Haven: Yale University Press.

———. 1967. *Pluralist Democracy in the United States: Conflict and Consent*. Chicago: Rand McNally.

———. 2006. *On Political Equality*. New Haven, CT: Yale University Press.

Dawson, Michael C. 1994. *Behind the Mule: Race and Class in African-American Politics*. Princeton, NJ: Princeton University Press.

De la Garza. Rodolfo O. 2004. "Latino Politics." *Annual Review of Political Science* 7:91–123.

De la Garza, Rodolfo O., Louis Desipio, F. Chris Garcia, John Garcia, and Angelo Falcón. 1992. *Latino Voices: Mexican, Puerto Rican and Cuban Perspectives on American Politics*. Boulder, CO: Westview Press.

DeNardo, James. 1980. "Turnout and the Vote: The Joke's on the Democrats." *American Political Science Review* 74:406–20.

DeNavas-Walt, Carmen, Bernadette D. Proctor, and Robert J. Mills. 2004. *Income, Poverty, and Health Insurance Coverage in the United States: 2003.* U.S. Census Bureau, Current Populations Reports, P60-226. Washington, DC: U.S. Government Printing Office.

Dixon, Lloyd, and Rachel Kaganoff Stern. 2004. "Compensation for Losses from the 9/11 Attacks." Santa Monica, CA: RAND Institute for Civil Justice.

Dovi, Suzanne. 2002. "Preferable Descriptive Representatives: Will Just Any Woman, Black, or Latino Do?" *American Political Science Review* 96:729–43.

Downs, Anthony. 1957. *An Economic Theory of Democracy.* New York: Harper.

Eckel, Catherine, and Philip J.Grossman. 2001. "Chivalry and Solidarity in Ultimatum Games." *Economic Inquiry* 39:171–88.

Ellis, Chris, Joseph Ura, and Jenna Ashley-Robinson. 2006. "The Dynamic Consequences of Nonvoting in American National Elections." *Political Research Quarterly* 59:227–33.

Erikson, Robert S. 1978. "Constituency Opinion and Congressional Behavior: A Reexamination of the Miller-Stokes Representation Data." *American Journal of Political Science* 22:511–35.

———. 1990. "Roll Calls, Reputations, and Representation in the U. S. Senate." *Legislative Studies Quarterly* 15:623–42.

Erikson, Robert S., Michael B. MacKuen, and James A. Stimson. 2002. *The Macro Polity.* New York: Cambridge University Press.

Erikson, Robert S., and Gerald C. Wright. 2000. "Representation of Constituency Ideology in Congress." In *Continuity and Change in House Elections,* ed. David W. Brady, John F. Cogan, and Morris P. Fiorina, 148–77. Stanford, CA: Stanford University Press.

Erikson, Robert S., Gerald C. Wright, and John P. McIver. 1993. *Statehouse Democracy: Public Opinion and Policy in American States.* New York: Cambridge University Press.

Espino, Rodolfo. 2004. "Minority Agendas, Majority Rules: Representation of Latinos in the U.S. Congress." PhD diss., University of Wisconsin–Madison.

Fears, Darryl. 2003. "Draft Bill Stirs Debate Over the Military, Race and Equity." *Washington Post*, February 4, 2003, A3.

Feinberg, Kenneth R. 2004. *Final Report of the Special Master for the September 11th Victim Compensation Fund of 2001.* See the U.S. Department of Justice Web site: http://www.usdoj.gov/final_report.pdf.

Feldman, Stanley, and John Zaller. 1992. "The Political Culture of Ambivalence: Ideological Responses to the Welfare State." *American Journal of Political Science* 36:268–307.

Fenno, Richard F. 1973. *Congressmen in Committees.* Boston, MA: Little, Brown.

Fiorina, Morris P. 1974. *Representatives, Roll Calls, and Constituencies.* Lexington, MA: Lexington Books.

Fiss, Owen. 1976. "Groups and the Equal Protection Clause." *Philospohy and Public Affairs* 5:107–77.

———. 2004. "Another Equality." Issues in Legal Scholarship, The Origins and Fate of Antisubordination Theory: Article 20, at the Web site of the Berkeley Electronic Press: http://www.bepress.com/ils/iss2/art20.

Fowler, James. 2005. "Dynamic Responsiveness in the U.S. Senate." *American Journal of Political Science* 49:299–312.

Frymer, Paul. 1999. *Uneasy Alliances: Race and Party Competition in America*. Princeton, NJ: Princeton University Press.

———. 2003. "Acting When Elected Officials Won't: Federal Courts and Civil Rights Enforcement in U.S. Labor Unions, 1935–1985." *American Political Science Review* 97:483–99.

Gates, John B. and Jeffrey E. Cohen. 1988. "Presidents, Supreme Court Justices, and Racial Equality Cases: 1954–1984." *Political Behavior* 10:22–36.

Gay, Claudine. 2002. "Spirals of Trust? The Effect of Descriptive Representation on the Relationship between Citizens and Their Government." *American Journal of Political Science* 46:717–32.

———. 2004. "Putting Race in Context: Identifying the Environmental Determinants of Black Racial Attitudes." *American Political Science Review* 98:547–62.

Gerber, Alan S., Donald P. Green, and Ron Shachar. 2003. "Voting May be Habit-Forming: Evidence from a Randomized Field Experiment." *American Journal of Political Science* 47:540–50.

Gerber, Elizabeth R., and John E. Jackson. 1992. "Endogenous Preferences and the Study of Institutions." *American Political Science Review* 87:639–56.

Gilens, Martin. 1999. *Why Americans Hate Welfare*. Chicago: University of Chicago Press.

———. 2001. "Political Ignorance and Collective Policy Preferences." *American Political Science Review* 95:379–96.

———. 2003. *Race and the Politics of Welfare Reform*. Ann Arbor: University of Michigan Press.

———. 2005. "Inequality and Democratic Responsiveness." *Public Opinion Quarterly* 69:778–96.

Giles, Michael, and Melanie A. Buckner. 1993. "David Duke and Black Threat: An Old Hypothesis Revisited." *Journal of Politics* 55:702–13.

Gilliam, Frank D., Jr. 1996. "Exploring Minority Empowerment: Symbolic Politics, Governing Coalitions and Traces of Political Style in Los Angeles." *American Journal of Political Science* 40:56–81.

Griffin, John D. 2006. "Senate Apportionment as a Source of Political Inequality." *Legislative Studies Quarterly* 31:405–32.

Griffin, John D., and Brian Newman. 2005. "Are Voters Better Represented?" *Journal of Politics* 67:1206–27.

Griffin, John D., Brian Newman, and Christina Wolbrecht. 2006. "Descriptive Representation, Political Equality, and Gender." Paper presented at the annual meeting of the American Political Science Association, Washington, D.C., August 31–September 2.

Grofman, Bernard, Robert Griffin, and Amihai Glazer. 1992. "The Effect of Black Population on Electing Democrats and Liberals to the House of Representatives." *Legislative Studies Quarterly* 17:365–79.

Guinier, Lani. 1994. *The Tyranny of the Majority: Fundamental Fairness in Representative Democracy*. New York: Free Press.

Gutmann, Amy and Dennis Thompson. 1996. *Democracy and Disagreement*. Cambridge, MA: Harvard University Press.

Hajnal, Zoltan, Elisabeth Gerber, and Hugh Louch. 2002. "Minorities and Direct Legislation: Evidence from California Ballot Propositions." *Journal of Politics* 64:154–77.

Hajnal, Zoltan, and Jessica Trounstine. 2005. "Where Turnout Matters: The Consequences of Uneven Turnout in City Politics." *Journal of Politics* 67:515–35.

Harris, Angela. 2000. "Equality Trouble: Sameness and Difference in Twentieth-Century Race Law." *California Law Review* 88:1923–2015.

Haynie, Kerry L. 2001. *African American Legislators in the American States.* New York: Columbia University Press.

Hero, Rodney E. 1998. *Faces of Inequality: Social Diversity in American Politics.* Oxford: Oxford University Press.

Hero, Rodney E., and Caroline J. Tolbert. 1995. "Latinos and Substantive Representation in the U.S. House of Representatives: Direct, Indirect, or Nonexistent?" *American Journal of Political Science* 39:640–52.

Highton, Benjamin, and Raymond E. Wolfinger. 2001. "The Political Implications of Higher Turnout." *British Journal of Political Science* 31:179–192.

Hill, Kim Quaile, and Jan Leighley. 1992. "The Policy Consequences of Class Bias in State Electorates." *American Journal of Political Science* 36:351–65.

Hill, Kim Quaile, and Patricia A. Hurley. 1999. "Dyadic Representation Reappraised." *American Journal of Political Science* 43:109–37.

Hochschild, Jennifer L. 1981. *What's Fair? American Beliefs about Distributive Justice.* Cambridge, MA: Harvard University Press.

Hong, Kessely, and Iris Bohnet. 2004. "Status and Distrust: The Relevance of Risk, Inequality, and Betrayal Aversion." Available online at http://ksghome.harvard.edu/~ibohnet/Hong_BohnetFinal10_21_05.pdf.

Hurley, Patricia A., and Kim Quaile Hill. 2003. "Beyond the Demand-Input Model: A Theory of Representational Linkages." *Journal of Politics* 65:304–26.

Hutchings, Vincent. 1998. "Issue Salience and Support for Civil Rights Legislation Among Southern Democrats." *Legislative Studies Quarterly* 23:521–44.

———. 2001. "Political Context, Issue Salience, and Selective Attentiveness: Constituent Knowledge of the Clarence Thomas Confirmation Vote." *Journal of Politics* 63:846–68.

———. 2003. *Public Opinion and Democratic Accountability: How Citizens Learn about Politics.* Princeton, NJ: Princeton University Press.

Hutchings, Vincent L., Harwood K. McClerking, and Guy-Uriel Charles. 2004. "Congressional Representation of Black Interests: Recognizing the Importance of Stability." *Journal of Politics* 66:450–68.

Hutchings, Vincent L., and Nicholas A. Valentino. 2004. "The Centrality of Race in American Politics." *American Review of Political Science* 7:383–408.

Issacharoff, Samuel, and Pamela S. Karlan. 2003. "Groups, Politics, and the Equal Protection Clause." Issues in Legal Scholarship, The Origins and Fate of Antisubordination Theory: Article 19, at the Web site of the Berkeley Electronic Press: http://www.bepress.com/ils/iss2/art19.

Iyengar, Shanto. 1990. "Shortcuts to Political Knowledge: The Role of Selective Attention and Accessibility." In *Information and Democratic Processes*, ed. John A. Ferejohn and James H. Kuklinski, 160–85, Urbana: University of Illinois Press.

Jacobs, Lawrence R. 1993. *The Health of Nations.* Ithaca, NY: Cornell University Press.

Jacobs, Lawrence R., and Benjamin I. Page. 2005. "Who Influences U.S. Foreign Policy?" *American Political Science Review* 99:107–23.

Jacobs, Lawrence R., and Theda Skocpol. 2005. *Inequality and American Democracy: What We Know and What We Need to Learn.* New York: Russell Sage.

Jefferson, Thomas. 1955. *Notes on the State of Virginia.* Ed. William Peden. Chapel Hill, NC: University of North Carolina Press.

Johnson, Martin. 2001. "The Impact of Social Diversity and Racial Attitudes on Social Welfare Policy." *State Politics and Policy Quarterly* 1:27–49.

Jones, Bradford S., and Barbara Norrander. 1996. "The Reliability of Aggregated Public Opinion Measures." *American Journal of Political Science* 40:295–309.

Kaufmann, Karen M. 2003. "Black and Latino Voters in Denver: Responses to Each Other's Political Leadership." *Political Science Quarterly* 118:107–25.

Keech, William R. 1968. *The Impact of Negro Voting: The Role of the Vote in the Quest for Equality.* Chicago: Rand McNally.

Kelley, Stanley. 1983. *Interpreting Elections.* Princeton, NJ: Princeton University Press.

Kendall, Willmoore, and George W. Carey. 1968. "The 'Intensity' Problem and Democratic Theory." *American Political Science Review* 62:5–24.

Key, V. O. 1949. *Southern Politics in State and Nation.* New York: Alfred A. Knopf.

———. 1961. *Public Opinion and American Democracy.* New York: Alfred A. Knopf.

Kinder, Donald R., and Lynn M. Sanders. 1996. *Divided by Color: Racial Politics and Democratic Ideals.* Chicago: University of Chicago Press.

Kinder, Donald R., and D. O. Sears. 1981. "Prejudice and Politics: Symbolic Racism Versus Racial Threats to the Good Life." *Journal of Personality and Social Psychology* 40:414–31.

Kinder, Donald R., and Nicholas Winter. 2001. "Exploring the Racial Divide: Blacks, Whites, and Opinion on National Policy." *American Journal of Political Science* 45:439–56.

Kingdon, John W. 1984. *Agendas, Alternatives, and Public Policies.* Boston, MA: Little, Brown.

Kousser, J. Morgan. 1974. *The Shaping of Southern Politics: Suffrage Restriction and the Establishment of the One-Party South, 1880–1910.* New Haven, CT: Yale University Press.

———. 1999. *Colorblind Injustice: Minority Voting Rights and the Undoing of the Second Reconstruction.* Chapel Hill, NC: University of North Carolina Press.

Krosnick, J. A. 1988. "Attitude Importance and Attitude Change." *Journal of Experimental Social Psychology* 24:240–55.

———. 1990. "Government Policy and Citizen Passion: A Study of Issue Publics in Contemporary America." *Political Behavior* 12:59–92.

Krosnick, Jon, and Shibley Telhami. 1995. "Public Attitudes toward Israel: A Study of the Attentive and Issue Publics." *International Studies Quarterly* 39:535–54.

Kuklinski, James H. 1978. "Representativeness and Elections: A Policy Analysis." *American Political Science Review* 72:165–77.

Lardner, James, and David Smith, eds. 2005. *Inequality Matters: The Growing Economic Divide in America and Its Poisonous Consequences.* New York: New Press.

Leal, David L. 2002. "Latino Political Opinion: Is It Unique?" Paper presented at the annual meeting of the American Political Science Association. Boston, MA, August 29–September 1.

Lee, Frances E., and Bruce I. Oppenheimer. 1999. *Sizing Up the Senate: The Unequal Consequences of Equal Representation.* Chicago: University of Chicago Press.

Lewis, Jeffrey, and Keith T. Poole. 2004. "Measuring Bias and Uncertainty in Ideal Point Estimates via the Parametric Bootstrap." *Political Analysis* 12:105–27.

Lijphart, Arend. 1997. "Unequal Participation: Democracy's Unresolved Dilemma." *American Political Science Review* 91:1–14.

Lincoln, Abraham. 1953. *The Collected Works of Abraham Lincoln.* Ed. Roy P. Basler. Vol. 3. New Brunswick, NJ: Rutgers University Press.

Lindblom, Charles E. 1977. *Politics and Markets.* New York: Basic Books.

Lowi, Theodore J. 1969. *The End of Liberalism; Ideology, Policy, and the Crisis of Public Authority.* New York: W. W. Norton.

Lublin, David. 1997. *The Paradox of Representation: Racial Gerrymandering and Minority Interests in Congress.* Princeton, NJ: Princeton University Press.

Lyman, Rick. 2006. "Extension of Voting Act is Likely Despite Criticism." *New York Times*, March 27, A14.

MacKinnon, Catherine A. 1987. *Feminism Unmodified: Discourses on Life and Law.* Cambridge, MA: Harvard University Press.

Madison, James, Alexander Hamilton, and John Jay. 1987. *The Federalist Papers.* Ed. Isaac Kramnick. New York: Penguin Books.

Manin, Bernard. 1997. *The Principles of Representative Government.* New York: Cambridge University Press.

Manley, John F. 1983. "Neo-Pluralism: A Class Analysis of Pluralism I and Pluralism II." *American Political Science Review* 77:368–83.

Mansbridge, Jane. 1999. "Should Blacks Represent Blacks, and Women Represent Women? A Contingent 'Yes.'" *Journal of Politics* 61:628–57.

Manzano, Sylvia, and Barbara Norrander. 2007. "Latino Public Opinion, Influence and Policy Outcomes." Paper presented at the annual meeting of the Midwest Political Science Association, April 11–13, Chicago, IL.

Martin, Gary. 2000. "Pollsters See GOP Gains Among Hispanic Voters." *San Antonio Express News*, March 2.

Martin, Paul S. 2003. "Voting's Rewards: Voter Turnout, Attentive Publics, and Congressional Allocation of Federal Money." *American Journal of Political Science* 47: 110–27.

Mayer, Kenneth R. 2001. *With the Stroke of a Pen: Executive Orders and Presidential Power.* Princeton, NJ: Princeton University Press.

Mayhew, David R. 1974. *Congress: The Electoral Connection.* New Haven, CT: Yale University Press.

Mayo, H. B. 1960. *An Introduction to Democratic Theory.* New York: Oxford University Press.

McClain, Paula D., and Albert K. Karnig. 1990. "Black and Hispanic Socioeconomic and Political Competition." *American Political Science Review* 84:535–45.

McClain, Paula D., and Joseph Stewart. 2002. *Can We All Get Along? Racial and Ethnic Minorities in American Politics.* 2nd ed. Boulder, CO: Westview Press.

McClosky, Herbert. 1964. "Consensus and Ideology in American Politics." *American Political Science Review* 58:361–82.

McCrone, Donald J., and James H. Kuklinski. 1979. "The Delegate Theory of Representation." *American Journal of Political Science* 23:278–300.

Meier, Kenneth J., Paula D. McClain, J. L. Polinard, and Robert D. Wrinkle. 2004. "Divided or Together? Conflict and Cooperation between African Americans and Latinos." *Political Research Quarterly* 57 (September): 399–409.

Miller, Warren E. 1964. "Majority Rule and the Representative System of Government." In *Cleavages, Ideologies, and Party Systems*, ed. Erik Allardt and Yrjo Littunen, 343–76. Contributions to Comparative Political Sociology, Transactions of the Westermarck Society, vol. 10. Helsinki, Finland: Academic Bookstore.

Miller, Warren E., and Donald E. Stokes. 1963. "Constituency Influence in Congress." *American Political Science Review* 57:45–56.

Monroe, Alan D. 1979. "Consistency between Public Preferences and National Policy Decisions." *American Politics Quarterly* 7:3–19.

———. 1998. "Public Opinion and Public Policy." *Public Opinion Quarterly* 62:6–28.

Nagel, Jack H., and John E. McNulty. 1996. "Partisan Effects of Voter Turnout in Senatorial and Gubernatorial Elections." *American Political Science Review* 90:780–93.

National Advisory Commission on Civil Disturbances. 1968. *Report of the National Advisory Commission on Civil Disturbances.* New York: Bantam Books.

Norrander, Barbara. 2005. "Measuring State Public Opinion with the Senate National Election Study." *State Politics and Policy Quarterly* 1:111–25.

Office of Management and Budget. 2004. *Historical Tables: Budget of the United States Government, Fiscal Year 2005.* Washington, DC: U.S. Government Printing Office.

Page, Benjamin I., and Marshall M. Bouton. 2006. *The Foreign Policy Disconnect: What Americans Want from Our Leaders but Don't Get.* Chicago: University of Chicago Press.

Page, Benjamin I., and Robert Shapiro. 1983. "Effects of Public Opinion on Policy." *American Political Science Review* 77:175–90.

Pantoja, Adrian D., and Gary M. Segura. 2003. "Does Ethnicity Matter? Descriptive Representation in Legislatures and Political Alienation among Latinos." *Social Science Quarterly* 84:441–60.

Pildes, Richard H. 2000. "Diffusion of Political Power and the Voting Rights Act." *Harvard Journal of Law and Public Policy* 24:119–39.

Pitkin, Hannah. 1967. *The Concept of Representation.* Berkeley and Los Angeles: University of California Press.

Polsby, Nelson. 1980. *Community Power and Political Theory.* New Haven, CT: Yale University Press.

Poole, Keith T., and Howard Rosenthal. 1997. *Congress : A Political-Economic History of Roll Call Voting.* New York: Oxford University Press.

Powell, Lynda W. 1982. "Issue Representation in Congress." *Journal of Politics* 44: 658–78.

———. 1989. "Analyzing Misinformation: Perceptions of Congressional Candidates' Ideologies." *American Journal of Political Science* 33:272–93.

Primus, Richard A. 2003. "Equal Protection and Disparate Impact: Round Three." *Harvard Law Review* 117, no. 2:493–587.

Prior, Markus. 2005. "News vs. Entertainment: How Increasing Media Choice Widens Gaps in Political Knowledge and Turnout." *American Journal of Political Science* 49:577–92.

Radcliff, Benjamin, and Martin Saiz. 1995. "Race, Turnout, and Public Policy in the American States." *Political Research Quarterly* 48:775–94.

Riley, Russell L. 1999. *The Presidency and the Politics of Racial Inequality: Nation-Keeping from 1831-1965*. New York: Columbia University Press.

Romer, Daniel, Kate Kenski, Paul Waldman, Christopher Adasiewicz, and Kathleen Hall Jamieson. 2004. *Capturing Campaign Dynamics: The National Annenberg Election Survey Design, Method, and Data*. New York: Oxford University Press.

Rosenstone, Steven J., and John Mark Hansen. 1993. *Mobilization, Participation, and Democracy in America*. New York: Macmillan.

Schattschneider, Elmer Eric. 1960. *The Semisovereign People; A Realist's View of Democracy in America*. New York: Holt, Rinehart and Winston.

Schumaker, Paul D., and Russel W. Getter. 1977. "Responsiveness Bias in 51 American Communities." *American Journal of Political Science* 21:247–81.

Schuman, H., and S. Presser. 1981. *Questions and Answers in Attitude Surveys*. New York: Academic Press.

Schwartz, S. P., W. Li, L. Berenson, and R. D. Williams. 2002. "Deaths in World Trade Center Terrorist Attacks—New York City 2001." Office of Vital Statistics, New York City Department of Health and Mental Hygiene, New York. Centers for Disease Control Weekly Morbidity and Mortality Weekly Report, vol. 51, September 11, 2002. Available at http://www.cdc.gov/mmwr/preview/mmwrhtml/mm51SPa6.htm#tab1.

Sigelman, Lee. 1982. "The Nonvoting Voter in Voting Research." *American Journal of Political Science* 26:47–56.

Silver, Brian D., Barbara A. Anderson, and Paul R. Abramson. 1986. "Who Overreports Voting?" *American Political Science Review* 80:613–24.

Smith, Tom W. 1985a. "The Polls: America's Most Important Problems. Part 1. National and International." *Public Opinion Quarterly* 49:264–74.

———. 1985b. "The Polls: America's Most Important Problems. Part 2. Regional, Community, and Personal." *Public Opinion Quarterly* 49:403–10.

Smith, Rogers M. 2003. "'Black' and 'White' in Brown: Equal Protection and the Legal Construction of Racial Identities." Issues in Legal Scholarship, The Origins and Fate of Antisubordination Theory, Article 16, at the Web site of the Berkeley Electronic Press: http://www.bepress.com/ils/iss2/art16.

Sniderman, Paul M., and Edward G. Carmines. 1997. *Reaching Beyond Race*. Cambridge, MA: Harvard University Press.

Sniderman, Paul M., and Thomas Piazza. 1993. *The Scar of Race*. Cambridge, MA: Belknap Press of Harvard University Press.

Steiner, Jurg. 1971. "The Principles of Majority and Proportionality." *British Journal of Political Science* 1:63–70.

Sullivan, John L. 1973. "Political Correlates of Social, Economic, and Religious Diversity in the American States." *Journal of Politics*, 35:70–84.

Sunstein, Cass R. 1994. "The Anticaste Principle." *Michigan Law Review* 92:2410–55.

Swain, Carol. 1993. *Black Face, Black Interests: The Representation of African Americans in Congress*. Cambridge, MA: Harvard University Press.

Swarns, Rachel L. 2006. "Immigrants Rally in Scores of Cities for Legal Status." *New York Times*, April 11, A1.

Swers, Michelle. 2002. *The Difference Women Make: The Policy Impact of Women in Congress*. Chicago: University of Chicago Press.

Tate, Katherine. 1993. *From Protest to Politics: The New Black Voters in American Elections.* Cambridge, MA: Harvard University Press.

———. 2003a. *Black Faces in the Mirror: African Americans and their Representatives in the U.S. Congress.* Princeton, NJ: Princeton University Press.

———. 2003b. "Black Opinion on the Legitimacy of Racial Redistricting and Minority-Majority Districts." *American Political Science Review,* 97:45–56.

———. 2007. *Critical Transformations of Black Public Opinion.* Unpublished manuscript. University of California–Irvine.

Terhune, Lea. 2006. "Incoming 110th Congress Reflects American Diversity." See "Current Issues" section of the U.S. Department of State Web site: http://usinfo.state .gov/xarchives/display.html?p=washfile-english&y=2006&m=December&x=20061 214135453mlenuhreto.6124994. Accessed May 12, 2007.

Thernstrom, Abigail M. 1987. *Whose Votes Count? Affirmative Action and Minority Voting Rights.* Cambridge, MA: Harvard University Press.

Tomz, Michael, Jason Wittenberg, and Gary King 2003. CLARIFY: Software for Interpreting Statistical Results. Version 2.1. Stanford University, University of Wisconsin, and Harvard University. January 5.

Tribe, Lawrence H. 1988. *American Constitutional Law.* Mineola, NY: Foundation Press.

Tucker, Harvey J., Arnold Vedlitz, and James DeNardo. 1986. "Does Heavy Turnout Help Democrats in Presidential Elections?" *American Political Science Review* 80:1291–1304.

Uhlaner, Carol Jean, and F. Chris Garcia. 2002. "Latino Public Opinion." In *Understanding Public Opinion,* ed. Barbara Norrander and Clyde Wilcox, 77–101. Washington, DC: CQ Press.

Uhlaner, Carole Jean, Mark M. Gray, and F. Chris Garcia. 2000. "Ideology, Issues, And Partisanship Among Latinos." Paper presented at the annual meeting of the Western Political Science Association, March 24–26, San Jose, CA.

Verba, Sidney. 1996. "The Citizen as Respondent: Sample Surveys and American Democracy. Presidential Address, American Political Science Association, 1995." *American Political Science Review* 90:1–7.

———. 2003. "Would the Dream of Political Equality Turn Out to Be a Nightmare?" *Perspectives on Politics* 1:663–79.

Verba, Sidney, and Norman H. Nie. 1972. *Participation in America: Political Democracy and Social Equality.* New York: Harper and Row.

Verba, Sidney, and Gary R. Orren. 1985. *Equality in America: The View from the Top.* Cambridge, MA: Harvard University Press.

Verba, Sidney, Kay L. Schlozman, and Henry E. Brady. 1995. *Voice and Equality: Civic Voluntarism in American Politics.* Cambridge, MA: Harvard University Press.

Visser, Penny S., Jon A. Krosnick, and Joseph P. Simmons. 2003. "Distinguishing the Cognitive and Behavioral Consequences of Attitude Importance and Certainty: A New Approach to Testing the Common Factor Hypothesis." *Journal of Experimental Social Psychology* 39:118–41.

Weissberg, Robert. 1978. "Collective vs. Dyadic Representation in Congress." *American Political Science Review* 72:535–47.

Whitby, Kenny J. 1998. *The Color of Representation: Congressional Behavior and Black Interests.* Ann Arbor: University of Michigan Press.

Whitby, Kenny J., and George A. Krause. 2001. "Race, Issue Heterogeneity, and Public Policy: The Republican Revolution of the 104th U.S. Congress and the Representation of African–American Policy Interests." *British Journal of Political Science* 31 (July): 555–72.

Wilson G. K. 1981. *Interest Groups in the United States.* New York: Oxford University Press.

Wlezien, Christopher. 2004. "Patterns of Representation: Dynamics of Public Preferences and Policy." *Journal of Politics* 66:1–24.

Wolfinger, Raymond E., and Steven J. Rosenstone. 1980. *Who Votes?* New Haven, CT: Yale University Press.

Wood, B. Dan, and Angela Hinton Andersson. 1998. "The Dynamics of Senatorial Representation, 1952–1991." *Journal of Politics* 60:705–36.

Wright, Gerald C. 1977. "Racism and Welfare Policy in America." *Social Science Quarterly* 57:718–30.

———. 1978. "Candidates' Policy Positions and Voting in U. S. Congressional Elections." *Legislative Studies Quarterly* 3:445–64.

———. 1989. "Policy Voting in the U.S. Senate: Who Is Represented?" *Legislative Studies Quarterly* 14:465–86.

Wright, John R. 1996. *Interest Groups and Congress: Lobbying, Contributions, and Influence.* Bostonm, MA: Allyn and Bacon.

Young, Iris Marion. 2002. "Status Inequality and Social Groups." Issues in Legal Scholarship, The Origins and Fate of Antisubordination Theory: Article 9, at the Web site of the Berkeley Electronic Press: http://www.bepress.com/ils/iss2/art9.

Index